Eileen aged 10

In Memorian

Eileen Mary Webb
(neé: Salmon)
1928–2005

Eileen sadly passed away at her home in Hastings on 29th September, 2005 after a long battle against cancer and is buried in the local cemetery.

Her *hiraeth* (extreme yearning) for Nant Gwrtheyrn did not lessen over the years and like all the Valley's children, the longing to return did not cease.

In writing *This Valley was Ours* she introduced thousands of people to this magical place. Many have been touched by the writings in the book and had the great desire to visit Nant, and after fulfilling this desire wrote to Eileen to tell her that they also experienced the magnetism and tranquillity of the Valley that captures one's heart.

This Valley was Ours has brought together people from all walks of life and Eileen herself enjoyed and valued the deep lasting friendships formed through the book, which enriched her life.

This Valley was Ours

Eileen M. Webb

First published in hardback by Gwasg Tŷ ar y Graig: 1983
First published in paperback by Gwasg Carreg Gwalch: 1997
New edition: 2007
Second new edition: 2016

ISBN: 978-1-84524-255-5

Cover image: David Graham
Cover design: Eleri Owen

Sketches and village plan by Dennis A. Webb

Published by Gwasg Carreg Gwalch,
12 Iard yr Orsaf, Llanrwst, Wales LL26 0EH
tel: 01492 642031
email: books@carreg-gwalch.com
website: www.carreg-gwalch.com

Dedicated to
The Children of the Valley
and
In Fond Memory of
Gwilym Rees Parry

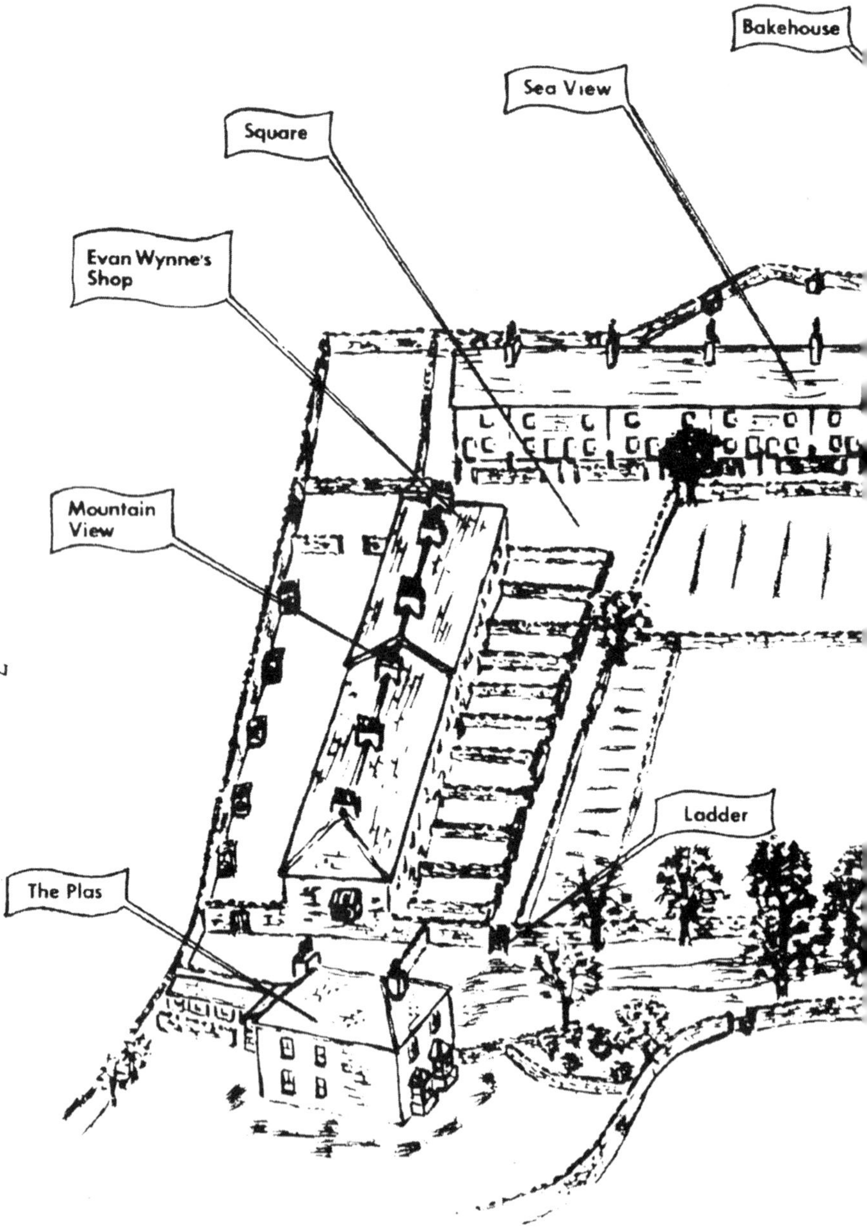
Bakehouse
Sea View
Square
Evan Wynne's Shop
Mountain View
Ladder
The Plas

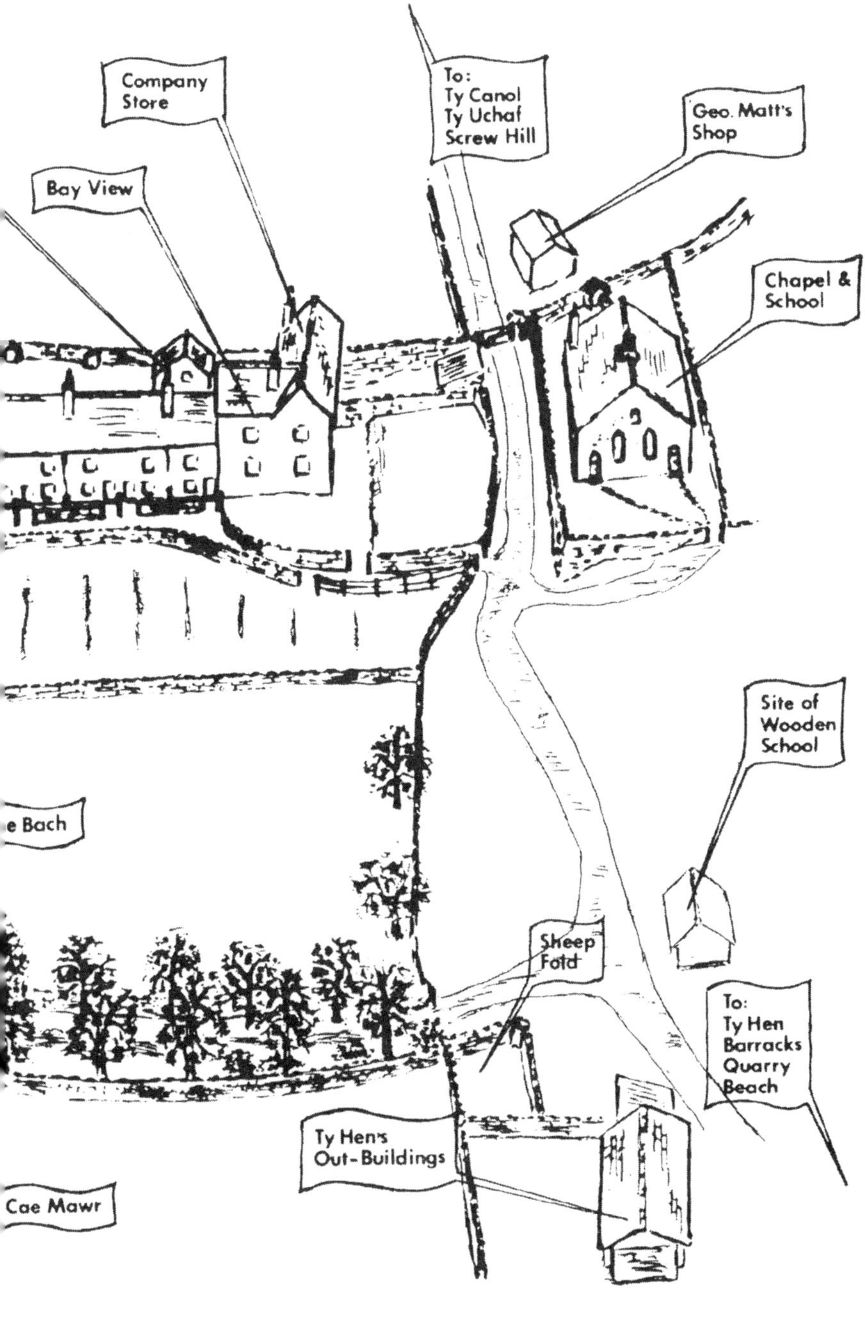
Company Store
To: Ty Canol Ty Uchaf Screw Hill
Geo. Matt's Shop
Bay View
Chapel & School
Site of Wooden School
e Bach
Sheep Fold
To: Ty Hen Barracks Quarry Beach
Ty Hen's Out-Buildings
Cae Mawr

Contents

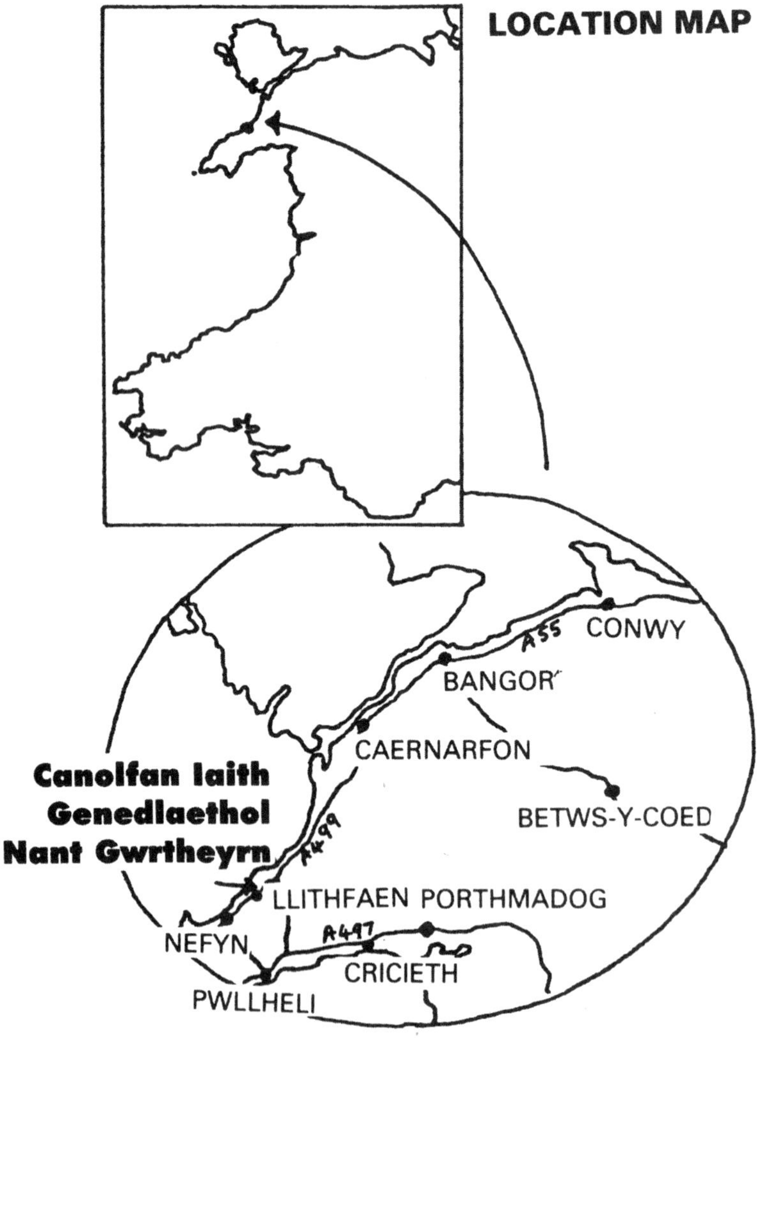
LOCATION MAP
A55
CONWY
BANGOR
CAERNARFON
BETWS-Y-COED
Canolfan Iaith
Genedlaethol
Nant Gwrtheyrn
A499
LLITHFAEN
PORTHMADOG
NEFYN
A497
CRICIETH
PWLLHELI

Acknowledgements

I should like to express my thanks to the following, without whose help this book could not have been written.

Mr John Dafydd Davies, Captain F. W. G. Grant, Mrs A. Herbert, Mr Will Eifion Jones, Mrs Olwen Jones (in recognition of the invaluable help given by her and her late husband, Mr Goronwy Jones). Mr J. Kidd, Miss Florence Lewis, Mr N. McSween [of John Kelly Ltd (Ship Owners)]. Mr K. R. Monroe [of Monroe Brothers (Ship Owners)]. Mrs J. Morris, Captain H. C. Ryding, Mr & Mrs John Roberts, Mr & Mrs Sam Roberts, Mr & Mrs Tom Alun Roberts (whose encouragement and efforts gave birth to the idea of compiling this book), Captain O. G. Spargo, Mr M. L. Summerfield [of Summerfield & Lang Ltd (Granite Merchants)], Mrs A. Mair Williams, Mr Griff Williams, Mrs Hannah Williams, Mrs Rebecca Williams, Mr Robin Ellis Williams, Mr William B. Williams and last but not least, my thanks to my so patient husband and family for their unwavering support and encouragement throughout the writing of this book.

Foreword

Until recently, Nant Gwrtheyrn was an isolated and long deserted little valley situated on a plateau above the sea on the western side of the Rivals Mountains (*Yr Eifl*) on the Llŷn Peninsula. Until my marriage the place meant nothing to me other than that I vaguely knew of its existence, that it was off the beaten track and was not easily accessible. However, to my wife, Phyllis, who had spent two years of her childhood there, it was a very special place. Although at first I was indifferent to her constant references to it, I gradually came to realise that underlying those references was not only an inordinate love for the little valley but a deep longing to return there. It seemed that she could not get the place out of her mind which, in view of her short residency, appeared to me to be somewhat illogical.

I then discovered that her brother was similarly affected and I noticed how at every opportunity the two talked about it and about the people they had known there. An indication of the subject arising yet again was the bringing out of the school group photograph which then led to hours of reminiscing.

As time went by, they longed more and more to know what had become of those friends of so long ago and in particular those in the photograph among whom they had spent their happiest days. The situation finally came to a head when they decided to put an end to that longing by doing something constructive about it. Their plan, which was immediately put into action, was a request to the local press to publish the school photograph, together with notice of their intention to arrange a reunion for interested ex-pupils.

My own feelings about the plan were highly sceptical as I

felt that the response, if any, would bring them nothing but dire disappointment. To my amazement, within hours of the publication, there came an excited telephone response from an ex-pupil. Happily, she knew the whereabouts of a few of the others and from that call came a chain reaction. What had begun as a plan to contact a few people now snowballed into daily responses by letter and by telephone, not only from those in the photograph but from almost every still living ex-resident of the valley, many of whom were complete strangers to my wife and her brother, each one desiring to attend the reunion and confessing to the same inexplicable longing to return to the valley.

The planned reunion for just a small number now became one of banqueting proportions, with people prepared to travel long distances to attend. By this time my indifference had vanished and I readily acknowledged that there was much more to this valley than I had realised and something that affected all those who had lived there. They seemed to be held by some invisible bond which caused even those that had never before heard of each other, let alone met, to be not just new acquaintances but members of one big family, the like of which I had never before experienced.

The reunion was a complete success and proved to be one of the happiest occasions I had ever attended. Shortly afterwards it was decided that the story of the valley, its people and its strange power over those people, should be recorded but, unlike previous articles by outsiders, should be written by someone who had been on the inside.

Here, then, is that story.

Tom Alun Roberts

Part 1:

History

Chapter I

As it was in the Beginning

It was a little after three in the morning as we settled ourselves in the car to begin our journey, a last minute check that nothing had been forgotten and we fastened our safety belts. There was no moon or stars that night and not a glimmer of light could be seen in any window for everyone was in bed. The silence and the darkness seemed to engulf us. The ignition was turned on but care was taken not to rev. up the engine for fear of disturbing the sleeping neighbourhood.

As we slowly and quietly moved off it began to rain, it was not a nice night to be starting on a journey of ever three hundred miles. Approaching London, the rain that had accompanied us became torrential and on reaching the West end of the City the streets were awash. Here half the world seemed to be awake and on the move despite the early hour. The silence of the countryside we had left behind such a short time ago was now replaced by the thundering of traffic and the drumming of the incessant rain on the roof of the car. Lights came at us from all directions and reflected in the gushing water of the streets, neon lights and traffic lights flashed eerily, horns blared and water almost enveloped the car as monster vehicles tore by. Everyone seemed to be taking part in a mad race with no end, appearing to be bent on self destruction and on the morrow doubtless the situation would be repeated. Was this all there was to life, this maniacal race run by dark silhouettes seated like robots in mechanical monsters, this dreadful cacophony of sound and the pollution of our very breath of life.

As we moved on with the traffic and left London behind my thoughts turned to the reason for this journey, a journey that had been planned some time before. It was to be the culmination of months of excitement caused by over forty years of indefinable longing, a longing to return to an isolated, almost inaccessible and now long deserted little Welsh valley. This longing had defined all logic and reason, increasing as the years passed by to become a never ending ache at the back of my mind. All my efforts to cure it had failed, nothing had any effect and now at last I had discovered that I was not alone in this, others too it seemed suffered from this strange malady.

This discovery, although pleasurable, served only to confuse me. What was it about this valley that held its children forever, this seemingly indestructible force that never let one go and strong enough to bring its people together again after forty years and more. They were coming from different climes and walks of life but united by the one common factor, the valley. Were we all under some spell, was it some form of magic or was there more fact in the legends of the valley than we realised? It was impossible to determine. I could be sure of only one thing and that was that on the next evening we were all to meet again and some for the first time at a reunion dinner and social.

We were now travelling steadily along the motorway. Dawn did not make an appearance that morning, the torrential rain seemed determined to blot out everything and only the time on my wristwatch proved that the night was over. The moving mass of traffic hemmed us in on all sides, spray from their spinning wheels showered against the windscreen defying the overworked wipers and the noise of it all was deafening. There would be no let up for some time as we still had many miles to cover and in an effort to blot it out my thoughts turned again to the valley.

I began to muse on the people who had lived there before my time, generations before, back as far as 450A.D. to the first known inhabitant, the Celtic King Vortigern. I closed my eyes and as though in a dream the scene unfolded before me and I saw the valley as it must have appeared to him in that time so long ago.

* * *

Peace is dominant, broken only by the sounds of the birds, the bleating of the mountain goats and the cry of the occasional seagull wheeling in from the sea. This wild luxuriant valley lies hidden and protected on three sides by the Rivals mountains, the highest of its three peaks rising to almost two thousand feet. Open only to the sea, the valley is raised some two hundred feet above sea level on a plateau, with to one side several raised mounds interlaced with miniature ravines and a fast flowing mountain stream.

Oak, hazel and willow trees skirt the stream and on the western slope of the mountain trees form a dense wood running almost to the shoreline. Shingle and shells of many

View of Headland – Trwyn y Gorlech – Vortigen's castle believed to be sited on the plateau in middle ground of photo

View of beach below Trwyn y Gorlech

varieties are scattered along and above the high tide mark. Low tide reveals golden sand and an occasional large rock beneath which crabs and lobsters take shelter. The water here is not shallow, in a short distance the sea bed drops away sharply. A small bay is formed between two headlands, Trwyn y Gorlech and Birds Rock. The latter seen from seawards as a moving mass of black and white, home of the guillemot, cormorant, razor bill, shag and many species of gulls, their activities leisurely observed by the basking seals on the rocky ledges below.

Only the seasons rule here. Spring brings forth the new life, the catkins, pussy willow, primroses, bluebells, fox and wolf cubs, goat kids, all the flora and fauna of the valley. The sun rises higher and summer brings a dramatic change of scene. The stark mountain slopes become a vision in colour with heather of many hues, harebells, roseroots and rock plants in profusion and in perfect co-existence with the fruits of these mountains the sweet succulent bilberry. The lower slopes complete the picture with a wide fringe of tall green ferns. Ferns grow, too, like miniature forests on the valley floor and in their shelter snakes glide silently seeking their prey, occasionally emerging from the gloom to climb up on to the rocks to bathe in the warmth of the sun. In the bay mackerel and pollock break the glassy surface of the water, seals' heads appear and disappear and schools of porpoise play.

Autumn steals in and has a special quality here. Slowly the shadows of the mountains lengthen across the valley, the trees are now a blaze of copper and gold, the brambles heavy with fruit and the hazels display their bountiful crop. No longer green, the lower slopes have turned to the rich brown bracken. The earlier setting sun gives way to the harvest and hunters moons bringing delight to the carnivores, their barks and howls echoing eerily from crag to crag.

The days shorten and autumn gives way to winter. Cold air now clings to the mountain tops. The lowering clouds burst on the peaks, the water spreading out like the fingers of a giant hand forming white cascading streams that rush down the rock face to the valley. Snow falls fast and furiously, the peaks are virgin white, little moves on the mountain save for the hungry predators. The goats have moved down to the valley for here there is shelter from the icy winds, seldom does snow penetrate to the plateau. The sea can no longer be likened to a mirror, waves pound the shore and rocks throwing spume high into the air from where it falls to build up on the shoreline like snowdrifts. Despite the fury above and below, the peace of the valley is undisturbed.

This, then, was the valley that revealed itself to King Vortigern and his faithful followers. Looking down from the mountain he recognised it as the refuge he had sought over so many weary miles. A king dispossessed, he had trekked wounded and dispirited across the land from distant Wessex. What had been his fortunes, had caused the loss of his kingdom and brought him to this inaccessible place? The place that henceforth would bear his name, that of Vortigerns' valley and in Welsh Nant Gwrtheyrn.

* * *

Vortigern, a Celt, ruled as King of Wessex. His was the first rule to unite the tribes under one leader and as a result he organised the first form of Council in Britain. The Council was made up of the accepted elders of the various tribes. His aim in uniting the tribes was to discourage persistent attacks by the Picts and the Irish who repeatedly sent out raiding parties to sack and pillage and generally create havoc in the settlements. The scheme proved to be highly successful and was admired by many but it also brought resentment from those who were jealous of his success and popularity.

All went well for him until news reached him of an Irish intent to invade in force. Fearing that he had insufficient forces to quell such an invasion as well as deal with the Picts he decided to seek help from the Jutes, Hengist and Horsa, whom he believed were his friends. In return for their assistance he invited them to settle with their warriors in Thanet. Hardly able to believe their good fortune but delighted, the Jutes readily accepted, seeing it as an ideal opportunity to get a foot-hold in Wessex.

As expected, the Irish attempted to invade but Vortigern's fears and resultant invitation to the Jutes proved unnecessary as he subdued the Irish without their assistance. Regrettably for him that invitation was also to prove to be one of his greatest mistakes and was eventually to cost him his kingdom.

Having settled and gained Vortigern's trust, Hengist, a cunning man, plotted with the Picts to stage an invasion by massing their forces on the border. This accomplished, he hurried with news of the threat to Vortigern, suggesting that a larger force than they could muster would be needed to deal with it and the only remedy would be to bring in more of his men. Vortigern, trusting Hengist implicitly, readily agreed to his suggestion. Hengist, losing no time, immediately brought in a large force of Saxon warriors and kinsmen and also his daughter, Rowena. With this force supporting them the two Jutes had set the stage to gain control and get rid of the King.

Their next move was that of ensuring Vortigern's continued trust and to this end they planned an elaborate banquet in his honour. The banquet took place as arranged and from the Jutes' point of view was a complete success. Wine flowed freely and eventually everyone but themselves became very drunk. At this point Hengist presented his beautiful daughter to the King and he, enchanted by her beauty, fell instantly and deeply in love with her. Without hesitation Vortigern asked Hengist for her hand in marriage adding, 'ask of me what you will and it shall be yours'. Hengist cunningly feigning surprise, replied that he would consider the matter and at once hurried away to consult his advisors. In a short time he returned to inform the King that he would agree to the marriage on condition that he was given the rule of Kent. Vortigern, man of his word, agreed to the condition without hesitation.

When news of the King's foolhardiness spread throughout the Kingdom those who had resented his skills and courage now jumped at the opportunity to openly criticise him. Hearing of this, the Jutes became confident that the time was ripe to overthrow him. Impatient to achieve his end, Hengist set about picking a fight with the King. He accused him of failing to supply sufficient food and money to support his warriors and threateningly demanded immediate availability of larger supplies. As expected, the King, shocked and distressed and not least by Hengist's manner, denied the accusation. At once Hengist turned nasty and a fight ensued. The fight became a bitter one and continued relentlessly until Vortigern's son Vortimer killed Horsa and as a result Hengist was contained.

Not long afterwards Vortimer died suddenly. By this time the Elders, tired of so much strife and suffering, wanted a lasting peace in the land. Vortigern, too, wanted peace and wanted only to live happily with Rowena whom he had made his wife and with whom he was still deeply in love. Bearing no malice, he readily forgave Hengist his treachery and again offered him his friendship. Hengist eagerly responded, saying that he, too, was weary of conflict and was only too willing to play his part in making every effort to keep the peace.

Agreement seemed finally to have been reached and all was quiet in the kingdom for a time. Regrettably for the King, that peace was to be short lived, for Hengist, treacherous and cunning as ever, had prepared a plan to rid himself of Vortigern once and for all. Calling his men together, he told them of his plan. He explained that he would invite the King and his Elders to a banquet of friendship. At the banquet each Briton was to be seated next to a Saxon and each Saxon was to be armed with a dagger hidden in his shoe. At Hengist's command, they were to rise and slaughter the Elders, but Vortigern, for whom he had other plans, was not to be harmed.

Seeing the invitation as a genuine attempt to further their friendship, the King happily looked forward to the occasion. The banquet took place and the seating arrangements were accepted with complete trust. Halfway through the feast Hengist signalled to his men and the assault began. Such was the surprise and speed of the attack that the Elders stood no chance of escape and all were slaughtered. Vortigern, helpless and stunned by the carnage, was taken prisoner. Any fears he may have had as to why he alone had been allowed to survive must soon have been confirmed when Hengist played his final card, that of offering Vortigern his freedom in exchange for the rule of Essex and Sussex. The King, horrified by the thought but now a broken man, shamefully agreed.

With nothing left but dishonour and a handful of still loyal subjects, he wandered away, bewildered, into what had become a hostile land, for news of the massacre and his shameful failure had travelled before him. An outcast and hounded by those he had served so well he fled, knowing not where to find refuge. Reaching the Rivals Mountains, he saw beneath him the uninhabited and so peaceful valley and knew that he need travel no more.

How long he survived in the valley is unknown but legend has it that he built a wooden castle on a raised mound above the shore. One night, some years later, a terrible storm broke and a thunderbolt struck the puny castle. The whole structure went up in flames and the deposed King was burned to death.

Whatever the truth of the legend, it is fact that some centuries later a large slab of rough hewn granite was discovered in the valley, inscribed upon it in Celtic form was the name Vortigern. On investigation it was found to be a grave containing the skeleton of a very tall man, which the King was reputed to have been.

The Chronicler Bede wrote a great deal about Vortigern and branded him as a coward. Understandably Bede's opinion was highly prejudiced as Vortigern was not of his faith and had openly rejected his dogma, he preferred a more simple but nonetheless sincere form of belief. Others who wrote at the time and earlier, such as Gildas, respected Vortigern and claimed that he was a well meaning and brave leader.

Chapter II

The Three Curses

After Vortigern's death his followers deserted the valley and it was left to its own devices until the sixth century when the Abbey of St Mary was founded on Bardsey Island by St Cadfan. Pilgrims coming from the North travelled across the Rivals Mountain and some, desiring shelter and rest, saw the valley as a welcome oasis. These travellers lingered only long enough to satisfy this need then moved on, leaving no trace of their visit save for the track worn by their weary feet which remained to be used by future generations.

Apart from this intrusion, the valley remained undisturbed until the coming of the fisher-folk. Little is known of these folk but that they formed a close community, their livelihood depended on their fishing and hunting skills and the harvests of nature. Abundant trees provided material for their primitive dwellings and boats and ample supplies of fresh water came from the mountain streams. This Pagan community lived contentedly and undisturbed for many years, knowing little or nothing of Christianity but secure in their own beliefs.

A century or so after the founding of the Abbey on Bardsey another monastic house was founded by St Beuno at Clynnog Fawr. This new abbey soon became established and Monks set forth from there to spread the gospel and gain converts to the faith. During their travels they heard of the isolated valley and its little community and so made plans to carry the gospel there. To this end three Monks set out on the long trek.

Reaching the Rivals, they sat to rest while observing the valley below. Seeing no sign of movement or human habitation they began to wonder whether they had been misled but then in the distance they noticed wisps of smoke curling lazily upwards from a fire just above the shore. Rising to their feet they then saw that near the fire and partly hidden by trees was what appeared to be a settlement. Anxious to delay no further they looked around and soon found the path leading down.

Eventually they came in sight of the settlement and saw to their relief that it was not deserted. Outside the dwellings was gathered a large group of people who seemed to be waiting for them. Realising that their progress down the mountain had been observed and feeling that the group must be a welcoming party, the Monks hurried along with confidence. That confidence soon deserted them when, as they drew near, they recognised not a welcoming party but a human barrier. Confronting them was a long line of men formed in close ranks with the women and children at a safe distance behind and no movement or gesture was offered to greet them. The Monks stepped forward apprehensively but careful to show no sign of their apprehension. Instead, they adopted an air of confidence, armed with the thought that all would surely be well when these simple folk realised that they brought with them the greatest news on earth. A further step forward with warm smiles and arms raised in greeting brought no response other than stony faces and obvious signs of hostility.

It was not surprising that the community reacted in this way for they were not used to outsiders and as a result were suspicious of any stranger. These three strangers, dressed as they were, presented a frightening sight to them. Their long black hooded robes, leather thonged belts from which hung large wooden crosses and the long staves they carried suggested nothing but an evil threat. They had already heard disturbing rumours of such men who travelled around the countryside interfering in people's lives, frightening them with talk of spirits and devils, of burning in fires and other horrific things and the arrival of these three filled them with fear.

They determined to rid themselves of these strangers as quickly as possible and without allowing the Monks a chance to explain their mission, one of the group, who appeared to be a leader, ordered them to leave. Seeming to ignore the hostility and still smiling warmly, the Monks advanced a pace. Immediately the mood of the settlers became ugly. One of them picked up a stone and threw it. At once more stones were thrown and the women and children began jeering. It was now obvious that the time had come for the Monks to beat a hasty retreat. Without delay they turned and ran towards the mountain. Hopes that their retreat would satisfy their aggressors were dashed when they saw that the whole population of the settlement was in pursuit.

They reached the foot of the mountain but still their pursuers, close on their heels and warmed to the chase, kept up the attack. By this time the Monks feared for their lives but this fear served to spur them on to greater efforts to gain safety. On and on they climbed with lungs almost bursting and on and on came the jeers and threats echoing ominously from the surrounding crags. On, too, came the endless hail of stones, many still finding their target. It seemed that they would not survive when to their great relief they reached the last bend. This sight encouraged a final effort and minutes later they gained level ground.

Suddenly the jeering became muted and stones no longer rained around them. Turning, they saw their attackers gathered some way down the track, still threatening and jeering but no longer in pursuit. The shouts and jeers then died away completely and, watching from the shelter of huge boulders, the Monks saw their enemies turn and retrace their steps down the mountain.

Only on seeing them reach the bottom did the Monks relax. They collapsed to the ground, exhausted, bruised and bleeding, unable to take another step and filled with anger at the ignorance of these pagans, for pagans they must surely be to attack such holy men as they. So incensed were they that they decided that these people and their valley must be punished and punished in some lasting form. For some time they lay nursing their wounds and recovering from their ordeal while considering what action to take.

Finally refreshed and having made up his mind, the elder of the three rose to his full height and, raising his staff to the heavens he called out for witness to the curse he was to lay on the valley. As though possessed he cried out, 'Never shall any ground in this accursed valley be consecrated'. The second Monk, revitalised by his elder's vehemence, arose in the same manner and proceeded to lay his curse, crying out, 'Never shall a marriage be solemnized between any man and woman born in this valley'. No sooner had his words died away than the third Monk arose and likewise raised his staff and proceeded to lay the final curse. 'This valley shall live three times and die three times and at the last will become a deserted ruin forever'. For some moments afterwards they did not move and then, satisfied that their curses were justified, they began the long trek back to the Abbey, leaving the valley to its accursed fate.

Unaware of the events taking place on the mountain top, the fisher-folk returned triumphantly to the settlement. Life went on as before until one day, whilst the men were out fishing, a great storm arose, whipping the sea into a fury. Never before had they experienced such a storm and such was the ferocity of the elements that every boat foundered and every man was lost. The women waited for their men-folk in vain. Without their support they could not survive in the valley and in a short time were forced to leave their homes and seek refuge elsewhere.

Once more the valley was deserted. Was this disaster the result of the Monk's curse and, therefore, the end of its first life? Would there be a further two as foretold in the final curse? Time alone would tell.

Chapter III

A Legend of Love

Deserted by the fisher-folk the valley returned to its former solitude and remained so for centuries until the coming of the Meredith family. These were farming folk and seeing the fertile valley, they recognised its potential. As a result two picturesque cottages arose, built from the local granite and so blending perfectly with the valley scenery they stood side by side overlooking a shimmering little stream. With yards at the rear, gardens at the front and the necessary outbuildings ranged around them, they presented an attractive sight. Once complete the families moved in and having acquired their stock, farming on the virgin land began in earnest.

These then were the pioneers of the valley's agricultural industry, its second life. If the Merediths knew of the Monks' curses they would hardly have given them credence, so idyllic were their circumstances and surroundings. It did not take them long to settle and although isolated they were happy and content with just each other's company. The men were kept busy tilling the land, building up their stock and attending to the innumerable tasks involved with farming while the women committed themselves to looking after their homes.

The farms prospered and as time passed were handed down through the generations from father to son. So it was that sometime in the eighteenth century the farms were still in the hands of the same family. In one cottage was a widower and his only child, a daughter named Meinir. In the other, the widower's nephew, Rhys, and two nieces, Gwyneth and Gwendolen. Meinir was but a few months younger than Rhys and although an only child, was never lonely as she was treated like a sister by her cousins.

As the years went by Meinir grew into a comely young maiden. With the delicate pink of roses in her cheeks, a shy and gentle disposition, she was admired by everyone. Gwendolen, too, was pleasing of countenance, unlike her sister who was plain and sour tempered while Rhys developed into a handsome young man of fine physique and honest of nature.

As Meinir and Rhys reached their late teens they began seeking each other's company more and more and accompanied by Rhys's faithful sheep-dog, would spend their time walking among the mountains or along the sea shore. Their favourite spot was a little copse of tall oaks and there in the shade they would sit and dream away the hours. Before either realised what was happening, they had fallen deeply in love. What had dawned on them with surprise had to their families been obvious for some time. So it was with even greater surprise, when they nervously announced their wish to marry, they were greeted not with amazement but with joy and the air of their news being a foregone conclusion. Ecstatic with delight and seeing no reason for delay, they began excitedly to discuss their forthcoming wedding. After much discussion July the fifth was chosen for the great day. As Meinir's parents had married at Clynnog Fawr church, eight miles distant, her father expressed the wish that she would marry in the same church. This she readily agreed to and plans for the wedding went ahead.

One evening while walking in the little copse, approaching their favourite oak beneath which they always sat, Meinir noticed some markings on the old tree. Immediately curious, she ran forward and there saw, beautifully carved in the trunk, her name and the date of their wedding. As Rhys joined her he confessed that he had secretly carved it there earlier that day. Fighting back tears of happiness, Meinir embraced him and vowed that she would love him to eternity.

News of the forthcoming wedding soon spread to neighbouring villages and the little valley became host to a constant stream of people coming and going up and down the mountain. Friends and relatives, many having travelled miles, made the journey to congratulate the young lovers and each one was warmly welcomed and offered nourishment before facing the long trek home.

All was bustle in the two cottages as much had to be done. Visits to the Vicar and to the harpist who, in keeping with tradition, would play for the couple outside the church. Preparations for the inevitably large reception for, being a popular couple, folk from miles around would attend. The making of the wedding finery for the family and most important, Meinir's dress. As time went by panic set in that all would not be ready in time but despite their fears all was complete when the great day dawned and as fine a day as they could have wished.

In those days tradition played an important part in all that was done and Rhys and Meinir's wedding was no exception. That bride and groom should set eyes on each other before the ceremony was unthinkable and although living in such close proximity, this rule was strictly adhered to. Tradition also demanded that as soon as the groom had left for the church, the bride should hide and remain in hiding until found by local young men. These would be appointed by the groom and would escort her to his side at the altar. The better the hiding place the longer the groom would have to wait, thus ensuring the couple of a long and happy marriage.

Rhys and the family left in good time for the church and as soon as they were out of sight Meinir made her way to her chosen hiding place. She had earlier told her father, taking care not to divulge the location, that quite by accident she had found the perfect place.

In due course Rhys and his relatives arrived at the church gate to shouts of cheer and goodwill and a festive scene of welcome. There seemed to be hundreds of people, all smartly dressed in their Sunday best. The trees around the Church were beautifully decorated and even the borders of the footpath which led to the door had been decorated with flowers and gay ribbons by the children. Appreciation for the children's efforts would be shown when pennies were thrown to them by the groom as he and his bride left the Church. Among the decorations in the trees were posted several young people. These acted as look-outs to signal to the waiting crowd the moment the bride and her escorts came into view. Outside the door the harpist was in position, tuning his instrument to perfect pitch.

Shyly but happily Rhys made his way along the path, turning first to one side and then the other to smile and nod to the well-wishers. Suddenly a figure rushed out of the crowd and, standing before Rhys and his family, began cursing and abusing them loudly. Everyone at once recognised the figure as that of a local half wit and just as suddenly as he had appeared he was quickly but gently pulled back into the crowd and silenced. For a moment all was quiet and no-one stirred and not just a few felt a sense of foreboding and unease that what they had witnessed may have been a bad omen. However, the brief interruption was soon dismissed from mind as they saw Rhys enter the Church. The chief guests followed and then a number from the crowd who wished to choose a seat that would allow a good view of the ceremony. Others preferred waiting outside where they could greet and cheer the bride on her arrival.

The appointed time arrived and an air of excitement and anticipation filled the Church. Hushed ripples of conversation reached Rhys as he stood nervously at the altar. Making every effort to control his nervousness, he contented himself to wait for the strains of the harp that would announce Meinir's arrival. Patiently he waited but as time passed no sounds of music reached him and he could sense the growing impatience of the congregation as they coughed and fidgeted. He was becoming increasingly anxious and kept glancing at his best man when, with relief, he heard footsteps coming down the aisle. His relief was short lived when he was joined, not by Meinir but by one of the appointed escorts. Breathlessly and with a worried expression the newcomer informed him that despite a thorough search he and his companions had failed to find Meinir. Rhys for a moment was shocked and speechless but almost at once regained his composure. In a whisper he told the young man that it was obvious that Meinir was playing a game with them. He begged him to hurry back to the valley where she would be waiting and urged him to bring her back before it was too late for the ceremony. Making no move the still breathless young man insisted that they had searched every possible place and found no sign of her. Rhys could not believe that she was not there and without another word ran from the Church to carry out the search for himself.

Reaching the valley he frantically searched everywhere

he could think of but met with no success. He then thought that she must be hiding somewhere on the mountain and immediately dashed back up the track. By this time his anguish and desperation had taken its toll and he collapsed, unconscious, to the ground.

Having waited in the Church for beyond a reasonable time his family and friends hurried back to the valley for news. As they made their way down the mountain they found Rhys and carried him home. At once search parties were organised and these spread out across the valley, the sea-shore and the mountains but as darkness fell no sign of Meinir had been found. Throughout the night lantern lights flashed along the mountains and across the length and breadth of the valley as the search continued. Voices echoed back and forth as they repeatedly called her name. Dawn broke with still no sign of where she could be and no-one knew what to do next or where else to search. Rhys, now distraught and thinking that he would go mad, suddenly remembered an old witch who lived in a cottage high up on the Rivals and who was reputed to be a good fortune teller. He decided that he would go at once to consult her. Worried about his state of mind, his sister Gwendolen bade him wait at home as news may come during his absence, adding that she would go in his place. Much to her surprise he agreed without argument.

Gwendolen was greeted with suspicion by the old woman but when she explained the circumstances the witch became sympathetic and ushered her in. For some time there was silence while the fortune teller seemed to be deep in thought, then breaking the silence she asked Gwendolen what it was that she wanted to know. Seizing the opportunity the young woman asked, 'Will Meinir be found?'

The answer came without hesitation. 'Yes.'

Gwendolen continued, 'Will Rhys find her?'

Again the answer was yes.

'Where will she be found?'

The fortune teller did not answer but just shook her head.

Gwendolen persisted, 'Will it be in heaven or on earth?'

'On earth,' came the immediate reply.

'When will she be found?'

This time the old woman did not reply at once but again seemed to be deep in thought. Patiently the young woman waited and eventually, slowly and clearly, the reply came.

'Tell your brother to search no longer for the maiden but to wait until a light comes from heaven to direct him.'

Gwendolen asked, 'Is she far away?'

The answer came immediately. 'No, she is not.'

The fortune teller then turned away, making clear that the consultation was at an end. Anxious not to antagonise her Gwendolen thanked her then left to hurry home with the news.

The result of the consultation was discussed by everyone with the exception of Rhys who uttered not a word but seemed to be listening intently. Try as they might they could glean little sense from the answers and they decided that there was nothing more they could do but wait and pray that Meinir would return safely. At this Rhys arose and went to bed, his only companion his faithful old sheep-dog. Throughout the night, the next day and the following night he did not stir from his bed. When eventually he did join the others, he spoke to no-one and answered only when absolutely necessary and then as briefly as possible. As the days went by he became completely withdrawn, speaking only to his dog and, faithful as ever, the dog did not leave his side.

The year came to an end and without any clue to the mystery. Meinir's father was heartbroken and it was not long before he succumbed to his broken heart and joined her long departed mother. Rhys continued to avoid all companionship but that of his dog. Silently he went about his duties but with no heart for anything.

Spring came and went with no change in the situation. In early summer a tragedy befell the young man, when suddenly his faithful old companion died. His year of suffering and now this new loss was more than he could bear and he lost his reason. No longer could he work but every day wandered off in his madness, walking back and forth along the sea-shore, believing that Meinir had drowned and calling to the waves to give him back his beloved. Eventually tiring of the shore he chose each day to visit the cops where he and Meinir had spent so many happy hours. There beneath their oak he sat crying and screaming for her and refusing even to return home for his meals. Despite his family's pleading nothing would move him so each day his sisters took it in turns to take him food.

This situation continued for some weeks until one day as Gwyneth approached the cops she realised that she could not hear his usual anguished cries. Hurrying forward in fear of what she may find, she was relieved to see that Rhys was still there. She gave him his lunch and was about to turn away when, for the first time for over a year, he spoke to her voluntarily. Her hopes rose immediately but just as quickly were dashed when she heard what he had to say. In a calm and steady voice he informed her that he would no longer return home to sleep. He intended to remain where he was for the rest of his life. Gwyneth begged him to come home and even cried while she pleaded with him but Rhys was adamant, saying that this was the place where he and Meinir had been together so often, where they had first declared their love and later planned their future. In despair Gwyneth no longer knew what to do or say to persuade him to return home. Helplessly she begged him to at least eat the meal she had brought. This, too, he refused saying that he appreciated her efforts but that he no longer wished to eat. Sick at heart Gwyneth turned away and left him.

Some days went by until one hot and sultry afternoon a severe storm broke over the mountains. So violent was it that the young women feared for their brother's life and because of it knew that somehow he must be persuaded to come home. Gwendolen at once prepared to go to him but as she did so Gwyneth rushed past her, calling as she went that she would go and would bring him home.

As she reached the little copse she could hear, above the storm, his voice raised in prayer. Almost deafened by the crashing and rolling of the thunder and near blinded by the vivid flashes of lightning, she ran forward and knelt at his feet, pleading with him to return home with her. Ignoring her pleadings, Rhys urged her to leave, saying that it was too dangerous for her to remain, adding that he had no fear of the storm himself as a far greater storm raged within his heart.

Realising that she could do nothing, Gwyneth rose to her feet and as she did so there came another tremendous flash accompanied by a thunderous crash. So close was it that she felt its heat. At that same moment she saw Rhys fall to the ground and, terrified, she closed her eyes. When she opened them again she saw a sight that horrified her. Rhys was on his feet, smiling the smile of a madman, babbling incomprehensibly and pointing to the tree beneath which he had kept his long vigil. There before them and split asunder lay the oak, revealing the remains of a wedding dress and a skeleton. The position of the skeleton with the arms raised above the head told its own tragic story. Rhys indicated that she should come no nearer, screaming that at last he had found his beloved bride and now they would be together to eternity. Saying no more he moved towards the fallen tree and as he bent over the skeleton he suddenly dropped and fell upon it. Gwyneth ran forward and saw immediately that he was dead. At last his troubled soul had left his tortured body. With great sadness in her heart she slowly turned and made her way home.

The two sisters now alone carried on farming for a time but then Gwendolen fell ill. She had contracted tuberculosis and after a short illness she succumbed to the disease.

After such tragedy and great sorrow Gwyneth's personality changed completely. She became a much kinder and considerate young woman. Later she was to find happiness with the man who, as Rhys's best man, had stood beside him at the altar on that ill-fated wedding day. Her going once again left the valley to its own devices.

The years went by and the once so meticulous little cottages fell into disrepair and dereliction and the land so carefully and lovingly tended returned to nature. It seemed that the valley's agricultural industry had come to an end until some generations later another farming couple moved in. Unlike the Merediths they built their home higher up the valley in a sheltered little copse of oak. Strangely they had chosen the very copse where Meinir and Rhys had so tragically died.

The couple settled happily and over the years many children were born to them. Their last born, a little boy whom they named Ellis, bore no resemblance at all to his brothers and sisters and did not grow and develop physically as a normal child. Instead he became a dwarf and because of it was known to everyone as Ellis bach. So short was he that with each step that he took when running down the mountain his bottom bumped against the ground. His mother, wearying of constantly tending to his bruises and renewing the seats of his breeches, in desperation to save the garments, sewed leather patches on to the most vulnerable areas.

Ellis was a strange little boy. He was a dreamer and spent many hours away from the family, saying that he had been with the fairies with whom he claimed to have an affiliation. Not surprisingly these claims led to speculation by many that he was a changeling.

Despite his lack of height he was as agile as the wild mountain goats that roamed above his home and well earned his keep by catching the nannies and milking them. Such was his agility that no rock or ledge on the mountain was inaccessible to him. When from time to time stray sheep became trapped on some of those ledges his agility proved invaluable. Mentally, too, he was agile, enabling him to produce fine poetry which gained him local recognition as something of a bard.

What eventually became of the family is not known other than that Ellis was the last surviving member to remain in the valley until his death in the early part of the nineteenth century. His name, however, has lived on in that the little copse, where the remains of his home can still be seen to this day, is known to everyone as Coed Ellis bach.

Ellis's passing did not leave the valley deserted for long. By eighteen fifty farming was again being carried out and this time on a larger scale. Three new farms had sprung up: Tŷ Hen, *Old house,* a strange name for a new building; Tŷ Uchaf, *Highest house,* and Tŷ Canol, *Middle house.* Stone walls now separated the land and the valley took on an ordered appearance. The little farms soon became established and prospered although no-one could have known at the time how important their activities were to become, or that two of them would outlive the next much larger industry which was to change the face of the valley for all time.

Chapter IV

A Village is Born

In 1861 the valley became host to a completely different industry. An industry that was to tear at its very bastions, to extract its very nature and, when finished, leave deep scars as witness to its activities. That industry was the quarrying of granite for the new roads being constructed throughout the kingdom. Prospectors on the prowl found the Rivals Mountains an ideal source as not only were they composed of granite but one of the finest grades of the mineral.

Mineral rights were acquired by the Kneeshaw Lupton Company and they, without delay, set about opening up a quarry on the south side of the valley, erecting a jetty for transporting the stone by sea and the building of accommodation for their pioneer work force. This accommodation was built on the main plateau and formally named Holyhead View but this title did not last long.

Nant in 1910

Instead it became known as the Barracks and was even registered as such in the Census of that year.

The Barracks was built in the shape of a capital letter I with a large house at each end and at right angles to thirteen smaller houses between. The larger houses were to accommodate the manager and the foreman and the smaller for the workers. Each of the smaller dwellings consisted of four rooms, two up and two down. These were sparsely furnished by the Company and with just a table, a chair, a bed and cooking facilities. Outside was a large garden with to one side a number of pigsties in which some of the residents kept pigs.

At first the houses were occupied by men only, two or three to a unit and each man cooking for himself. A number of the men came from as far away as Ireland and came by ship to the newly erected jetty. They would stay only for a period to earn a little money and then return home the same way, coming back again when their funds had run out. Other workers came from all parts of the peninsula and many of these were farm labourers whose wages at that time were so piteously small they welcomed the opportunity to try their hand at quarrying and so earn a little more money, farm wages in those days being seven shillings and sixpence per week as against quarry wages of ten shillings.

The men would arrive at the Barracks late on a Sunday evening or in the early hours of Monday morning, depending on how far they had to travel, carrying their sustenance on their backs as food was not available in the valley at that time. By mid week their supplies would be running low and to replenish would necessitate a visit home for the Welsh and to Llithfaen for the Irish, Llithfaen being the nearest village some two miles over the mountain. For anything other than the basic needs a further seven mile journey to Pwllheli was necessary. These must have been hardy men as in many cases the fetching and carrying of supplies involved trekking miles over rough terrain and that journey, home and back again in time for work the following morning, would be undertaken after a long and exhausting day's work at the quarry. Walking was their only means as lifts as we know them today were almost non-existent apart from the remote chance of a lift on a farmer's cart.

With the opening of the quarry the name Nant Gwrtheyrn was considered to be unsuitable from an industrial and commercial point of view and as it had become a port it was decided that the name Portnant would be more practical.

As the quarry became established the married men quartering at the Barracks decided to bring their wives and families to the valley and so whenever one of the houses became vacant a family would move in. The result was the forming of the first quarrying community which quickly grew and thrived with Welsh, Irish and English families living side by side in harmony. Once again the mountains echoed to the sounds of human activity and children's laughter and no-one at that time gave any thought to the fact that this was the valley's third community and prophesied to be the last by the Monks when laying their curse. These were early days and to speculate on the death of the valley when its new life had only just begun would not only have been ridiculous but impossible.

As the quarry developed so a larger work force was brought in. By the mid eighteen seventies the Barracks overflowed and again many men were obliged to travel long distances, not just twice weekly but morning and evening to and from their work. In 1878 the Company decided that further accommodation must be provided and so it was that a little village was born.

The new village provided twenty-four houses in two terraces. Built at right angles to one another they were aptly named Sea View and Mountain View. Attached to one end of Sea View terrace was a larger house. This was Bay View and to its rear was another building which was to serve as a shop cum bakehouse. Lastly, standing apart in its own grounds and surrounded by a high stone wall was a much larger property, The Plas. With the houses completed thought was given to providing a place of worship and as a result a little Presbyterian Chapel was erected on raised ground just outside the village compound. To what at first had been a minute and fluid community was added the now established Barrack families and twenty-six new village families, raising the population from a mere sixty or so to three times that number. The rent for the terraced properties, at four shillings and twopence per fortnight, was considered by the tenants to be a fair price to pay for such fine dwellings.

The newcomers were welcomed by their predecessors as

their coming meant not only the enlarging of their hitherto limited social life but also by the swelling of their numbers the Company saw the need for services that previously had been lacking. The first of these was the opening of the Company store cum bakehouse, to be followed shortly after by a coal yard. This was situated below the plateau at a point about half-way to the beach. The coal and stock for the store was brought in by ship and these ships, three in all, also belonged to the Company, their names indicating their trade: the Galchfaen, *Limestone*; Gwynfaen, *Whitestone* and the Ithfaen, *Granite*. The Gwynfaen was to come to a sorry end one foggy night some forty years later when, running in to Porthdinllaen for safe anchorage, she struck a submerged rock and sank within minutes.

These services were a great advantage as no longer would the people have to trek up the mountain to Llithfaen and face the seemingly longer trek when heavily laden back to 'Nant'. The shop was well-stocked and bread made at home could be taken to the bakehouse to be baked for a small charge. Coal was purchased at a hundredweight and sometimes half a hundredweight at a time. It was then carried home on one's back or on homemade trolleys and the cost added to the purchaser's account at the shop. Wages were paid on alternate Saturday afternoons so shop accounts were settled on the Monday following. For each pound spent at the shop the Company paid a dividend in the form of metal coins known as tallies. These were marked with their value of anything from a penny to half a crown. They were then saved by the purchaser and later exchanged for goods at the shop.

The Plas was the last house to be built and its first residents were a honeymoon couple. One of the sons of the Kneeshaw Lupton Brothers married soon after its completion and brought his bride there for a month long honeymoon. The honeymoon over, the new Manager, a Mr

Jones, moved in, occupying all but two of the rooms which had to be kept in readiness for visiting directors.

Among Mr Jones's duties was the weekly task of collecting money for wages which had been deposited by the Company at a bank in Pwllheli. This necessitated a special journey to the town, one week for the actual wages and alternate weeks for cash to be paid in advance of wages which was known as subs. Every week regularly and at the same time of day, the Manager would be seen setting off on his errand and returning with the bag of money. Not surprisingly, one day when returning from the bank, he was set upon by someone who attempted to rob him and only with difficulty did he manage to foil the attempt. After reporting the incident to the Company who then immediately informed the police, it was agreed that he be authorised to carry a defensive weapon and thereafter he carried a revolver. Whether he would have used the weapon is open to question but as its acquisition was well publicised, it is not surprising that he had no occasion to do so.

Mr Jones was a strong character and had a keen eye for business. Seeing Tŷ Hen and its outbuildings deserted he seized the opportunity of making use of them. Without delay he installed cows, pigs and hens and soon had a profitable sideline going selling the produce to the villagers. This was somewhat of a blow to the other two farms and caused some heart searching among the villagers as to where their loyalties lay.

With the community growing so fast thought had to be given to providing at hand some form of education for the children. To this end a wooden school was erected halfway between the village and the Barracks. With both school and Chapel now ready, a teacher and Minister were needed so the Company appointed a Minister who also agreed to take on the position of headmaster at the school.

The Chapel proved to be very popular and on Sundays was filled to capacity with not only Nant residents but people from Llithfaen who, having heard of the fine sermons, came to join in the worship and songs of praise. For the minority who were of the Roman Catholic faith a Priest visited the valley on alternate Monday evenings to hold confessionals. The Chapel also played an important part in the Community's social life for there on several evenings during the week prayer meetings, singing practices and Band of Hope meetings took place.

One service which was not provided was a form of hostelry or inn, but this posed no problem as those that felt they needed the liquid refreshment provided by this type of establishment, were happy to make the journey to the Victoria Hotel in Llithfaen. The journey home after a merry evening, and usually in full song, was not as difficult as at other times as once having gained the top of the track it was down hill all the way, and in their state steady legs were not always essential to reach the bottom.

Among those who made regular visits to the 'Vic' were Mr & Mrs Butler who after closing time would be seen unsteadily but merrily making their way home. One winter Saturday, having been shopping in Pwllheli earlier in the day, they called at the 'Vic' on their way home and stayed as usual until closing time. It was bitterly cold and freezing hard as they set off for Nant carrying their shopping in sacks on their backs and well under the influence of an evening's hard drinking. Slithering and sliding they reached the top of the track and began their descent. Reaching the second and steepest bend they stopped to rest on the bank. Having rested a few minutes, Mr Butler, now feeling the severity of the cold, rose unsteadily to his feet and urged his wife to do the same. Mrs Butler, still exhausted, begged him to wait while she rested for just a little longer. Patiently her husband agreed and settled to wait for her. Finally, urging her yet again to make a move and seeing her make no effort to do so, he decided to go on, telling her that he was much too cold to wait any longer and advising her not to delay. Reaching home and still in a befuddled state, he went straight to bed, imagining that his wife would soon join him.

Awaking in the morning with his usual Sunday morning hangover, he was a little angry to see that his wife was not beside him. Dressing hurriedly, he ran downstairs and began searching for her. Finding no sign of her he then recalled the events of the night before. Immediately and with alarm he realised that she must still be somewhere on the mountain and perhaps was lying there injured. Stopping for nothing he rushed off. As he climbed up the track he repeatedly called out her name but to his dismay there was no answering call. Reaching the bend where he had left her he saw to his relief that she was still there, sitting in a huddled position on the bank. He ran towards her and thinking that she was asleep he touched her gently but to his horror she slowly keeled over. Desperately he tried, as best he knew, to revive her but it was far too late, she was frozen stiff and had frozen to death. Not knowing what to do and in shock and utter despair, he picked up her frozen body and, putting it in the sack which had held the shopping, he carried it down to the village. As a result of the tragedy that particular bend from that day forward became knows as Butler's bend and was thought to be haunted by Mrs Butler's ghost. For the children, including my generation, it was an awesome spot to pass after dark.

A large number of the Irish contingent in the community were regular visitors to the 'Vic' and particularly on pay Saturdays when they would liven up any gathering. On these Saturday nights the more sober residents of Llithfaen would stay out of sight and firmly lock their doors well before closing time as some of these men, when having imbibed well over the eight, would in their happy and carefree state be inclined to believe that the world was their friend and was waiting to embrace them. Any refusal or rebuff to sharing their bonhomie would not be taken too kindly but due to the level-headedness of the locals and the general goodwill of the Irish, no unpleasantness did arise and good relations were maintained.

One of their number, a Mr Barlow, having spent an enjoyable evening at the 'Vic', delayed so long in returning home that he was left to make the journey alone. It was a fine night and between scudding clouds the moon shone brightly. All went well until he had travelled some three quarters of the way down the mountain when he saw on the bank ahead of him a figure standing motionless with arms outstretched. He stopped in his tracks and, frozen with fear, he watched the strange and eerie figure. At first he saw no movement and heard not a sound other than the drumming of his fast beating heart and his panting breath. Rooted to the spot he continued watching and then suddenly he was sure that he saw a faint movement of the arms. This sight convinced him that he was in the presence of a ghost and the shock brought instant mobility. He raced back up the mountain at a speed he would never have believed possible. On reaching the first house on the summit he banged on the door and screamed to be let in. Such was the noise that several doors flew open and people rushed out. Mr Barlow, now on the verge of collapse, and gasping for breath, was taken into one of the houses. After being given a drink and regaining a little breath but still pale and shaking with fear, he told the astonished gathering what he had seen, adding that nothing would ever induce him to go back down there again.

Quite some time was spent in calming him down and when it was thought that he was more reasonable two of the men volunteered to accompany him home. At first he would not entertain the idea but after a great deal of persuasion he nervously agreed. The two men set off with Mr Barlow in the middle, apprehensively clutching the arms of his companions. Approaching the spot from where he had observed the apparition, Mr Barlow pulled them back and in a whisper begged them to go no further. His companions, not now so sceptical, hesitated but only for a moment then, telling him to stay where he was, they advanced around the bend. At the same moment the moon came out from behind the clouds and they, too, saw Mr Barlow's ghost. Unlike Mr Barlow, both men were stone sober and so immediately recognised the ghost for what it really was, an inoffensive little hawthorn tree growing innocently on the grassy bank. Unable to control themselves they burst out laughing and, hearing their obvious merriment, Mr Barlow gained sufficient courage to creep forward cautiously. On reaching the dreaded spot one of the men kindly put his arm around his shoulders whilst the other jumped up on to the bank and embraced the little tree to prove to him that there was nothing to fear. However, despite that proof, never again when having had a few drinks would Mr Barlow risk being alone when passing that tree after dark.

News of this night's event was to travel the length and breadth of the peninsula and locally yet another spot on the hill, that had now become known as the Screw Hill, was to achieve fame with the little tree thenceforth being known as Bwgan Barlow, *Barlow's Ghost*. Strange to say that at the time of writing – over ninety years after the event – the little hawthorn still stands proudly on the bank and, stranger still, has not grown one perceptible inch since that night.

During the preparation of this book numerous requests were made for the inclusion of a plea to future planners and owners of the land that the little hawthorn should not be disturbed.

Chapter V

As Time Goes By

The Quarry's output increased as the workings bit deeper into the mountain and this was reflected by the increase in shipping calling at the little Port. Not only were the vessels vital for transporting the granite but at times also useful to the community. On occasions when a ship was known to be Liverpool bound and returning directly to Nant after unloading, some of the women would seize the opportunity to beg a lift. Once in Liverpool they would scurry around the big stores purchasing goods, not only for themselves but also on behalf of their neighbours, spending their hard saved money and taking advantage of the so much greater variety of goods than that available to them in the rural towns back home. Arriving home, they would proudly display their purchases and tell of their journey and the great city, to which the youngsters in particular listened with wide-eyed wonder.

As time passed, houses changed hands and as properties in the village became vacant so families from the Barracks would move in to the better accommodation.

Although the Chapel fulfilled a number of spiritually social needs, the Company decided to provide premises for pastimes during the long winter evenings. Soon afterwards two adjacent houses in Sea View became vacant and as these seemed ideal for the purpose, work began immediately on their adaption. One house was fitted out as a library and reading room, supplying a large selection of books as well as daily and weekly newspapers and the other fitted out as a games room where such games as dominoes, draughts, chess and cards could be played. These premises were a great success and much appreciated.

For some years the wooden school served its people well until one winter's night when a severe north-westerly gale hit the village. Arising the next morning everyone was shocked and dismayed to see that the little building had been ripped from its base and blown to pieces, its broken timbers scattered far and wide. It was obviously irreparable and its loss brought great concern and even sadness to the villagers. The Company was informed immediately and to everyone's relief they promised that another building would be provided as soon as possible. Not long afterwards numbers three and four Mountain View became vacant and, true to their promise, the Company arranged for the two houses to be adapted into one and fitted out as a school.

In the early days postal services to the valley were non-existent so mail had to be collected by the addresses from the Post Office in Llithfaen. With the growing of the community the postal authorities agreed that the numbers were sufficient to warrant a daily service. As a result a letter box was set into the outside wall of the Plas drive and a hut erected between the village and the Barracks for the postman. Everyone was highly excited about the new service and some, wishing to be among the first to receive a delivery, had arranged for letters to be posted in time to arrive on that first day. Certainly the postman must have felt his journey worthwhile when he saw at least half the population on their doorsteps waiting to greet him.

The service, whilst of great advantage to the residents, made for the postman a rather unusual and somewhat difficult round. Having first sorted the mail at Pwllheli he would then cycle the seven miles across the peninsula to Llithfaen, arriving there soon after eight o'clock. His first call was to the Post Office where he would leave his bicycle and some of the mail for that village. Having rested for five minutes he would proceed on foot, delivering mail to the houses en route and would arrive in Nant at about ten o'clock. Considering the journey, his time-keeping was commendable as, whatever the weather, he regularly arrived within a few minutes of that hour. Having completed his delivery in the village he would retire to the little hut to await his next duty at three o'clock. The hut was cosy and compact, housing a seat, a stove and a few cooking utensils and there he would while away the hours reading and producing some fine wood carvings. That waiting time was unavoidable for no-one could have made that journey back and forth twice a day with a deadline of a three o'clock collection in Nant, four o'clock in Llithfaen and be back again in Pwllheli in time for the mail train.

In 1906 Mr Jones left Nant and a Mr Chenall from Buckinghamshire was appointed as Manager. His stay in the village was short as after only about eighteen months he was transferred to another of the Company's quarries. After his departure the Foreman, a Mr Watkin Williams, was promoted to Manager and as a result he and his wife and their three children moved from Bay View and took up residence in the Plas. The new Manager was a popular and just man and life in the valley settled down once more. Under his management a safe was installed in the Plas where the money for subs was deposited so cutting by half the number of journeys to the Bank. Another improvement was the hiring of an hotel room where the wages money could be left whilst he was engaged in paying the Company's bills in the town. Although this did not dispense with the need to carry a revolver, it did relieve him of carrying around large sums of money.

The first birth in the Plas was when their third daughter was born. It was a joyful event and, as with all such events in the village, was welcomed with pleasure. So, too was the arrival of their next child, a little boy. Sadly this baby, when only three months old, fell ill with whooping cough and in only a short time succumbed to the disease. The family's grief, as had been their joy, was shared by everyone.

In 1910 the Prince of Wales was to be invested at Caernarfon Castle. The Manager and his wife dearly wished to be able to witness the ceremony but knew no means of getting there. They then heard that a coach had been hired to leave Llanaelhaearn, a village over three miles away, very early on the morning of the great day and without a second thought promptly reserved seats on it. The fact that to be in Llanaelhaearn on time meant leaving Nant at four o'clock in the morning to walk there did nothing to deter them. Surely, no Prince could wish for more loyal subjects. Whilst they were on the spot paying homage to their Prince, the people of the valley celebrated with a memorable party in his honour.

All went well with the family until December of the following year when it was discovered that the jetty was damaged and in urgent need of repair. To enable the work to be carried out the Company decided to close the quarry whilst one of their employees, a Mr Richard Williams, carried out the repairs. Scaffolding was erected to enable him to reach the damage but, nevertheless, it was no easy task in such an exposed position as the weather had turned bitterly cold with a strong wind causing heavy seas. Although the quarry was at a stop the Manager still had certain duties to attend to and among these was checking that all was well in various parts of the quarry as well as on the jetty.

On the morning of the fourth of December, he set off with his usual large and heavy bunch of keys in his pocket. As he left the house his wife called out to him, saying that as it was such a rough and cold day she would like him to invite Mr Williams to join them for lunch. Her husband promised to do so and with a wave of his hand set off for the quarry.

Having completed his round and checked that all was well, he joined Mr Williams on the scaffolding. The two men had been conversing for only a few minutes when suddenly an enormous wave hit the jetty with such force that the scaffolding collapsed and they were hurled into the sea. The rough sea and their heavy winter clothing made the struggle to save themselves extremely difficult. For the Manager the danger was even greater for he was a non-swimmer and was being pulled down by the weight of the keys in his pocket. The only factor in their favour was that although Mr Richard Williams was not a particularly good swimmer, he was a strong and well-built man. An ex-sailor, he knew only too well that it was imperative to get out of the water as quickly as possible as survival time in such low temperatures was very short. Despite this knowledge and disregarding his own safety, he struck out for the Manager and with seemingly superhuman strength managed to grab him and bring him to one of the jetty piles. From there they were able, with difficulty, to climb up on to the jetty. Resting only to regain their breath and shivering with cold, they hurried in their sorry state for the Plas where Mrs Williams was shocked to see their condition and hear the reason for it. Quickly she provided dry clothing, warmth and nourishment and expressed her gratitude to Mr Williams for saving her husband's life.

The following day the Manager was unable to resume his duties, being confined to bed suffering from what at first appeared to be a heavy chill. Blessed with a loving family he was given every care but, nevertheless, his condition deteriorated. Without delay the Doctor was sent for and he diagnosed pneumonia which in those days, when such life savers as penicillin were undiscovered, was a serious illness. The Doctor did everything possible but in spite of his efforts the battle was lost and because of it the family lost a loving husband and father and the community a just and kindly friend.

Mr Richard Williams's courage and disregard for personal safety did not go unnoticed. A short time afterwards he was awarded a certificate from the Royal Humane Society in recognition of his bravery. Two years after the accident he was suddenly taken ill and suffered a fatal heart attack. Sadly the autopsy showed that the attack had most likely been precipitated by the enormous strain undergone when struggling to save the Manager from drowning.

After the Manager's death the family had to leave Nant and so moved to Pwllheli. To this day the surviving children, some of them now grandparents, like those who left before and after them, still long to return to their beloved valley.

Following their departure the late Manager's brother moved into the Plas as caretaker of both village and quarry. Contrary to expectations, the quarry did not re-open and so the men dispersed to other quarries such as Caernant,

Carreg-y-Llam and Trefor, the latter employing up to nine hundred men. Life went on but with a complete reversal of earlier times for now men went away to work and returned to the valley at the end of the day. The shop and bakehouse closed, the coal ran out in the yard and the last of the Barrack families moved into available houses in the village. Once again the necessities of life had to be carried down the Screw Hill but despite the difficulties most people were content to stay where they were.

Two years later war broke out and so most of the men had to leave the industry to serve in the armed forces. With the hope that the quarry would re-open at the end of the war their families remained in the valley but when peace did come that hope was not realised and again work had to be sought elsewhere.

For some years little changed in the valley until one morning in 1925. There had been torrential rain for some days and as a result the mountain streams overflowed into one another, cascading over the rock face in one enormous waterfall. At Tŷ Canol, Mrs Griffiths, the farmer's wife, was busy churning butter when the Postman arrived with a letter for her young daughter, Rebecca. The letter, together with a certificate and a ten shilling note, was to inform Rebecca that she had been awarded first prize in a Local Education Authority competition for an English essay on hygiene. The family were excitedly discussing the pleasing news with the Postman when suddenly their conversation was disturbed by a loud and ominous rumbling sound coming from the direction of the village. So frightening was it that for a moment no-one moved and in her fear Mrs Griffiths began quoting the Bible. They then realised that, whatever had happened, their help may be needed and so without wasting another moment they ran as fast as they could towards the village. As they approached they saw a large gathering of people a short distance beyond Tŷ Hen. They hurried towards them and then saw to their horror that there was no sign of the Barracks. Unable to believe their eyes, they went further forward and then saw that a large piece of land had broken away from the plateau and had plunged down to an area above the beach, taking the Barracks with it. As everyone gazed with almost disbelief at the now torn and ragged edge, thankful that the buildings had been unoccupied, speculation arose as to whether there would be a further slide and one which may even threaten their homes. Not only were the residents worried but the Company, too, was concerned, to such an extent that a few days later letters arrived warning the householders that, should another landslide occur, the Company would bear no responsibility for their safety; their residency would continue but at their own risk. Understandably, for some years afterwards, whenever heavy rain descended on the valley, everyone was fearful of a further slide and a few people did leave but the majority of those left for reasons other than fear.

It was certainly not from fear that an eighty-five year old stalwart decided to leave in 1929. He was a retired baker and storekeeper whose wife had died in the village many years before and, having taken a fancy to a Llithfaen lady, decided it was time he married again. The lady willingly accepted his proposal and plans for their wedding in Llithfaen went ahead. There was, however, one problem; that of his getting up the Screw Hill. Determined that nothing would stand in his way he solved the problem by hiring a pony to pull him up on a sledge. The marriage took place as planned and the couple were very happy but, sadly, not for long for only a few months later the old man suddenly passed away.

For the stout-hearted that refused to leave the valley, fortune was to turn in their favour for not only were their fears of another landslide proved unfounded but by the turn of the decade the quarry would be open again under new ownership.

Part 2:

Childhood

Chapter VI

Our First Day

I do not remember anything at all about our move from Dorset to North Wales as I was too young at the time. Neither do I remember living at Miss Jones's house Ty'n Parc in Llithfaen whilst the Plas, our new home, was being redecorated and prepared for us. I do, however, remember quite well the day of our move to Nant a few months later. That day for me was the dawn of my awareness and so the beginning of my life.

That beginning was in springtime and was a fine, sunny day. I arrived with my Mother and other members of the family at the top of the Screw Hill and saw that the furniture van was already there and men were busy unloading. It did not seem at all strange to me that as the furniture was unloaded on to the rough track it was then re-loaded on to sledges to which horses were harnessed.

View from the top of the Screw-hill

Panoramic view from top of valley

While the family were busy talking to the men I looked around and, seeing nothing but the mountains and grazing sheep, I wondered where our house was. As I gazed about me, impatient to see our new home, I heard a miaow and saw coming towards us across the heather a very pretty and colourful cat. It reached the track and came up to me purring loudly and began brushing itself back and forth against my leg. It was then I noticed that, unlike the few other cats I had seen, it had no tail. I was trying to draw the family's attention to the new arrival when one of the men picked me up and swung me on to his shoulders.

The next moment we were off down the mountain with the family following behind. Down and down we went, around bend after bend but there was no sign of any house. I could see and hear the water rushing down the crags on the other side of the valley and thought how nice it looked. After what seemed a long time we reached level ground and from there I could see in the distance, nestling at the foot of one of the mountains, a house with outbuildings nearby and surrounded by small, neat fields in which cows were grazing. I called out excitedly that I could see our house but to my disappointment was told that it was not the Plas but was Tŷ Uchaf farm from where we would get our milk.

Continuing our journey we rounded yet more bends and eventually came to a building with its back to us and its roof almost level with the track. This it seemed was Tŷ Canol where there were also cows and where some of the sledge horses lived. As we left Tŷ Canol behind I could see ahead of us a cluster of roofs and beyond them the beautiful blue of the sea.

A glance behind confirmed that the cat was still following us. Now the valley seemed to become wider. We had reached the edge of the village. Up on the bank to our left was a neat red wooden hut. In answer to my question my patient carrier informed me that it was a shop and would be open on the next day when I would be able to buy sweets and many other nice things to eat. We then passed between two stone walls; the one on the left seemed to tower above us and beyond it I could see the roof of a building. This he told me was the Chapel and also the school, in front of which was a yard where the children played at playtime. The other wall surrounded a fine-looking house and neat garden. At last this must be our house but, no, it was not; it was Bay View. A few yards further and we came out into the open again. Now I could see all the houses and on our immediate right a little iron gate which opened into the village. On the other side of the gate was a well-worn footpath which led past Bay View and Sea View terrace to the little village square and from there turned left along Mountain View. In front of the houses were neat flower gardens and opposite, across the footpath, were vegetable gardens, each with its own little gate. At the lower end of Mountain View was a high wall beyond which stood a large house and at last I was told that this was the Plas.

Leaving the village gate we continued our journey, skirting a small field, until we reached a large white iron gate and standing there awaiting us were some children. My carrier gently lifted me down from his shoulders and as he did so a big boy stepped forward and handed me a bunch of pink flowers. My Mother, now at hand, spoke to the children and thanked the boy for his kindness. In answer to her enquiry he shyly told her that his name was Robin Ellis Williams and that he lived in the village. The gate was then politely opened for us by the children and we entered a wide drive-way flanked by grass verges on which grew tall pines with here and there a number of privet and May bushes. The May was in full bloom and was so bright and welcoming. Releasing my Mother's hand, I ran along the drive and,

Plas y Nant

rounding a corner, saw my Father coming out of the house to meet us.

We entered the house and inside were greeted by two young women who had prepared tea and sandwiches for us. Having eaten and drunk as much as I could, I began exploring the house. It was great fun rushing from room to room. At the end of the hall on the right was a funny door, not at all like other doors. It was dark green and warm to my touch and all round the edges were large, round, shiny studs. I pushed it open and, going through, found myself in a small area with two doors leading from it. I tried the first and saw that it opened on to a flight of stairs. It was very dark there so I did not venture further. The other led to the kitchen so I decided to take a look in there.

The kitchen was large and I noticed above the door a lot of bells with numbers beneath them. I asked what they were for and was told that there was a bell for each room and when a button was pressed in any one room, that bell would ring in the kitchen and the maid, by looking at the number, would know where she was wanted. I immediately went to one of the rooms, found a button and pressed it then waited. To my disappointment nothing happened and no-one came so I ran back to the kitchen where I was told that they did not work at the moment.

Losing interest in the bells, I left the kitchen and entered a smaller room where there was sink and taps. This was the scullery and it was most uninteresting but there was another door which was ajar and well worth investigating. Pulling the door open, I stepped through and found myself in a large area which was enclosed on three sides. To my right was the driveway and facing me was a very high wall with a door in it and what seemed to be the end of a house. This I realised later was the gable end of number eleven Mountain View. I tried the door but it was bolted so turned my attention to the left where the wall continued and noticed that in the wall was a large, square hole. I ran to look through but it was too high. After several attempts to reach it and painfully scraping my knees in the process, I gave up the struggle. There was, however, still another door worthy of my interest and luckily it was wide open. I went through and on the other side found a row of four small outbuildings. Poking my nose into the first, I saw only a large amount of coal. The second and third were empty and very dusty; nothing interesting there. I was, therefore, surprised to see that the last was exceptionally clean, with snow-white walls. It, too, was empty except for a long sort of wooden box running along its length. The box I thought must be a seat but then I noticed that in the middle of the seat was a large round hole. Immediately curious, I climbed up on to the box and peered down the hole and there, to my surprise, saw a large bucket. I could not imagine what it was doing there but then came to the conclusion that someone must have hidden it there. Feeling that I had discovered something important, I excitedly thought of how surprised everyone would be when I told them about it.

Having exhausted my exploration of the outhouses, I retraced my steps and turned into the garden. The garden extended around three sides of the house and along the high wall surrounding it were some peculiarly shaped trees growing flat against the wall. Some months later I was to enjoy the apples and pears produced by these trees. Sloping down from the house were lawns and below them the vegetable and fruit garden. Overlooking the lawn, between two bay windows, was a solid stone seat with a stone back rest so I climbed up and sat on it but it was too hard and too cold to stay on it for long. Lastly, at the far side of the vegetable garden was a large, somewhat rough, grassy area where sometime later my youngest brother was to keep his pet rabbit and, later still, a mini-tragedy was to take place.

Looking up at the house, I realised that I had not yet been upstairs and so returned indoors immediately. Inside seemed to be all noise and bustle so, quickly getting out of the way, I made for the stairs. Up on the landing were several doors. As I looked into each room, the same scene presented itself; nothing but a lot of jumbled-up furniture. There were even boxes in the bathroom. Obviously there was nothing exciting up there so I returned downstairs.

With nothing much left to explore, I looked for my Mother and found her in the kitchen. She was talking to one of the young women who had earlier given us the tea and sandwiches. Seeing me come in, my Mother introduced me, saying that the young woman's name was Lizzie and that she was to be our maid and would live with us. I thought it was a very good idea as Lizzie looked very nice and perhaps she would play with me sometimes.

The hours passed by, interspersed with stand-up snacks

and drinks of milk. I was tiring but determined not to show it as someone may have remembered that it was well past my bedtime and because of it I may have missed something vital. By nightfall the last load had been unloaded and everyone agreed that only a meal and a night's rest would restore the energy needed on the next day to make order out of the remaining chaos. Soon afterwards Lizzie brought in our meal and we sat down to enjoy it.

It was whilst we were enjoying the meal that the dining room door slowly opened and in walked the cat, miaowing softly. In my earlier excitement I had completely forgotten about her. Now I tried to tell everyone that she had followed us but it was unnecessary as my Mother had also noticed her on the mountain. I asked why she had no tail and was told that it was because she was a Manx cat, which meant that she came from the Isle of Man. I wondered where the Isle of Man was but thought it better not to pursue that as, far more important, I wanted to know whether we could keep her. In reply to my question my Mother said that as she seemed to have moved in already she had better stay.

The cat soon settled down as a member of the family and answered to the name of Puss. Enquiries were made as to any previous owners but nothing could be discovered about her origin. She certainly was not house-trained but she soon became accustomed to her own toilet facilities. No training was necessary for hunting mice and she well earned her keep in this way. A box lined with a piece of blanket was provided as a bed but, despite all encouragement and enticement, she ignored it, choosing her own sleeping quarters when the lower door of the airing cupboard next to the kitchen range was left open. Several attempts were made to evict her but all ended in failure.

Some months after her arrival she began spending more and more time in the cupboard and one morning Lizzie informed us that Puss had given birth to four kittens. We all rushed to the kitchen and there she lay, purring proudly. They were tortoiseshell, exactly like their mother and one was ginger. My Father said that it would be impossible to keep them so homes would have to be found for them as soon as they were old enough to leave their mother. This litter was the first of dozens of litters in the years to come.

Puss stayed with us until the day we left Nant. On that day she left the valley with us but on our arrival at the top of the Screw Hill, much to our sorrow, she suddenly and mysteriously disappeared and despite our searching and calling she was nowhere to be found. She was never seen again. Having come from nowhere on our first day, she had seemingly returned there on our last.

Chapter VII

Settling In

The house now became our home and was comfortable and cosy. Downstairs was the dining room, the lounge, breakfast room, a room with cupboards along the length of one wall, which was the larder and beyond the green baize door, the kitchen and scullery. The breakfast room was allocated to my eldest brother, William Stanley, and his wife, Ethel, to serve as their lounge/diner and it was made very clear to me that, should I wish to enter that room, I must always knock first and wait for an answer and also that this was not to happen too often.

Upstairs were five bedrooms, the bathroom and lavatory. I was not at first allowed a bedroom of my own as a short time before I had developed a habit of sleep-walking. Lizzie occupied the bedroom at the farthest end of the landing and I later discovered that she had been given a key to protect her privacy from me. This cleared up the mystery of why I had always failed to open it.

The next few weeks were filled with activity for the grown-ups in settling in to our new home so no exact pattern was formed. I, too, was not inactive for there were many new things to do and see. One of my first impressions was walking up to the sounds of sheep and lambs bleating, getting out of bed and struggling up on to the window sill to see through the bedroom window the many sheep and gambolling lambs in the big field on the other side of our garden wall. Going out into the drive, I could hear the sound of children playing but, because of the high walls, I could not see them. I longed to play with them but was told that I was not yet big enough.

A few days after moving in, my Father took me along the drive and showed me the stone stile that went over the wall and down into the big field. We climbed over and I was able to see the sheep and lambs at close quarters. I wanted so much to pick up the lambs but at each attempt they moved just out of reach. Some children were playing there and my Father spoke to them but I did not understand anything he said or their replies. He then asked me to say hello to them but I was too shy to utter a word. We left the children and crossed to the farthest end of the field. There the edge of the field was ragged and dropped sharply away to a shelf lower down and lower still was the beach. In the distance to our left and just above the beach was a building that looked like a small, neat house with a chimney and which reminded me of an ink bottle. Pointing to it, my Father said that it was the office where he worked. Almost opposite the office was a long, wooden structure running out into the see and this he told me was the jetty where the ships came to collect the stone from the quarry.

So many things were strange to me and some were

frightening. The first time I heard the hooter sound, followed by big bangs coming from the direction of the quarry, I raced breathlessly indoors where my Mother calmed my fears, saying that there was no need to be frightened. She went on to explain that the bangs were caused by things like fireworks used by the men in the quarry to break big rocks away from the mountain-side, adding that it was only dangerous when anyone went too near when they were blasting. To ensure that no-one did, the hooter was sounded and a red flag was hoisted on a pole with a warning beneath it, saying that no-one should proceed further than that point. When it was safe, the hooter would sound again and the flag would be taken down. She then took me upstairs and through the bedroom window I could see the flag not far away.

We had not been in Nant many weeks when I was presented with a lovely little puppy by one of the men from the village. After much thought, it was decided that the name Mickey suited him best. Mickey was mainly terrier with a slight sprinkling of 'fifty-seven varieties'. He was an independent little character from the start with a ginger coat, pointed ears and a tail that curled permanently upwards. I was thrilled with him but Puss, despite his playful advances, did not at all appreciate the newcomer and after a few hefty cuffs from her he gave up his efforts to be friendly. What did concern me was that whenever I wanted to play with him, he ran away from me. As the weeks went by, he began growling every time I went near and it became clear that the only person he was interested in was my brother, Will. A short time afterwards he moved permanently into the breakfast room and from that time on left Will's side only when forced to do so and after much protest. Even Ethel was only just tolerated by him. Until he died, fourteen years later, he remained Will's faithful and constant companion.

It was during this time that I discovered that the little red hut, George Matt's shop, was not the only shop in the village. There was another, known as Evan Wynne's shop. This one was at number ten Mountain View and was rented solely for that purpose. Evan Wynne's opened not only on Tuesdays, as did George Matt's, but Fridays and Saturdays as well.

My first visits to the shops were accompanied by my Mother and what wonders I beheld there. At Evan Wynne's there were shelves all around the walls laden with all kinds of goods; tins with attractive pictures of their contents, bottles of all shapes and sizes, colourful packets and a variety of exciting-looking boxes. On the floor stood large packing cases with shiny silver linings, containing brown and white loaves which gave out the most appetising smell. Near the packing cases were several tins of biscuits with glass lids, through which I could see the different varieties. Here and there on the walls hung large cards, attached to which were numerous small bottles, tins and packets. These, I learned, contained pills, medicines, iodine, powders, vaseline and other ointments. The soothing vaseline and stinging iodine I was already well acquainted with.

At both establishments the wooden counters were rather high and particularly Evan Wynne's but by standing on tip-toe and grasping the edge, I could just see on top. At the end of his counter were huge pieces of cheese, lumps of butter and lard. To cut the cheese he used a long wire with a piece of wood at the end which he pulled down through the cheese. Also on the counter was a large object with buttons at the front. Every time he pressed the buttons a bell rang and a drawer at the bottom flew open, into which he then put our money. This, I was told, was a till. George Matt had a different and much smaller till, more like a box with a drawer at the bottom and a slit at the top where he would write something then turn a handle every time he wanted to open the drawer.

On both counters were machines that had two flat plates suspended by chains from a long bar and next to the machines were kept some round, metal objects of varying sizes. The purchase was placed on one plate whilst on the other the round objects were tried in turn until the two moved to the same level. These, I discovered, were scales but it was some time before I could understand why both men had never learned to pick up the correct weight first instead of having to try several before choosing the right one.

It was also quite some time before I learned that George Matt was, in fact, a Mr George Williams but had become known as such because his uncle, who owned the shop, was a Mathew Williams. This means of identification was, and still is, common practice in some areas of Wales where so few surnames are shared by so many. In Mr Owen's case the use of his forenames, Evan Wynne, solved the problem.

The most interesting part of the shops for me were the shelves that held the large bottles and boxes of sweets and chocolates. In the bottles were sweets of every kind and in the boxes were lollipops of all colours, liquorice in a variety of shapes such as pipes with red ends meant to resemble burning tobacco, shoe laces, wheels with a coloured sweet in the middle, bars and hard sticks. Chocolate also in many shapes, sherbert dabs, bars of nougat and what, in fact, to me was every kind of sweet and chocolate imaginable. With such great variety, choosing the best and largest quantity that I could get for my penny was an important and lengthy business and often involved several changes of mind. Fortunately both men were kind and patient and so allowed me as much time as I wanted to make the final decision.

My youngest brother Garnie, or Ces as he became

known in the village, was due to start at the village school soon after our move. He was not at all keen on the idea, having had an unhappy term or two in Llithfaen school while we were at Ty'n Parc. That unhappiness had been due to the fact that he did not understand the language and was made worse because he had attended the school wearing the uniform of his previous school, a private school in Dorset. The uniform itself may well have been accepted by the children had it not been for the head-gear which was a beret. Never before in that locality had a boy been seen wearing such a thing and to them it meant that he must be a sissy. The result was that he was constantly teased and tormented. In the light of that experience, small wonder that he was not willing to expose himself to a repeat performance at Nant. The dreaded day arrived, however, and he had to go but at least by this time a new cap had replaced the offending beret.

On his return at lunch time we were most surprised to hear him whistling happily as he ran along the drive. The moment he came in, it was obvious that all had gone well and he lost no time in telling us about it. It had been a wonderful morning. Everyone had been very nice to him and he had made hundreds of friends – a miraculous feat as the school's compliment at the most was no more than twenty-five. The teacher was a Miss Lewis and was the prettiest and kindest teacher he had ever seen. So anxious was he to return that the moment he had finished his dinner, he rushed off, calling as he went that it was all due to his new cap which matched the other boys' caps. No mention was made of the language difficulty and to my parents' relief, he was never again reluctant to attend school.

The next addition to the family was to be a six weeks old Collie puppy. Any thoughts I may have had that he was to be mine were soon dismissed when I was told that he was to be the family's guard dog. Unlike Mickey, he was to live outside so a fine kennel was made for him by Johnny Price, the Company joiner. The kennel was placed at the house end of the drive and half filled with straw and hay to await its new occupant.

The puppy eventually arrived and turned out to be a little, fat ball of black fur with a beautiful white ruff and white paws. He soon settled down in his new home which then left only one problem, that of choosing a name for him. Several suggestions were made but could not be agreed upon and this in spite of the fact that I thought that some of mine were particularly good. Finally, but for no reason that I could see, the name Moss was chosen.

Moss grew a great deal faster than I and in no time had surpassed me in height. When standing on his back legs to put his paws affectionately on my shoulders, as he often did, he towered above me. On one occasion after a heavy shower, becoming over enthusiastic, he jumped up as usual but this time knocked me face down into a squelchy patch of mud. Realising what he had done and instantly concerned, he did his best to pick me up by sinking his teeth into my jumper and pulling whilst in between barking to attract attention. His efforts did bring my Mother rushing out but also tore my jumper in several places. However, his motives were understood and so all as well.

Puss, surprisingly, made instant friends with him, spending many hours sleeping by his side but Mickey, with his usual aloofness, took a little longer. When he did eventually decide to relax his reserve, the two dogs became firm friends.

As a guard dog his qualities were unquestionable for not only did he alert the whole household the moment a stranger set foot on the property but also quickly sent off those who were unwelcome. An example of this occurred one afternoon when three gypsies, two men and a woman, came walking down the drive. Moss, as usual, barked furiously until my mother came to the door then, seeing her talking to them, he settled down quietly to watch.

The gypsies, having successfully sold my Mother some pegs and lace, then asked for a sum of money. My Mother refused and began to close the door, but as she did so, one of the men pushed against it whilst the other raised his hand in attempt to strike her. Before he could deliver the blow, Moss although firmly chained to his kennel, came rushing towards them, hair standing up on his back, barking and snarling, with teeth bared and his kennel dragging behind. Immediately frightened, the gypsies turned and ran up the drive with Moss and his kennel in hot pursuit. Only when they were all clear of the gate did he stop and, having satisfied himself that they were not returning, he settled down to await removal back to his usual site. This was done when my father and Will returned home, as the kennel was too heavy for the ladies of the household.

With the growing season well advanced, our garden was in danger of becoming a wilderness, and so it was arranged that Mr Rowland Davies from Sea View would look after it. Mr Davies was a strong-looking man who sported a large, white moustache. He turned out to be an excellent gardener, growing most of the vegetables we needed and caring for the fruit trees and bushes. He was friendly and had a ready smile, but I was later to find that when it came to what my friends and I considered was fruit-picking time, but in his opinion was weeks too early, he was capable of getting very angry, and so was a man to be respected, especially as my father always favoured his point of view.

Slowly I got to know the families in the village, but I was confused when, although I understood what they said to me, I did not at all understand them when they spoke to each other. By the time I realised that this was because they were speaking in Welsh, I was beginning to speak and understand the language myself.

By this time we were into our first summer in the valley. At this time of the year the beach was the most popular place for the children and Garnie and I were no exception. He, of course, was old enough to go with his friends whenever he liked and had the advantage of being taken with the other children by Miss Lewis during term-time. As a result, he soon learned to swim, I too, was lucky in that my sister-in-law, Ethel, was a keen swimmer and did not need much encouragement to take me with her.

Going to the beach had many attractions for me. There was the walk down the rough, winding track, stepping off the track as we often did among the rocks and bracken where on occasions we momentarily caught a glimpse of an adder basking on the hot stones, the next moment to be gone, slithering silently away. Newts and frogs too, were common in this area. When our beach outing included a picnic, so delaying our return until early evening, we frequently caught sight of weasels moving about among the rocks. At times they would sit up on their hind quarters, staring motionlessly at us and showing to the full their snow-white underparts.

Also on our route was the Crusher, where the stone was crushed and where Will worked while Mickey sat outside throughout the day, waiting to accompany him home. We usually called in to have a word with Will and the other men, but did not stay long as it was a very noisy and dusty place and one had to shout to be heard. The only interest there for me was to watch him when he was acetylene welding. The large, dark green glasses he wore and which made him look so strange, and the rainbow coloured sparks that showered all over the place, never failed to fascinate me.

The next and biggest attraction was calling at the office where I would see my Father, Mr Lewis and Richard. Mr Lewis was the shipping clerk. He was short in stature and because of it was endearingly known to everyone as Lewis Bach. Richard was a trainee and among his tasks was the job of coming up to our house at mid-morning to collect my Father's lunch, so I got to know him quite well and looked forward to his daily visits.

Mr Lewis was very kind to me and, on reflection, I realise also most tolerant, for my arrival surely could not have filled him with joy. Within minutes I would want to use the typewriter and my ever indulgent Father would go into the outer office to ask if I could 'have a go soon'. Invariably, 'soon' was almost at once and even though at times he would be busy using the machine himself, he never once refused me, but with a smile allowed me to 'have a go'. Having exhausted my enthusiasm for the typewriter, there was always plenty of paper and pencils to amuse myself with, as well as the rubber stamps with their outlines of ships and important-looking numbers which I later discovered were tonnages.

Eventually Ethel would become impatient to get to the beach, which was only a few yards down the bank, so we would take leave of the office. She did not have to worry about my safety while she swam as there were always a number of children there with whom I could play and as two of the office windows overlooked the sea, some supervision was also carried out from there.

One of the most enchanting sights I have ever seen took place on that beach and was brought about by a group of young mothers from the village. On some fine afternoons during the summer months, these young women, carrying their babies in shawls wound round their bodies, would come down to the beach and, whilst there, would sing lullabies as they strolled along. So fine were their voices and their harmony that the air seemed to fill with melodious music and those of us on the beach would stop whatever we were doing to listen.

We humans were not the only appreciative audience for, no sooner had the singing begun than the water around Birds Rock erupted with activity and within moments a number of bobbing heads would be seen, hastily making for the shore. These were the grey seals from the colony on the ledges at the foot of that headland and, attracted by the melodious sound drifting across the water, would come rushing in to the shallows.

Having come as close in as they dared, they would then turn and swim abreast of the singers, while all the time seeming to be listening intently. This procession on the beach and its counterpart in the water would continue until the young women tired and turned for home. As they left the beach, the seals, with their large, soulful eyes, would watch until they were out of sight then, as one, themselves turn and disappear.

Another advantage of being on the beach was able to see the ships come in to the jetty and watch them being loaded. My first sight of them had been from the bedroom windows as they steamed across the bay, but that could in no way compare with seeing them at close quarters. The ultimate came later when, on several occasions, my father took me aboard the vessels. Little did I realise then how important those vessels were to our livelihood and if, for any reason, they stopped coming, then our life in the valley would come to an end.

Chapter VIII

Jacqueline

It was sometime in mid-summer that Jacqueline joined us. I do not remember her surname, but I do remember very clearly her stay with us, that she was in her early twenties and was the daughter of a French Army officer. She had come to this country to further her knowledge of the English language and, deciding that this would be best accomplished in a family situation, took up the position of Governess to the children of Carreg-y-Llam's quarry manager, Carreg-y-Llam being Nant's sister quarry half a mile south of us along the beach. When those children left for boarding school it was arranged that Jacqueline would come to us.

Any addition to the family was always popular with me, but when I was told that her coming was solely for my benefit, I was a little apprehensive as I was not sure what it would mean. As far as I could see we already had enough grown-ups in the house and so another one could well mean an extension of the do's and don'ts that were becoming so familiar to me. In particular, those involved with washing my hands and cleaning my teeth so frequently that those parts of me were in danger of wearing away, the eating of large portions of those things which were not very nice but which I was told would do me good and even make my hair curl, while on the other hand, those that were delicious were allowed only in limited quantities because it seemed they would ruin my teeth and stunt my growth. Ethel had already begun making remarks such as, 'This child should improve once Jacqueline takes a hand,' so all in all, I was not looking forward to the lady's arrival.

The moment I set eyes on Jacqueline my apprehension melted away and I took an instant liking to her. She was young and pretty and although she spoke in a peculiar way I quite liked it. We very quickly made friends and she proved to be a wonderful companion. No longer did I have to amuse myself and wait for my mother or Ethel to take me out, for Jacqueline spent almost all her time with me. She took me for long walks and for picnics, and while on those walks, told me many stories and also told me about her home and family in Paris. There were also frequent outings to the beach as she was a keen and proficient swimmer and when no-one was on the jetty, she would thrill me by diving off the end. She, like Ethel had done, tried to teach me to swim but to her disappointment, her efforts were in vain.

Included in Jacqueline's duties was the task of teaching me some basic conversational French. In this, too, she proved to be proficient for in just a short time I was able to string together a few simple sentences and not long afterwards to carry on a limited conversation with her. Ethel was particularly pleased about it as, having finished her education in France, she was fairly fluent in that language and so looked forward to being able to make use of it with me. Regrettably, after Jacqueline left I soon forgot most of what I had learned and the little I did retain, such as the French song, 'Apres le guerre finis', the roundelay, 'Frere Jacques', together with, 'le cheval est noir', and the same description of a cow, did nothing to help me when I later began studying the language at school. Ethel did attempt to further that earlier grounding but, not being blessed with infinite patience and dogged by the disadvantage of being just a sister-in-law, she did not really stand a fair chance.

During Jacqueline's stay with us we discovered that not only was she pretty but also had a kind and sensitive nature and a deep sense of spiritual faith. This became apparent in so many ways and none less than when she heard of the death of Mr and Mrs Hughes, Tŷ Uchaf's baby son. She immediately went to the farm to offer her condolences and whilst there asked the family's permission to offer up a prayer for the departed's little soul. So touched were they by her sincerity and the understanding of one so young, that they not only agreed but joined her as she knelt to pray.

One of her possessions which greatly impressed me was a fine-looking tennis racquet and frame. I told her that as soon as I was old enough I hoped to have one like it and I would learn to play the game. To my delight she said that she would teach me, and so a small racquet was bought for me by my mother. The lessons, which I thoroughly enjoyed, took place in the drive but, because of my early years and corresponding size, her efforts were not a resounding success. However, to her credit, she did achieve a condition whereby I invariably managed to return the ball in her general direction and she also taught me the rudiments of scoring which I used to the full when she was in doubt. Recognising that my interest was not temporary, she promised that when the time came for her to leave, she would give me her racquet and frame as a momento. That time was to come much sooner than any of us expected but, nevertheless, she kept her promise. Regrettably and much to my sorrow, I was not to own that racquet and frame for as long as I had imagined.

When Jacqueline had been with us for some four months or so, a letter arrived from her home, telling her that her father was very ill and requesting that she returned home. She left on the next day and I believe that she was sorry to leave. We were certainly sorry to see her go. Some correspondence passed between her and my parents for some time after she left, but eventually contact was lost. Over the years I have often thought about her and wondered what became of her. I sincerely hope that she survived the last war and that all went well for her.

Chapter IX

A Minor Challenge

Visits to Pwllheli were necessary for the family from time to time. I had not been included in the outings as it was considered that the climb up the Screw Hill, followed by another walk of over half a mile from the mountain top to Llithfaen to catch the bus would be too much for me. At first I had no desire to go, but with Jacqueline gone and autumn well advanced, so putting paid to beach outings, I became keen to accompany my mother and Ethel. They, on the other hand, were not at all keen to take me but, after much pleading by me and warnings by them that no-one would carry me, they agreed to let me try it.

We set off almost an hour and a half before the bus was due to leave, with me marching confidently along in front. After what seemed a long walk, we reached the bottom of the Screw Hill and began the climb up the wide, stony track.

I did not know at the time that the gradient was approximately one in three but I soon found out how steep it was and how sharp the numerous bends were.

It was when I reached the second bend that I realized why they had been reluctant to take me with them. By this time I was puffing and panting and my legs ached so much that I could not take another step so I flopped down on to the grassy bank at the side of the track. My enthusiasm began to wane, perhaps I did not want to go after all. I turned to tell the others and was surprised to see that they had also stopped and were still only at the first bend. By the time they joined me I had regained my breath and the aches in my legs had gone so, with renewed enthusiasm, I attempted the next bit of the hill.

I achieved a further two stretches before once more being forced to stop. Looking down and seeing that my Mother and Ethel were only then beginning on the next stage, my confidence began to return. Perhaps it would be possible after all for me to gain the top without their assistance. Spurred on by this thought, I set off once more, but this time managed only one stretch and one bend before having to rest. I was about to move off again when I heard a sort of rumbling and screeching sound coming from somewhere above. I looked up but could see nothing, yet the sounds seemed to be coming nearer. Suddenly, from around the next bend, a man came into sight, followed by a horse which was pulling a sledge. Not wishing to pass him on my own, I decided to wait for my Mother and Ethel. The man approached and I then saw that he was Mr Thomas, Tŷ Canol. Smiling pleasantly, he spoke to me and then exchanged a few words with the ladies who by that time had joined us. While they were busy talking I noticed that the sledge was the same as the one used to carry our furniture. It was made of wood, with a perfectly flat surface and running along underneath were strips of something very shiny. Neatly stacked on the sledge were several bags of coal which Mr Thomas was delivering to the village. Bidding him farewell, we continued our climb and as the sledge moved away, I again heard the screeching sound and, involuntarily, my teeth clenched and my hands flew up to cover my ears. On asking my Mother what caused it, she explained that it happened when the metal runners passed over a grit-covered stone. It was a horrible sound and, despite passing the sledge hundreds of times over the years, I was never able to overcome the effect of that screeching.

The short respite whilst talking to Mr Thomas had refreshed us and with renewed vigour we tackled the next two bends. Another short rest and then came a long stretch, but here the surface changed. No longer was it rock-strewn but much smoother and grey-blue in colour, composed mainly of large areas of slate. The slate was ridged here and there and along the mountain side of the track was a narrow ditch. Having rained fairly heavily a few hours earlier, the water in the ditch overflowed in some places and washed over the surface. My Mother remarked that it would be a very treacherous place in the winter.

The next bend was the steepest and sharpest of all and took a great deal of effort. This was the infamous Butler's bend. Having rounded Butler's bend, we faced another long haul. Although not quite as steep as the others, it seemed just as difficult as we were tiring but, determinedly, we carried on and turned the final bend. At last we had reached the top of the Screw Hill. Ahead of us the track continued, but was now almost level. We reached the stone boundary walls and passed between them. All around us was the heather, no longer green as I had first seen it, but turning brown with patches here and there of pink and purple, like little islands of colour in a dark sea.

On we trudged but to my dismay, the track began to slope uphill again. I had just decided that it would never end when suddenly the rough surface gave way to a smooth tarmacadam. Ahead of us, at the side of the road, was a row of cottages and this was the summit of our route. From the cottages it was downhill all the way to Llithfaen square.

We finally arrived at the square with several minutes to spare. As we stood there, waiting for the bus, a car and then a lorry sped past and I gazed at them with wonder. It had been such a long time since I had seen such things that I had almost forgotten they existed. Quite soon the bus arrived and we climbed aboard. The relief of sitting on that bus seat is something I will never forget for I was so tired, but I was also triumphant for I had made it and made it on my own two legs.

Chapter X

Winter Residents

Autumn faded and we were into our first winter in the valley. The change around us was dramatic. Where before the mountain slopes had been lush and green, with the gradual change through the shades to gold and brown, they now suddenly became stark and forbidding. Even the hardy and tenacious sheep were deserting them for the richer pastures and shelter of the valley. It was during this time that I witnessed an event that I was to look forward to thereafter every winter in Nant.

One afternoon Lizzie called me to the dining room window and, pointing to the top of 'Benclog', the mountain directly opposite, she asked me if I could see anything unusual. I looked up to where she pointed and there, silhouetted against the skyline, saw a largish, horned animal. I immediately wanted to know what it was and was told that it was a wild mountain goat.

While we stood watching, my Mother joined us and she, too, became interested. Some moments later, and seemingly for no apparent reason, as the weather was fine and clear, Lizzie remarked that bad weather must be on the way. My Mother, somewhat surprised by such a positive statement, asked her whatever made her say that. Lizzie, in reply, explained that every year, about this time, a herd of wild goats came to shelter in the valley and their arrival was a sure sign that bad weather was about to break on the mountains. She went on to say that the goat looking down on us would, without doubt, be their leader, a Billy goat that came in advance of the herd to observe the situation below and satisfy himself that there was no danger. She then added that if we were patient, we would eventually see him turn away and disappear, then re-appear a short time later with the herd.

This, I thought was very exciting and so I settled down to await events. The minutes ticked by but the goat did not make a move. I had just decided that it was never going to do so when, suddenly, it turned and disappeared from sight. Patiently and then impatiently, I waited for his return. I was about to give up my vigil when, to my delight, and just as Lizzie had predicted, he re-appeared, accompanied by several other goats. The newcomers were smaller than he and as each one came into sight, it took up position slightly behind him. I now became very excited, expecting to see them make their way down but, aggravatingly, they made no further move. Once again the Billy stood motionless, studying the valley. Time seemed to mean nothing to him until, finally, he seemed satisfied that all was well and he began the descent. Skilfully picking his way down between the rocks and boulders, he reached a ledge, where he stopped and again contemplated the valley. The herd made no attempt to follow him but remained on top, watching his every move. The Billy then turned and looked up at them and, as if by some signal, the herd, in order of size, with the smallest bringing up the rear, began moving down. When they had all gathered safely on the ledge, the performance was repeated in stages, exactly as before, until they reached the greenery on the lower slopes where they began grazing.

Now that they were so much nearer, I could see that some were brown, some white, whilst the others were a mixture of brown, black and white. The Billy was mainly white and was a magnificent animal with large, beautifully curved horns. Lizzie then told us that they would stay in the valley until their kids were born in the spring. Then as the days grew warmer and new growth spread slowly up and across the mountains, so the goats would follow the new pasture until, eventually, they would disappear from sight.

Occasionally during the summer months they would be seen among the rocks and crags on the higher slopes, but generally they disappeared and no-one seemed to know exactly where they were or how far they roamed. Wherever they spent their time, it was certain that the following winter, just before the onset of bad weather, a lone Billy would again appear on top of Benclog to view the situation before once again leading the herd down to the valley.

Lizzie's weather forecast proved to be accurate. Only two days later we awoke to see the surrounding peaks capped with the first snow of the winter, and the arrival of the goats each succeeding winter was as accurate a weather report as anyone could have forecast.

The goats had been coming to Nant for as long as anyone could remember. Despite the opening of the quarry and its noisy activities, the building of the houses and subsequent growth of the population, they continued to come and go in their quiet way, seemingly oblivious of mankind and his industry. But mankind was not oblivious of them and on occasions made good use of them.

Before my time in the valley, it was customary on occasions to shoot one or two of the goats. This was not done haphazardly and was usually carried out by Gwilym Hughes, Tŷ Uchaf, accompanied by his friend, Dafydd John Davies, from the village. Having accomplished the task, they then took the goats to the farm. There the meat, which was considered to be a delicacy, was cut up for sharing with the villagers and the fat kept by Gwilym's mother who rendered it down to make candles.

The candles were made in moulds which she bought from the tinkers who periodically came to the valley. Her method was simple and efficient and required only the moulds, some turnips, wicks and some nails. Having first made a hole in the centre of a turnip and threading a wick through it, she then fitted the mould upside down in the hole. This allowed the wick to pass through to the other end, where it was held in position by a nail resting across the top. With those preparations complete, she then poured in the melted fat and left it to set. Candle-making time at the farm was considered by the village children to be something of a social event so there was never a shortage of volunteers. With their help, hundreds of candles were produced and usually sufficient to last throughout the winter.

Dafydd John Davies's earlier experiences with goats was to gain him a pint of beer many years later when, as a member of the Merchant Navy, he was aboard a ship berthed at Constantinople. This is the story as he told it to me. It came about when he and his shipmates were collecting their dinner from the galley. As Dafydd John stepped forward with his plate, the cook/steward, who was busy carving a tender joint, remarked that he was sure that the meat would be enjoyed that day as it was an exceptionally fine piece of mutton. Dafydd John, taking a closer look at the joint and recognising what it was, immediately contradicted him, saying that it was certainly not mutton and never would be. It was goat's meat. The cook/steward, his face turning crimson, looked around to see whether anyone else had heard and then, looking extremely uncomfortable, signalled to Dafydd John to keep his voice down. Nothing more was said and Dafydd John left to eat this dinner. Some minutes later the cook/steward joined him and in a whisper asked him how he had known that it was goat's meat. Dafydd John replied that he would share his secret with him in return for a pint of beer when they went ashore.

That evening the two men met ashore and the cook/steward ordered two pints of Turkish beer. Handing one to his companion, he asked him to 'Spill the beans'. Dafydd John then explained to him that goats have double knee-caps, whereas sheep have not and he had recognised that part of the animal as the joint was being carved. He went on to say that the double knee-cap afforded protection for the goat when, in the event of it falling forward, only the upper joint would lock, so preventing its head hitting the ground. On the other hand, when grazing and in need of close contact with the ground, both joints would come into action. The cook/steward, having listened with interest, then begged him not to tell anyone on board as there would surely be trouble if the crew discovered what they had eaten, despite the fact that some had asked for a second helping. Dafydd John, with a smile, promised him that his lips were sealed.

During my years in Nant, I remember only one goat being shot and that was when Will shot one of the Billies, his purpose being to acquire the skin, but the moment the deed was done, he was filled with remorse and the rest of the family were not very pleased either. However, it was too late for regrets so he had no alternative but to skin the unfortunate animal. After quite some time, the successful cured skin became an elegant rug, but was not used as planned to grace Will and Ethel's domain. Instead we had to have it in the lounge as Will did not care to be reminded of his deed. Fortunately, this was not common practice and the goats survived to roam the valley every winter to this day.

Chapter XI

Starting School

As the days grew shorter and winter took a hold, going out to play in the drive and in the garden was restricted and I became very lonely. True, there was always someone to talk to but they were grown-ups. Even Garnie was not much company as he was seven years older than I and, besides, he was at school most days, and afterwards was always off somewhere with his friends. My Father was my best companion, but he too, was away all day. Even my little chats with Rowland Davies were limited as he now came only about once a week, so my only outlet was to watch for Richard and talk to him for the short time he had to spare.

With so little to occupy my time, it suddenly occurred to me that I could go to school and, feeling sure that my Mother would agree with me, as she had so often remarked that it would be a blessing for all concerned. I rushed off to ask her. To my surprise and disappointment my request was immediately turned down and for the same reason that I was given for so many things, that I was too young and would have to wait a while, in this case until I was five years old. The thought of having to wait that long was most upsetting, but then I realized that perhaps it would have been better to have asked my Father. There was a much greater chance that he would be more sympathetic and so I decided to put the question to him the moment he arrived home. This I did, but the result was utterly disappointing. His response was exactly that of my mother's, but with the rider that he did not want to hear any more about it. His tone of voice indicated a great deal more to me than his words, so I knew that however much I pleaded, he would not change his mind.

One evening, a few days later, Garnie was relating to some happening at school when I heard him say that the boy he was referring to could not help what he had done as he was only three years old. At once I pricked up my ears. If there was someone there of that age, then surely there was no reason why I could not also be there. The moment Garnie had finished speaking, I made my point, but in spite of such evidence, my parents still refused to discuss it further. However, the next morning, to my utter amazement, my Mother announced that she had thought things over and intended to go and see Miss Lewis to ask her advice.

When the time came, I quite thought that my Mother would take me with her so that I could show Miss Lewis what a big girl I was, but it appeared that such a thing was out of the question and she set off alone. She seemed to be away for hours and I had begun to think that she was never coming back when I heard her key in the door. I rushed to meet her and at once asked what Miss Lewis had said. To my delight I was told that Miss Lewis had agreed to have me and had said that quite a few of the children there had started at about my age.

With great excitement and without a moment's delay, I telephoned my Father to tell him the good news and then turned to my Mother to ask her what I would be wearing to school the following day. Her reply came as a bombshell, and I burst into tears when I heard her say that I would not be starting school until after Christmas, which was when Miss Lewis had agreed to enrol me. Seeing my tears, she added that if I was going to cry about such a small thing, as Christmas was only a very short time away, then perhaps I really was too young to start school. Instantly and as if by magic, my tears subsided. However, my Mother's assessment of a very short time proved, to my mind, to be very long time, but eventually Christmas did arrive and, surprisingly, passed even too quickly for me.

At last the great day came and I set off with my Mother. As we entered the playground, I saw that there were quite a few children playing there. Garnie was among them, but he took no notice whatsoever of us. One of the bigger girls spoke to us and volunteered to tell Miss Lewis that we were there and within moments Miss Lewis came and ushered us in to the school. After a few words with her, my Mother left, reminding me as she went that I was to do exactly as I was told. Miss Lewis then picked up a bell and took me with her to the door, where she rang the bell. At once the children stopped playing and formed into two lines, the girls in one and the boys in the other. They then filed into the school where the teacher introduced me and told them that I was a new pupil.

While the others sorted themselves out I was given a place to sit at a small table of which there were three directly in front of Miss Lewis's desk. I was then told that I should follow what the others did, but that I was not to turn around to look behind or talk to anyone during lessons. Miss Lewis then went behind her desk and everyone stood up to recite something in Welsh, which I later learned was the Lord's Prayer. When they had finished we all sat down and it became very quiet. I wanted to turn around to see what they were doing and see where Garnie was, but did not dare. At that moment Miss Lewis came to me and gave me a frame with coloured beads on it to play with. The little girl sitting next to me also had a frame so I copied what she was doing in between trying to take everything in.

In what seemed no time the bell rang and immediately everyone put their things away and we filed out through the chapel to the playground. The bigger girls were asked to look after me and so I had a wonderful time making friends and joining in their games.

Playtime was soon over and we returned to the schoolroom to take our places once again. The rest of the morning passed very quickly and then the bell rang, telling us that it was lunch time. When I got to the playground, I found Garnie waiting for me and we ran all the way home. I had so much to tell everyone that I could hardly wait to get indoors, and during lunch the 'never talk with your mouth full' rule was broken several times. I still had lots more to tell when Garnie announced that he was ready to go back and as I was just as anxious to return as he, I decided that the rest could wait until later.

Every moment of the afternoon was as enjoyable as the morning had been and by the time it was over, I was convinced that going to school was the best thing that had ever happened to me. During my years there my feelings about it did not change. Since then many years have gone by and much has happened, but I can remember clearly almost every detail of that little school where I learned so much and which was so special, not only to me, but to all the others who had the good fortune to be a part of it.

The school consisted of just one room situated at the far end of the chapel, and although not very wide, was reasonably long as its length incorporated the full width of the building. The room was separated from the chapel by a wooden partition which ran along behind the last row of pews and which was too high to see over unless one stood on one of the desks. This was sometimes resorted to by the children when, on occasions, the teacher received a visitor with whom she wished to converse in private.

The chapel had two entrances, both of which were at the front, one for men and the other for women. To reach the school-room, we children used the women's entrance which led to a small cloakroom where we hung our out-door clothes. From there we entered the chapel and, passing along the aisle, reached the door in the partition which opened directly into the schoolroom.

The focal point was the teacher's desk and big chair which stood at one end of the room and at the same end but in the corner was a large, round fuel-burning stove. The stove area was a popular place with the girls on cold winter mornings when we would be allowed to go in before the bell rang and there, pushing each other to get as near as possible, would gather to warm our frozen hands. The boys took advantage of this only when conditions were extreme as they prided themselves, even when their teeth were chattering and their hands turning blue, on being a tough and hardy breed.

The warmth from the stove was also utilised to start off our spring bulbs and when this took place, it allowed those hardy boys a good excuse to deviate from their determination and come inside a little earlier.

The bulbs, of which there were always three varieties,

hyacinth, daffodil and narcissus, were bought for us every year by our teacher. We were given one each, and from that moment on the bulbs became our responsibility. This was an exciting project and incurred a great deal of interest, especially as at first it was not always easy to be certain of the variety one had chosen. Apart from the end product, the honour of owning the first to sprout and then to flower, was extremely important. Care of the bulbs, such as watering and removing it each morning away from the stove where it had been placed the previous afternoon before leaving school, as well as staring at it and willing it to be the first to show, created a greater need than usual to get to school early as this had to be done before the bell rang.

Between the teacher's desk and forward of the stove was a blackboard and easel, in front of which were the small tables, and behind them were rows of desks with attached bench-type seats. Each desk accommodated two pupils. The school had just one teacher and catered for an age range of from three to fourteen years, fourteen being the school-leaving age at that time. The youngest pupils sat at the tables whilst the others occupied the desks. As they advanced educationally and correspondingly in age, they graduated along the rows and reached the last row in their final year.

Occupying one of the corners at the other end of the room was a large cupboard which housed the school stock and library. This cupboard was kept locked and opened only by the teacher, except on rare occasions when she would entrust one of the older pupils to fetch something under her direction. This was considered to be a great honour.

On the window sill behind the last row of desks stood a large, wooden shield, affixed to which were smaller, silver-like shields. These shields were highly prized as they were awarded by the local Education Authority to the school that had achieved the best attendance record over the period of the year, and we in Nant had been awarded a fair number of them. Also on the window sill was a much valued bottle, containing a scorpion, which my brother, Will, had brought from Egypt, and which he had presented to the school.

Most of our work was carried out on slates with slate pencils. These slates, in wooden frames, were most economical as they could be used time and time again, and with care they lasted for years. To clean them, pieces of cloth and bottles of water with perforated caps were kept on the shelf underneath our desks. We supplied our own bottles. Mine was usually a discarded tomato ketchup bottle, but I was constantly on the look-out for something more exotic for one-upmanship could be achieved by acquiring a bottle of unusual shape or one sporting an attractive label. Paper and copy books were also used, but these were generally kept for best or special work.

In front of the chapel was a square playground, and at the rear of the building was a further playing area. This area was divided by corrugated fencing, one side for the boys and the other for the girls and back to back, so allowing one in each area, were two little corrugated sheds which served as our lavatories. These were the bucket and box type.

Welsh was the first language and English taught as a subject. The end result produced a reasonable standard of bilingualism. When I started at the school there was a total of twenty three children on the register, but during my time there, this varied from as few as twenty to the grand sum of twenty-nine. This small complement was a handicap when competing for honours against the larger schools in the county, but because of it, much greater effort was put into everything that we did.

Such was the case when our pupils took the scholarship examination for entry to the County School at Pwllheli. The fact that rarely were we able to enter more than two candidates each year, and more often than not only one, made us all the more anxious to achieve a good success rate. Few candidates could have set out with such faith and hope invested in them as did ours. To their credit and our teacher's they generally obtained results which justified that faith and upheld our fierce pride in our little establishment.

In 1932, at the end of the summer term, our much-loved Miss Lewis left us to teach at a larger school. Her going made us all very sad and caused some trepidation as to what sort of teacher would take her place. It was not long before we heard that another lady teacher had been appointed, a Mrs Roberts, who was a widow and, according to the school governors, of which my Father was one, would be ideal for us. We also heard that, as her home was some miles away, arrangements had been made for her to stay at Tŷ Uchaf Farm during the school week.

We children were not entirely convinced by the reports that she would be ideal. Maybe she would be from our parents' point of view, but that did not necessarily mean that she would be from ours. Speculation went on throughout the holiday, with many rumours of pleasures and some of terrors in store for us with this new teacher, so it was with mixture of excitement and not a little trepidation that we returned to school.

It did not take us long to discover that we need not have had a moment's trepidation, for Mrs Roberts proved to be as perfect in every way as her predecessor. By the time the bell rang on that first day she had won us over completely, and as time went by she proved to be an excellent teacher and gained our respect and affection. For some there was one difficulty, that being the change from, 'Please Miss' to 'Please Mrs', but this was soon resolved when in our efforts to address her, it came out as 'Please S'miss' which, from that time on for most of us, became her title.

At the time of writing, Miss Lewis now in her eighties, is still enjoying her retirement and still remembers every one of her Nant pupils. Sadly, Mrs Roberts passed away recently, but to the end retained her interest in us and her affection for us all.

In retrospect, I am amazed that those two ladies not only coped with us all in that one room, but kept us under control, taught several different subjects at one and the same time, and maintained a good standard of education throughout. We children of Nant have a great deal to thank them for.

Nant Gwrtheyrn School group photograph 1933

Nant Gwrtheyrn School group photograph 1938

Pupils of Nant Gwrtheyrn School 1933 and 1938

1. Mrs Mary Roberts (S'miss)
2. Gwilym Owen (Bessie's brother) [XVIII*]
3. Lewis Trefor Owen
4. Cecil Garnon Salmon (Eileen's brother)
5. Robin Ellis Williams
6. Robert Banston
7. Gwilym Rees Parry •
8. William John Williams
9. Richard Edwin Williams
10. Phyllis Roberts •
11. Eileen Mary Salmon (Author)
12. Olwen Thomas (Tŷ Canol) [XVII*]
13. Eirlys Williams [XXIX*]
14. Annie Mair Jones [XXVIII*]
15. Rhiannon Williams [XXIX*]
16. Gwilym Thomas (Tŷ Canol)
17. John Jones [XXVIII*]
18. Trevor Earp
19. Kenneth Earp
20. Huw Williams
21. Samuel (Sam) Williams
22. Catherine Parry Jones
23. Maggie Olwen Jones
24. Robert Gwilym Jones
25. Emlyn Vaughan
26. Barbara Earp
27. June Williams
28. Betty Earp
29. Mary Earp (The Twins) [XIV*]
30. Gwynfor Thomas
31. Ieuan Thomas (Tŷ Canol)

* Chapter Reference
• Brother and Sister (see Foreword)

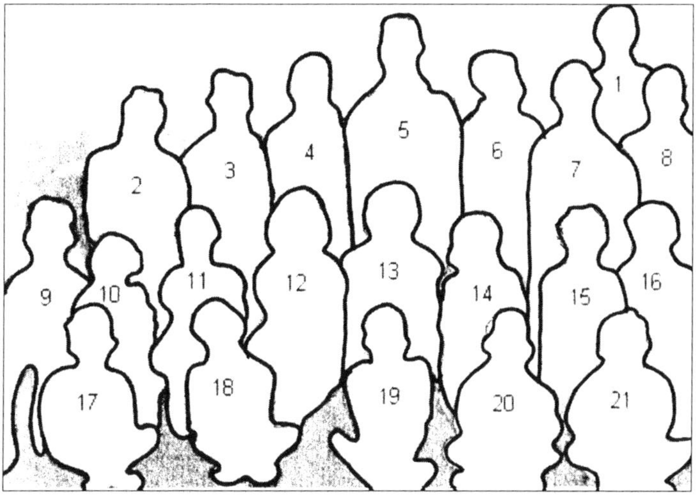

Silhouette of Nant Gwrtheyrn School group photograph 1933

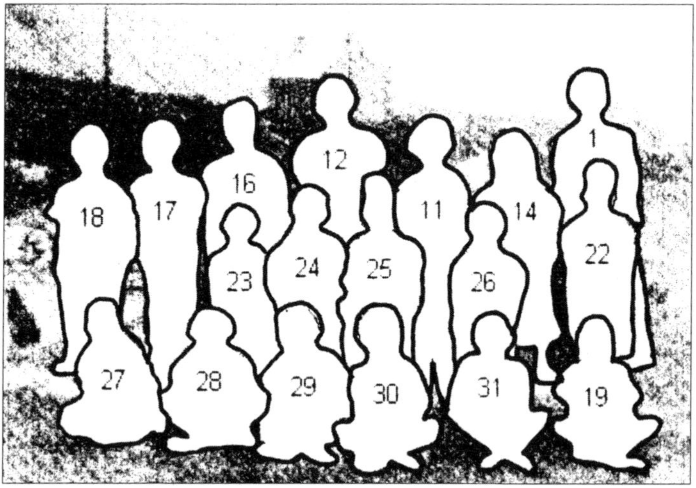

Silhouette of Nant Gwrtheyrn School group photograph 1938

Chapter XII

Over the Wall

Going to school and so meeting and making new friends with all the other children led to my wanting to play with them after school and at week-ends. During the first months it was dark in the evenings and as there was no form of outside lighting in Nant, playing out of doors was not possible for those of my age. I was, therefore, allowed to invite one or two children home, but week-ends were by far the best when I could have as many children as I liked to play in the drive.

For a time all went well until I wanted, in turn, to visit their homes in the village. As this involved going out of the drive and then up past the little field to reach the village gate, which from our house was at the other end of the village, my parents would not hear of it. Of course, the same route had to be taken by the children when they visited me, but they usually came in numbers, so the problem did not arise. Like children the world over, they would play for a while then wander off to engage in something different in the village, which left me on my own again. I begged and pleaded with my parents to be allowed to go with them, but it was to no avail.

It was whilst trying to amuse myself one day that I suddenly realized that getting into the village need not be a problem. There was the door in the wall across from our back door which Rowland Davies used and which I knew opened directly into the back area of Mountain View. I ran to the door to open it, but although the latch was within my reach, the bolt was not, so I went indoors to enlist Lizzie's help, only to be told that first I would have to get my Mother's permission.

As I ran off, Lizzie called after me, saying that she doubted that I would get that permission, but I took no notice as I was sure that my Mother would not object. Lizzie was right, my Mother did object, and strongly, saying that it was quite out of the question for any of us to use that door into the village as the back areas of the houses were private and it was unthinkable that we should violate that privacy. So that was that. My only hope, as usual, was to try my Father when he came home. To my disappointment he was of the same opinion as my Mother, and I could see that to keep on about it would be pointless. Indulgent though he often was, I had long since learned to recognise the signs of chance and no chance when dealing with him. Nevertheless, the problem remained and at times became acute when, after playing with me for a time, the children returned yet again to the village, and I could hear them playing so near and yet so far. These occasions more often than not brought tears and, although seeming to ignore my misery, my parents must have taken note of it, for not long afterwards my Father told me that he was arranging something that would solve the problem. He refused to tell me what was going to be done, saying that I would have to wait and see.

For days nothing happened until one afternoon, when returning from school, I was surprised to see, just across the drive from the front door, a long ladder with wide treads, leaning against the wall. Taking a closer look, I noticed that some of the capping stones had been removed from the top of the wall, leaving a flat surface. At once I climbed up the ladder and saw that on the other side was another ladder which led down to the footpath that ran along in front of Mountain View. This ladder was much shorter, as the ground on that side was at a higher level. I climbed down and excitedly rushed indoors to find out what it was all about. There I was told that the ladders were to be used as a short cut into the village, but I must promise never to go there without first asking permission. Delightedly I made the promise and then asked if I could go.

By the time I got back to the top of the wall, there were already a number of children inspecting the ladder on the other side. Everyone thought it was a great idea and most of that evening was spent in climbing up and down. The ladders had been made especially for the purpose by Johnny Price and were so sturdily built that despite the constant traffic over the years, they outlived our stay in the valley.

Having at last gained independent access to the village enabled me to visit the children's homes, and so get to know the people in my own right. All the houses, with the exception of Bay View, were of the same design and were welcoming and cosy. There was no electricity or gas, so lighting was provided by oil lamps and cooking was carried out on an open range, although some homes had primus stoves and oil stoves. Water was laid on to taps outside the houses and came from a small reservoir near the foot of

Graig Ddu, which was fed by streams that ran down the mountain. Each house had two rooms downstairs, a living room with a kitchen behind and two bedrooms upstairs. Almost without exception great pride was taken in keeping the houses and gardens clean and trim.

It was at this time that I realized the full value of the village square. This was the hub of the community where the children gathered to play, planned their activities or just sat on the wall and talked. Seldom out of school hours would the square be deserted, and being adjacent to Evan Wynne' shop, there was much coming and going, which allowed one to know whenever anyone had bought sweets. In most cases the purchaser was more often than not willing to share his or her bounty, but on the rare occasions when there seemed to be some reluctance this would generally be overcome with a little persuasion.

In what seemed to be no time, I got to know the whole population of the village as well as Mrs Thomas at Tŷ Canol Farm and Mr and Mrs Gwilym Hughes at Tŷ Uchaf. Mr and Mrs Thomas had four children, Olwen, Gwilym, Gwynfor and Ieuan. Olwen, the eldest, was some three years older than I but we often played together and became friends. At Tŷ Uchaf there was Hannah and Bobby, but I did not see very much of them as they stayed most of the time with their grandmother at the 'Vic' in Llithfaen. This made it easier for Hannah to travel each day to the County School. Mrs Hughes was a kind and gentle lady, and her husband was one of the most popular men in the valley, a very good sport and always willing to join in any activity.

My knowledge of Welsh was now increasing daily and it was not too long before I had a child's ability in both languages. English was kept for home. Although both my parents spoke Welsh and Will had some knowledge of it, Ethel had none and hardly made any progress with it throughout the years we were there. Outside our home Welsh was the order of the day.

With the ladders well and truly established, traffic over the wall was heavy and our drive became almost as popular as the square. It was about this time that a fine swing was put up for me in the drive. Suspended by chains from a stout branch of one of the trees, it was safe and almost indestructable. Being the only swing in Nant, it was very much in demand.

My Father now thought that a car would be an advantage, but first a garage would have to be provided. After some contemplation, it was decided to have one built at the top of the Screw Hill, just inside the Nant boundary wall. In due course the garage was ready and soon afterwards we acquired a very smart-looking little black Austin Seven. This car was to prove to be very useful, but also, at times, an absolute curse. The vehicle itself was most reliable, but my Father's forgetfulness regarding its fuel requirements caused many inconveniences as well as tired and sore feet. It was no joke, finding ourselves on a Sunday evening, with an empty petrol tank, half-way up a steep hill, miles from the nearest petrol pump, which in those days, in country areas, were few and far between, and with no-one about as most people were at worship. Should it also be raining, as it can only rain among the mountains, then it was even less funny. Nevertheless, the car was a great boon, even though we still had to climb up the Screw Hill.

It was after an outing in the car that I had my first contact with foxes. It was a dark night as we left the garage to begin our journey home and at once we switched on our torches. I was in front as usual, but only a few steps ahead as it was so dark. Suddenly, as if out of nowhere, something moved swiftly across my path. Caught momentarily in the beam of the torchlight, I saw two bright red eyes and a flash of browny fur. For a moment I was too startled to move, but then, frightened, I ran back to my parents. They, too, had seen it and told me that there was no need to be frightened as it was only a fox and it would not harm us. They explained that there were many living in and around the mountains and that they came out at night to search for food. By the time we reached the bottom, we had seen several others and, no longer frightened, I found it quite exciting to flash my torch around to try and catch them in the beam.

A few nights later I was awakened by the most eerie sound I had ever heard. It sounded as if someone or something was in terrible pain and that, whatever it was, it could not be far away. I opened my eyes and, although my bedroom was brightly illuminated by moonlight, I was too frightened to get up and look out. Instead, with fast beating heart, I pulled the bedclothes tightly over my head. Moments later, I heard another screech, this time very much nearer than before and this one quickly sent me scurrying off in fear to my parents' bedroom. To my relief they, too, were awake and soon calmed me down, explaining that it was the sound of foxes calling to each other. My Father then got out of bed and took me with him to the window. As we looked out, there came another screech and there, in the field only a short distance from the garden wall, and clearly defined in the moonlight, was a fox. As we stood there, watching, it was joined by another, but just then Moss started barking and Mickey immediately joined in, making enough noise to wake the whole village. The next second the foxes had gone.

As time passed we became used to these nocturnal disturbances which were frequent during the mating season, and were able to accept them as part of the price, or pleasure, depending on one's attitude, of living so close to nature. For me it was pure pleasure.

Chapter XIII

The More the Merrier

The next additions to the family were a dozen point of lay hens and two cockerels. These were housed in the out-buildings of the long-deserted Tŷ Hen Farm, just a short distance from the end of our drive. These hens and their descendants were to supply us with an abundance of eggs throughout our time in Nant, and when production was in full swing, allowed for sharing with the families in the village.

Eventually the hens became broody and, wishing to increase their numbers, my father put two of them to sit. Disappointingly, the success rate was not as high as he had hoped, with only nine hatching from each clutch of thirteen eggs. However, the chicks thrived and in turn became good layers.

The following year, still keen to increase and to improve on his original farm-yard variety, he decided to invest in two hundred Rhode Island Red x Light Sussex eggs, an incubator and hoover lamp. For this venture, new housing was required and with Johnny Price's help, he proceeded to erect a hen-house on the rough part of the garden. The new hen-house turned out to be a fine building and large enough, or so it seemed to me, to house several people. Finally, it was painted a redwood colour on the outside and became a worthy addition to the garden.

The incubator and lamp duly arrived, followed a few days later by the eggs. The eggs were immediately placed in the incubator and then began the twenty-one day wait. For me, the time seemed interminable, but at last we reached the twentieth day and, going with my Father to check on developments, we were delighted to see that a number of eggs were cracked and on the point of hatching. By evening, over sixty had hatched and by late the next day, the incubator drawers were a moving mass of cheeping, yellow fluff. Carefully, each was removed to the lamp area and then the rest of the family were called in to see and admire them. Very few eggs had failed and everyone was well pleased.

One fine but rather windy afternoon, just two or three weeks later, Rowland Davies came rushing in from the garden shouting, 'Fire, fire' at the top of his voice. My Mother, Lizzie, Ethel and I hurried to the scullery, wondering where the fire could be as there was no smell of smoke anywhere in the house. Breathlessly, he told us that the new hen-house was on fire and urged us to get as many buckets of water to the scene as quickly as possible.

Immediately, we were spurred into action and within moments, a chain of water carriers was organised between the five of us. Regrettably, we did not possess a hose but, nevertheless, we worked furiously with what we had. My job was to pick up the empty buckets thrown out by Rowland Davies and run as fast as my legs would carry me to Lizzie, who was in charge of filling at the tap. The smoke was rising in great black clouds from the roof of the building and billowing out through the door, at times completely enveloping Rowland Davies as he frantically threw in bucket after bucket of water. As I collected the empties, I could see the flames beyond him, dancing about inside the building. Despite our efforts, the situation did not seem to be improving. If anything it was getting worse.

It was no use telephoning my Father as he was too far away to get home in time to help. We continued to work away like demons with the buckets and any other suitable utensils we could lay our hands on, but the smoke kept coming thicker and thicker and the flames seemed to be spreading. Suddenly, the wind gusted and with a roar, long spears of flame leapt up out of the roof. There was nothing we could do but carry on what seemed to be becoming a fast losing battle in the remote hope that the next bucket would be the decisive one. The flames quickly ran along the roof and then, with an ear-splitting crack, the inside of the building burst into flames. The heat was now so intense that it was impossible for anyone to get near enough to do anything about it. Minutes later, it was all over. Where such a short time before had been a fine hen-house was now just a mangled heap of smouldering metal with an occasional flame dancing here and there. No sign was there that chicks, an incubator or lamp had ever been there. All had gone. For some time no-one spoke. We just stood, staring at the remains in incredulity. When we did eventually move, I could not help but notice that I was not the only one fighting back tears.

There was no point in informing my Father. He would know soon enough. Knowing how upset he would be, my Mother warned us to say nothing about the fire until he had finished his meal. However, when he arrived home, it took him only moments to realize that something was wrong. Despite our efforts to reassure him, he insisted on being told and so my Mother recounted the whole, sad story. Immediately, he rushed out to the garden and there stood staring in almost disbelief and sadness at the still smouldering ruins. Later that evening the grown-ups discussed the possible cause of the fire. Their conclusion was that one of the chicks had somehow got inside the lamp guard and, having caught fire, had then got out again and spread the flames.

It took us all quite a time to recover from the shock and it was many days later before Rowland Davies could bring himself to start clearing up the charred remains. No further hen-house was built to replace it. Instead, we fell back on our old faithfuls in the other buildings and they and their offspring served us well.

By this time Rowland Davies's green fingers were producing excellent results in the garden, with an abundance of fruit and vegetables and, together with the hens' efforts, we were enjoying the luxury of fresh home produce. It was this partial self-sufficiency that led to yet another addition to the family.

Arriving home from school one afternoon, I was asked by my Mother to accompany her to the garden, where she said there was something that she wanted me to see. Excitedly, I ran ahead, trying to guess what it could be. At first I could see nothing unusual, but then a movement caught my eye at the far end of the rough area. Going a little closer, I saw that it was a nanny goat, but quite different from any I had seen before. Unlike the wild goats, she had no horns and her ears were very long and flopped down each side of her face. Her coat at first glance appeared to be black but, seeing her at close quarters, I saw that over the black was a brown sheen, which caught the sunlight as she moved. Her face, too, was different but was quite pretty and as we approached she came running towards us. She could not reach us as she was tethered and I was warned not to go too near her as she would need a little time to get used to us. My Mother then told me that she was a Nubian goat and that she would provide us with a particularly nourishing type of milk.

The moment tea was over, I rushed off to the village to tell my friends about the new arrival and brought a number of them back to the garden to see her. They all admired her and wanted to know why she had no horns and such long, funny ears. With my newly acquired knowledge and the air of an expert, I told them that she was a Nubian goat. The piece of information probably meant no more to them than it did to me, but no-one questioned it.

It was when my Father came home that evening that I learned something about Nubian goats. He told me that they were natives of the east and had been brought to this country in the days of sail. In those days, the goats were taken aboard our ships to provide fresh milk for the crews. When the ships eventually arrived home, the crews were paid off and the goats then sold ashore. Pointing out the differences between the new goat and our Nant breed, he explained that without these differences, she would not survive in her native desert region. Her long, floppy ears served to protect her eyes when in sandstorms she would be able to fold them over her face. Her nose, too, had a dual purpose, in that not only did she breathe through it but could close the nostrils, so protecting her lungs from the penetrating sands when such storms blew up. Other important differences were her hooves, her flexible back-bone and even the shape of her face. He went on to explain that her hooves, unlike those of our wild goats, splayed outwards, so preventing her sinking into the sand and the flexibility of her back overcame the give of the soft ground, so allowing her to move without difficulty. As her desert diet consisted mainly of prickly type plants, such as cactus, her gently sloping face and slightly prominent teeth enabled her to avoid the prickly spines and so eat without risk of injury.

The new addition was to be called Jinny. Why, I cannot imagine unless perhaps she was already Jinny when she came to us. Having made short work of clearing the grass in the rough area, she was moved to Cae Mawr, which was to be her permanent home. There she settled down well with the sheep and, as expected, produced a good supply of milk.

She was soon to prove that she had a determined will of her own. Contrary to my expectations, she did not become my pet and for some time was not even friendly towards me. Instead, she developed an inordinate affection for my Father and a possessiveness that, whenever he came into sight, allowed for nothing but his undivided attention to her. This jealousy for his affection became a menace to me and resulted in both he and I having to take precautionary measures to outwit her.

I had developed a habit of going as far as the edge of the plateau to meet my Father when he came home in the evenings. As this involved passing Cae Mawr, Jinny, who missed nothing, soon became aware of my reason for going and seemed to know exactly what time to look out for me. If not tethered, which was generally the case, she would make a bee-line for me at a fair speed and, despite her lack of horns, would effectively bowl me over in a most undignified and painful manner. Not satisfied with that, she would then continue to butt and push me while I was still on the ground. The moment my Father came into sight, she would cease her attack and run to greet him with sheer adoration and unbelievable docility.

When tethered, she would watch until he appeared and

then bleat so piteously that, unable to resist, he would go at once and make a fuss of her. For some time he thought my complaints about her were little exaggerated until one day, arriving a little earlier than usual, he caught her in the act. At once he ran forward and picked me up, whilst at the same time loudly scolding Jinny. The effect of his scolding was instant. It made even me feel sorry for her for she laid down on the ground, folded her ears over her eyes and bleated so distressingly that there was no alternative but to forgive her and comfort her and even then it took some time. The result of the event was my Father's suggestion that I should take Jinny with me whenever I went to meet him and he, in turn, would take care to ignore me until he had made the necessary fuss of her. This, although a bit of a nuisance when I was in a hurry, turned out to be the answer, and because of it she became much more friendly towards me.

Jinny was with us for nearly three years until late one spring evening, she was seen in the company of the wild goats near the top of Benclog. That she would have anything at all to do with them was a great surprise as neither they nor Jinny had previously shown any interest in each other. My Father and Will immediately set off up the mountain to recapture her. It was not an easy feat at that point, and before they had reached half-way, the goats, including Jinny, had disappeared over the top. Nevertheless, the men struggled on and, gaining the summit, were dismayed to see no sign of the goats. In the fast fading light they searched and called, but failed to find any sign of her and had no alternative but to return home. The search was resumed the next evening but with no success. Our only hope then was that she would be seen by someone and so could be brought back or that she would return of her own accord.

Despite our hope, Jinny did not return. We waited, thinking that she may show up with the herd the following winter but, sadly, it was in vain. We were never to see or hear of her again.

Soon after Jinny's arrival, Garnie acquired two beautiful, white Angora rabbits and these were housed in a hutch on the rough area. With our livestock now composed of a goat, several hens, two rabbits, a tortoise (he or she had been acquired one Saturday in Caernarfon), two dogs and a cat, one would have thought that it was time to call it a day. But then Garnie came up with the idea of keeping fan-tail pigeons. At first my parents were not too keen but, after some discussion and laying down the law regarding their care, which was pointed out would be his sole responsibility, their housing which he would have to provide by building himself and which they insisted would have to be of a good standard, they finally agreed.

Anxious to prove his ability, he immediately set to work and for days was kept busy with the making of the dove-cote. The placing of the cote had to be given some thought and eventually, the gable end of eleven Mountain View was chosen as the sight. There was no danger of disturbing anyone as the house was unoccupied, being rented as a wash-house and store-house by Mrs Jenny Owen of number ten. In any case, it is doubtful that noise could have penetrated as the walls were so thick as to be almost sound-proof.

With the cote in position high up on the wall and a number of perches fixed around it, all was ready for the new occupants. A few days later, two young fan-tails arrived. These, like the hens, were fed on the finest Indian corn and they thrived on it. Inevitably, their numbers increased until, eventually, there were eight birds, which was as much as the cote could accommodate, so a halt was called. My Mother now remarked that she hoped that we were all satisfied, reminding us that what had at first been a home for one stray cat, had quickly grown to the proportions of a small menagerie. There must be no more as enough was enough and she was putting her foot down. Everyone nodded in agreement, little thinking that before very long there would be yet another addition.

As time went by, the pigeons became very tame and at feeding time would fly down to perch on Garnie's shoulders. Not only had they no fear of us but seemed to have complete trust in our other pets. On occasions, when their corn inadvertently landed between Moss's paws or bounced into his kennel, they would rush, without hesitation, to retrieve it whilst Moss sat, unconcernedly, watching them. The cat, too, held no fears for them for she often sat in on their feeding time and could be relied upon not to pounce.

The next, and what proved to be the last addition, was Judy, a lovely, black, cocker spaniel puppy. My Father bought her especially for me and I was delighted with her as at last I was to have my own personal pet. Judy was immediately friendly and full of life. She made instant friends with moss and Puss but his Lordship, as Mickey was often referred to out of Will's hearing, with his usual aloofness, at first totally ignored her. However, such was her charm that even he, after a few weeks, succumbed and they became life-long companions.

Although Judy was affectionate with us all, it was only a short time before it became clear that as a pet owner, I was to lose out yet again. Like Jinny, she chose my Father as her idol but, fortunately for me, she was not jealous of his attention to anyone else.

As soon as she was able, she followed him everywhere, which meant that she spent the best part of each day at the office. The only time she left him of her own accord was immediately after his lunch when she would make her way to the crusher to join Mickey. For just half an hour or so the two dogs would play together until suddenly, Judy, for all the world like someone having to 'clock on', would hurry back to the office. Throughout our years in Nant, this pattern varied only when she had pups and even then she attempted several times to carry them down to the office. When my Father had to go somewhere where it was not practical to take her, she would howl and go on howling for a long time after he had left. When the noise had practically driven us all mad and we could stand it no longer, she was firmly told off and as a result she would sulk and whimper until his return.

Jinny was terribly upset when Judy made her appearance and went for her at every opportunity. Having been butted and tossed into the air on a number of occasions, Judy became adept at avoiding the attacks. With my Father's care to show no preference for her, the goat finally accepted her presence and even greeted her with tolerance when she appeared with him on his return in the evenings. To any onlooker we must surely have looked a strange quartet, the man, the goat, the child and the dog.

Judy proved to be an excellent house-dog, giving ample warning, as did Moss, when any stranger approached. This service in return for bed and board was seldom offered by Mickey who appeared to consider it demeaning to his image to bark. Only when Will seemed threatened did he react and then left no doubt of his intentions.

Both dogs were good gun dogs, although Mickey had the more experience, as Will, at that time, was the hunter in the family. It was on one of their shooting expeditions that Mickey came close to losing his life. Running ahead as usual to flush out the game, he disappeared into some dense undergrowth. Suddenly, Will heard him yelp, followed by howls of pain. Rushing forward through the tangled mass of briars, long grass and bracken, oblivious of the pain of the thorns tearing at his hands and clothing, he found Mickey standing on three legs trembling violently and holding up what was obviously an injured paw.

Believing that a thorn had lodged in one of the pads, Will took the paw to examine it, when he noticed blood trickling down the fur from two areas on the lower part of the leg. Separating the fur, he saw to his horror the tell-tale marks of a viper's bite. Without stopping to examine the other area, but only to unload his rifle, which he then pushed under some bracken, he picked Mickey up and began to run as fast as he could for home. As he hurried along, Mickey's howls abated but then his breathing became extremely distressed and his leg was swelling more with every minute that passed. Desperately Will ran on over the rough and uneven ground, slipping and stumbling but determined to try and save his little companion or die in the attempt.

After what seemed a never-ending journey, he finally reached home but by that time he was almost on the point of collapse. Gasping out his story, he handed Mickey over to my Father who then, with Garnie, rushed off to Tŷ Uchaf farm. The farm was their only hope as only there was there the possibility of getting hold of anti-snake serum. Will, too exhausted to run any further, staggered along some distance behind them.

Mr Hughes, seeing them approach, at once guessed that something was wrong and hurried out to meet them. Seeing Mickey's condition, he needed no explanation. He was only too familiar with such symptoms in his cattle and dogs when, on occasions, they had suffered snake bites. Without wasting a moment, he produced the serum and proceeded to treat his little patient.

For a few days afterwards Mickey was very poorly and everyone was terribly upset but then he quickly improved and to our great relief made a complete recovery. There was no doubt that, between them, Will and Gwilym Hughes had saved his life, for which we were all so grateful, for had he not recovered, it would surely have broken Will's heart.

Strangely, not only we humans were affected by what happened, but also our other animals. During that time, their behaviour was so peculiar that it seemed impossible not to believe that they, too, realised that something was very wrong. Even Jinny was subdued and unusually well-behaved towards Judy and myself. Such individuals were they all and yet as one with us in times of trouble that it was impossible to think of them as anything other than members of the family.

Chapter XIV

The Twins

One morning at school S'miss called out our names as usual for the marking of the register. Reaching the letter 'E', she called out 'Kenneth Earp' but there was no response. Continuing down the register, she then called 'Trefor Earp' and again there was no response. Looking up from her marking, she asked if anyone knew why they were not present. Before anyone could answer we heard footsteps hurrying through the Chapel and the next moment the door opened and in came the two boys.

Being late for school was totally unacceptable and if persistent, called for punishment, unless one had a very good reason and a parental note to prove it. Seeing no note, we expected that they would at least look a little worried but to everyone's surprise, they did not seem at all concerned; in fact the very opposite. Both were looking pleased with themselves and were smiling broadly.

S'miss, looking a little stern, asked them to explain why they were late and we children, just as keen to know, kept very quiet and listened intently. Trefor, still smiling, apologised then said that the reason was that two baby sisters had arrived at their home that morning and because of it their breakfast had been delayed.

To several of us it was a complete surprise and a quiet ripple of excitement ran through the schoolroom. S'miss, however, remained quite calm and, looking kindly at the boys, congratulated them on acquiring two new sisters. Then, clapping her hands, she called our attention to remind us that there was work to be done.

While everyone else seemed to settle down and look busy, I just could not concentrate but kept thinking of how exciting it must be to have two brand new babies in the house. How the two boys had been able to come to school when so much was happening at home I could not imagine. Had we been so lucky as to have just one baby in our house, let alone two, I certainly would not have done so. The more I thought about the new babies, the more I wanted to know and could hardly contain myself until playtime when I hoped to find out all about them.

Eventually playtime arrived and we girls made a bee-line for Trefor and Kenneth to badger them with questions. However, it was all most disappointing for they could not spare a moment; they were far too busily occupied, playing with the other boys. By the time the bell rang we girls were none the wiser.

After what seemed an interminable morning, at last it was lunch-time. I raced home to tell everyone the news, only again to be disappointed when I found out that they already knew. During lunch my Mother and Ethel were discussing the new arrivals when I heard my Mother say that she intended to visit Mrs Earp and she suggested that Ethel may like to go with her. Before Ethel had a chance to reply, I quickly piped up that I would willingly go with her. I did not think for a moment that my offer would be accepted as everything worthwhile seemed to be reserved for grown-ups. However, to my surprise and delight I was told that I could also go.

The visit took place a few days later and I was surprised to see Mrs Earp in bed. I thought it most odd that she was in bed at that time of the day and at once asked her if she was ill. With a smile she assured me that she was not but as it was essential to keep the new babies warm, staying in bed with them was the best way of doing so.

The twins were lovely and I was allowed, with my Mother's help, to hold each one in turn for a few moments. It was whilst holding one of them that I began to wish that we had a baby and I wondered how we could get one. Someone had said that they came from special shops yet I had never seen such a shop. I was pretty sure that there were none of that kind anywhere near us or I would surely have seen them. Perhaps they were in the big towns like Liverpool. My Father had told me that there was a very big shop there that sold parrots so perhaps that was also the 'baby shop'! Well, I could easily find out by asking Mrs Earp and I decided to do so at the first opportunity.

Whilst waiting for a lull in the conversation, I sat quietly, watching the babies. The conversation, which seemed to go on and on, held no interest for me until I heard Mrs Earp say that looking after the twins as well as the two boys was going to be hard work. She was, therefore, glad of the opportunity to rest beforehand. At once it occurred to me that there would be no need to ask the whereabouts of the 'baby shop' for it would be much easier for Mrs Earp if she let us have one of her babies. There were plenty of grown-ups in our house to look after a baby and I would certainly do all I could to help. It seemed to me to be the perfect solution and so, without wasting another moment, I plucked up my courage and asked her.

My Mother and Ethel looked absolutely astonished and for a moment there was complete silence. When I had begun to think that no-one was going to say a word, my Mother, with a very uncomfortable look on her face, said that although it was a very nice idea, she was sure that Mrs Earp would not dream of giving away one of her babies. However, Mrs Earp's reaction was not so positive. Smiling kindly at me, she said that she did not think that we really wanted a baby in our house. I immediately tried to convince her that we did and said that I was certain that my Father would agree with me. Hoping that perhaps Ethel would back me up, I looked towards her but all she did was laugh. She seemed to think that it was a very funny idea and that I could not possibly be serious. How wrong she was. I had never been more serious but it seemed that no-one would support me. Mrs Earp then said that she would ask her husband for his views on the matter, so there was still a glimmer of hope.

A few minutes later, in answer to his wife's call, Mr Earp came into the bedroom and my suggestion was put to him. To say that he looked surprised would be an understatement and I was very much afraid that he was going to refuse. For some moments he did not respond but stood, considering the suggestion. Then, with a smile, he turned to me and said that we could have one of the twins in exchange for a sack of potatoes. Before I had really had a chance to take in what he had said, he asked me which one I wanted. I was so confused that I did not know what to say but then he pointed out that the baby on the left was Betty and the other was Mary. Afraid that if I did not quickly make up my mind he might change his, I pointed to Betty.

Shortly afterwards we left and we said goodbye I promised that I would bring the potatoes just as soon as my Father came home. I skipped and danced all the way home and could think of nothing but that we were going to have a baby. The moment my Father arrived I told him the exciting news but his reaction was not exactly as I had imagined. He was, of course, very surprised but he also seemed most uncertain and brought up all sorts of reasons against the idea. Finally, he said that he wanted a private discussion with my Mother before coming to a decision. The discussion took place in the dining-room whilst I waited outside in the hall. It seemed to be never ending but, eventually, I was called in and told that I could have a bag of potatoes to take to Mr Earp in exchange for Betty.

Will was asked to carry the potatoes for me but he was obviously unwilling, saying that he thought the whole idea was quite ridiculous. However, after a little persuasion by my Father, he reluctantly agreed and we set off for Sea View. As Will struggled up the ladder with the sack on his back, he made the most peculiar faces and kept mumbling under his breath. What he said was a mystery to me as the little I did hear clearly were words that I had never heard before.

Mr Earp answered the door and ushered us in, telling me to go straight upstairs. As I climbed the stairs I could hear the babies crying and such was the noise that it was almost deafening. Mrs Earp was sitting up in bed with one of the twins on her lap, busily changing its napkin. She made no attempt to compete with the noise but smiled at me and indicated that I should sit down. Having attended to the one baby, she then proceeded to see to the other and all the while the twins continued to cry at the tops of their voices. Mrs Earp did not seem at all perturbed but the noise was certainly affecting me and getting on my nerves.

After what seemed an interminable time, the twins at last

became quiet and fell asleep. Only then was it possible to speak and be heard so I asked Mrs Earp if the babies often cried like that. She replied that they did and that it was perfectly natural. She then added that sometimes babies cried nearly all night and when that happened, someone had to get up and nurse them also feed them and frequently change their napkins. Before she could say anything further, the crying started again.

It was at that moment that I began to think that perhaps having a baby was not such a good idea after all. I realised that my parents would not be very pleased if they had to get up in the middle of the night and, certainly, Will and Ethel would be sure to complain if they were disturbed. There was also the problem of changing napkins. I was sure that I could not do it but as I had promised to help with looking after the baby, I may well be asked to do so. At once my mind was made up. The whole thing was out of the question but what on earth was I going to say to Mrs Earp.

Once again the twins settled down quietly and Mrs Earp, sitting back against the pillows, looked at me expectantly. Feeling extremely uncomfortable and with my face becoming hotter and hotter. I stumbled out every excuse I could think of. The more I said, the less convincing I became but I had no choice other than to go on. Having exhausted my excuses, I paused in the hope that Mrs Earp would say something but she remained silent. Desperately, I tried to think of one really good reason which would convince her and my mind raced around in panic. Suddenly and like manna from heaven, came the realisation that we did not posses a pram and I hastened to inform Mrs Earp of this major deficiency. To my surprise she did not respond and, thinking that she had not heard, I began to repeat myself, when she interrupted and, smilingly, assured me that she quite understood and agreed that without a pram, it would be impossible for us to have Betty. The fact that prams were impracticable in Nant, due to our rough and stony paths and that most mothers managed very well without them, did not occur to me at the time which, on reflection, was probably just as well.

A few minutes later I joined Will and Mr Earp downstairs and told them that we were not having Betty after all. Will looked somewhat relieved and Mr Earp did not seem at all surprised or upset. In fact, like his wife, he was smiling broadly. Some whispered conversation then took place between the two men, followed by ill-disguised laughter, the cause of which it was obvious that I was not meant to share. Will then told Mr Earp that he would like him to keep the potatoes as he did not fancy struggling back home with that weight and we then left the house.

When we arrived home, everyone wanted to know where the baby was. I explained what had happened and they all seemed to understand. I could not help but notice that no-one appeared to be disappointed but then decided that it was just as well. The twins grew into lovely little girls and later Mr & Mrs Earp were blessed with a third daughter.

Many years after we had all left the valley – the Earp family being one of the last to leave – I was saddened but not surprised to read in a letter written by Mrs Earp that she had not for a moment been truly happy since leaving Nant, her birth-place, and had longed to return there. Sadly, not long after the writing of the letter, both Mrs Earp and her husband passed away and that longing was never to be fulfilled.

Chapter XV

Taking to the Water

Living so close to the sea, the ability to swim was important and most of the children of Nant learned this skill at an early age. I, too, was keen to learn but despite Ethel's and Jacqueline's efforts, I had failed to master the art.

My Father was concerned about my inability and, having given the problem some thought, asked one of the men in the quarry if he would volunteer to help us. The man, whom I knew well and liked, was Ifan Lan-y-Môr of Nefyn. I believe his surname was Roberts but cannot be sure, as it was seldom used. Ifan, a kindly and willing man, gamely agreed to help in any way that he could. My Father's plan was that I should be secured in a form of harness made of stout rope. The end of the rope would then be thrown up to the jetty, where Ifan would be waiting to receive it and he then, whilst walking back and forth, would tow me along the surface. Small wonder that, having first agreed and then been told of what the plan entailed, he looked absolutely astonished. He quickly regained his composure, however, and went to find a suitable rope.

In a short time he returned, carrying a long length of rope and, with my Father's help, it was fashioned into a harness and fitted over my shoulders. I then made my way down to the beach while Ifan took up his position on the jetty. The rope was thrown up and I entered the water. When I had reached what I considered to be a suitable depth, I called up to tell him that I was ready. Immediately, he took up my weight and I enthusiastically spread out my arms and legs, making the motions of what I thought to be the breast stroke. Next I tried the butterfly, the crawl and even swimming on my back as I had seen the other children do. This was really wonderful. My enjoyment was such that I gave no thought to the fact that Ifan was tiring and so was most surprised when he called down to me that time was up. I did not think that I had had half enough practice and begged him to allow me a little longer. He agreed to another five minutes and pointedly looked at his watch. The five minutes seemed to be gone in a flash and he began walking back along the jetty, determinedly taking me back to the shore. Most unwilling to co-operate, I began struggling to pull back seawards but, despite my efforts, he brought me back to the beach. Once out of the water, I waved to my Father, who was still watching from the office window. He then came down and, looking quite pleased, asked me if I had enjoyed myself. I replied that I had but felt that it was over so quickly that I had not really had much chance to get used to it and I pleaded to be allowed to have just a little more practice. Indulgently, he agreed and, calling up to Ifan, he asked him to carry on for just a little while longer. Ifan made no comment but just nodded and dutifully began another session of walking back and forth.

The second session seemed much shorter than the first for, in no time, Ifan again signalled that it was time to stop. Stupidly, I was still not satisfied and indicated that I was not ready yet. To my surprise, he made no objection but instead, readily agreed to carry on. Just at that time he had noticed something that I was unaware of and that was that my Father had left the office window to attend to his affairs.

This time he took me much further out than before, to well beyond my depth but it did not worry me as I had every confidence in him. All went well until, some minutes later, I suddenly felt the rope slacken and at the same time felt myself sinking. For a moment I was completely submerged but, before I had time to think, I was back on the surface. I looked up at Ifan but he obviously did not think that anything was amiss for he waved and smiled back at me. Reassured, I carried on quite happily.

As before, all went well, until I again felt myself going down, this time like a stone and taking a mouthful of salt water. I did not like it at all and called up to Ifan to ask what had happened. He replied that he was sorry, a big wave had come along before he could avoid it. But there was nothing for me to worry about.

Once again full of confidence, I continued to enjoy myself and had just decided to try floating on my back when I was engulfed by the water. I found myself in a world of green and, looking up, saw the surface seemed a long way above me. Thinking that it must be another of those big waves, I waited for the tug of the rope that would bring me up again. The expected tug did not come. Instead, I was being pulled down even further by the weight of the wet rope and I could feel the slack knocking against my knees. I was now very frightened and began to panic. Gasping for breath and convinced that I was going to drown, I swallowed another mouthful of water. At that moment there was a sudden jerk. The rope became taut and I was literally whipped up on to the surface. Gasping for breath, I gulped down the so welcome fresh air and then looked up to Ifan. To my surprise, he was walking quite unconcernedly along the jetty as before and seemed totally unaware of the dramatic events that had taken place at my end of the rope. Waving to me and with a broad smile, he called down that he thought I was getting on so well, he was perfectly willing to carry on a little longer.

To carry on was the last thing I wanted. Having swallowed what I thought was at least half the ocean, I felt decidedly sick and wanted only to get out of the water. I called out that I had had enough and asked him to take me back to the beach. Instead of being pleased as I expected, he seemed very reluctant and keen that I should persevere, saying that it would be a pity to give up now, just when I was getting to grips with it. Despite all his encouragement, I wanted no more and eventually persuaded him to take me back to the shore.

As I sat on the beach while Ifan unharnessed me, we were joined by my Father and he asked how we had got on. Ifan replied at once, saying that he thought I had made an impressive start and that he would be pleased to assist again any time. My Father thanked him and began discussing plans for the next session but I intervened, saying that I would prefer to wait for a while. My Father was very surprised at my lack of enthusiasm but I did not think that Ifan appeared to be so.

During the weeks that followed, I was asked several times if I was ready for the next exercise but succeeded in putting it off. Eventually and much to my relief, for I certainly did not relish a repeat performance, the idea was dropped. Needless to say, the experience did nothing in the way of helping me to learn to swim. It was a year or so later when I finally mastered the art.

To the reader, Ifan's course of action may seem to have been a little drastic but, in fact, was not so. To have had to walk back and forth along that jetty, dangling a child on the end of a rope, in full view of so many of his workmates, must have taken a great deal of courage. He would have been aware of the ribbing he would later have to bear and so had little alternative but to make sure that he did not find himself in such a position a second time.

For me there was no embarrassment as few children were on the beach at the time and those that were thought that I was very lucky to have had what they thought had been such a lot of fun.

There was no doubt that my Father was disappointed by my early failure to learn to swim. Having himself learned almost as soon as he could walk and become a powerful swimmer, he considered it an essential as much as a pleasure. The sea for him was one of God's finest gifts. He had loved and also respected it all his life to the extent that in his youth he had run away to sea, to sail on the last of the Windjammers and before his eighteenth birthday had made three trips around the Horn. The fact that his career had led him away from the sea in no way lessened his love for it.

It was, therefore, not surprising that we had not long been in the valley when he acquired a boat. I do not remember much about that particular craft, other than that it was flat-bottomed and for some unfathomable reason became known as the 'old frog'. I do, however, recall quite clearly its two successors which he built in Tŷ Hen with a little help from Johnnie Price and Will Jordan, together with questionable aid from myself and some of my friends.

The first of these was a small rowing boat, only ten feet in length. She was, nevertheless, a stout and seaworthy little craft, constructed of a double skin of quarter inch timber with canvas and glue between. Her launching was quite an occasion, with the whole family attending the ceremony. My Mother, stifling her dislike of any form of maritime activity, and doing her best to look enthusiastic, broke a bottle of our best home-made 'champagne' on the little craft's bow and in the age-old tradition, blessed all who were to sail in her and named her 'Mary'.

For me, the 'Mary' opened up a whole new world of pleasure. As far as I know, seldom did my Father go out in her without me. Fortunately from my point of view, although Will and Garnie, too, were keen on boating and fishing, they were not as keen as I and so, generally, left the field clear for me. For the first few outings I had to suffer the indignity of being harnessed for safety to the stern seat. Happily, I soon developed my sea legs and the sense not to fall overboard, so that indignity was dispensed with.

It was inevitable that a manually operated boat would not satisfy my Father for very long and so, again, it was no

Tŷ Hen farmhouse where the boats were built with view of Carreg-y-Llam and Birds Rock

surprise when we saw him pouring over plans and calculations for a larger craft. This one, we were told, would be petrol driven. Soon afterwards, long, beautifully finished planks, boxes of copper nails, tins of paint and other materials, began arriving at Tŷ Hen. The old building was ideal for the purpose for, as well as its roominess, there was a large, old-style open fireplace, over which the timbers could be steamed into shape.

Work began the moment the last delivery had been made and from then on my Father spent his every spare moment at Tŷ Hen. I, too, spent a great deal of time there, watching all that went on and was delighted when I was found to be useful.

There were times when I was not so welcome there when, on occasions, I was allowed to hammer in the copper nails which, despite my care, frequently went into the wood, looking more like staples. The result would send me scurrying home to my Mother, vowing never again to offer my help. These vows were short-lived. Almost as soon as they were made, I would remember having left my handkerchief or something equally vital at Tŷ Hen and have to return without delay to retrieve it. As the injured party, the injury being purely to my pride, my return would be dignified but aloof. My Father, known to be quick-tempered and just as quick to calm down, would by then be all smiles and would practically stand on his head in his efforts to make friends again. Faced with such opposition, my wounded pride would be healed and my vows forgotten.

The work went on for many months until, finally, the boat was complete. Clinker-built, she was a little over fifteen feet long, with the footing for her mast set into the bow locker. A feature that pleased me was that the locker was big enough to accommodate me as well as the mast, as I had visions of riding out raging storms in there. There was also a stern locker for stowage of her sails and the engine bearers were set amidships.

The next task was getting her out of Tŷ Hen and down on to the beach. Trouble was expected in getting her down the steep and twisting track that led from the plateau but no problems were envisaged in getting her out of the building. What happened, in fact, was the very reverse and caused my Father some embarrassment. A number of men were there to assist with the move and after struggling for a little time, it was discovered that the doorway was one and a half inches too narrow to allow passage of the boat.

A short debate took place and it was agreed that there was no alternative but to remove the door posts. This done, she was out in minutes. The journey on rollers down the incline to the beach surprisingly presented very much less trouble.

During the following few days, she was checked for buoyancy, the mast heeled into position and the engine fitted. The engine was an Ailsa Craig which I was told was one of the best types of marine engine. Whether this was a fact, I do not know, but it certainly never once let us down or gave any trouble.

This new boat was named 'Elizabeth' and she, too, was launched in style. With her gleaming, white hull and green gunwale, she presented a fine picture as she took to the water. From that time on, summer evenings and week-ends took on a new dimension for me for when my Father was free and the weather permitted, we spent countless hours on the water. I learned to fish and in the winter evenings helped to make lobster pots and nets. The lobster pots we made from the tough and pliable branches of the Bay Willow which locally were known as Withies.

For my mother, our outings were sheer misery for she knew no peace until our return. On the occasions when it was decided that we would be going as far as Porthdinllaen, which was a few miles along the coast, from the time we were due back she would watch from the bedroom window until she saw the boat come into sight around the headland. My father frequently teased her about it but she insisted that it was purely in order that she would know when to tell Lizzie to put the frying pan on.

For me, going to Porthdinllaen was a mixed blessing. The fishing we did on the way was always enjoyable, so, too, was the tall glass and sometimes two, of lemonade that on our arrival I was given to drink outside Tŷ Coch Inn. The two hundred year old inn and the surrounding white-washed cottages, standing as they did on the very edge of its golden sandy beach and tucked into the cliffs behind, made this little Port of the past a place of unique beauty, which was not lost on me. What I did not like was the long wait while my Father was inside 'seeing a man about a dog'. As I grew older, I understood why my Mother was always more worried about us on those outings as my Father sometimes allowed himself to 'see too many men about too many dogs'. However, when this did occur it never once impaired his seamanship. In any case, we frequently had either Bob Vaughan or Bob Williams from the village with us, as both men were keen sea fishermen and seldom, if ever, did they see 'so many men about so many dogs'.

For me, the most exciting fishing was by line and spinner, fishing for mackerel and pollack. The season began with the warm weather which brought the sprats into the bay and, being the mackerel's main diet, their predators followed. On calm evenings in a good season the water, even close inshore, would appear to boil with the activities of the hunters, leaping out of the water. On rare occasions, the mackerel in their frenzy would become stranded in the shallows and sometimes land out of the water, providing a free meal for anyone who happened to be around. Of course, the news soon spread and in no time the beach would be a scene of frantic activity with adults and children having a wonderful time, rushing about filling their baskets.

Although catching fish on the beach was such fun, it could not compete with that done from the boat. Chugging slowly through the water with the lines, one end attached to the cleats on the gunwale, the other trailing behind us and, in my case, holding it between finger and thumb to feel that first pull that told one that something was on the other end. The excitement and anticipation of carefully pulling in the yards and yards of line and the hope that the tension would continue to the point where, with one's eyes glued to the water, one sighted that beautiful, flashing blue and silver body breaking the surface. The disappointment when the line went slack was almost unbearable. The loss of our quarry was not always due to it freeing itself but to the seagulls that followed us, their sharp eyes sighting the fish below the surface and so making it easy for them to dive in and steal it. Their skills never failed to impress me but when shoals were small it was annoying.

The most impressive sight of all was the seals who, as soon as they heard us approaching Birds Rock, slid so gracefully off the rocky ledges and made for the boat. They then kept station only a short distance behind, helping themselves to an easy meal as we drew in our catch. Some evenings, Will came with us and brought his guitar to play to them. The moment he began, they would gather around us, bumping against the boat and jostling with each other in their efforts to get as near as possible, their soulful eyes gazing at us as though mesmerized. At those times, the engine would be shut off while we slowly drifted through the water. The scene was one of unforgettable beauty with those dark, bobbing heads all around us, listening so obviously to the soft strains of the music, and the magnificent red of the setting sun, its rays reflecting like dancing flames across the flat calm of the sea. Even the birds, returning for the night to their lofty ledges on the rock, seemed to hesitate and appreciate the scene below them. Only as the sun met the horizon would we hurriedly make for home, usually arriving as the last rays of light died away from the sky.

An exciting but less enchanting incident involving one of the seals took place one morning at the end of the jetty. Goronwy Jones, the shipping clerk who had replaced Mr Lewis on his retirement, and who was as kind and tolerant as his predecessor, was busy attending to his duties in the office when he noticed severe turbulence of the water in that area. He drew my Father's attention to it and for some minutes they both stood watching. Unable to see any reason for it, they decided to go there to have a closer look.

Reaching the end of the jetty, they looked down and there, immediately below them, they saw one of the most unusual sights they had ever seen, that of a vicious fight between one of the seals and a conger eel of at least six feet in length. As they watched fascinatedly, the contestants lunged and bit ferociously at each other, at times leaping clear out of the water which, by then, was turning red with spilt blood. Suddenly, the fighting stopped and the blood-covered participants rested on the waves, for all the world like those in a boxing match when the bell rings at the end of a round. Having rested for a minute or so, the next round began and continued just as ferociously as before until they again retired to rest. This pattern went on for at least half an hour until the seal, turning swiftly, managed to grab the conger across its back and hold it. For a moment all movement ceased and the onlookers thought it was all over when, like lightning, the conger brought its head round and savagely bit into the seal. However, the seal, despite the agony it must have been suffering, did not yield and, slowly but surely, the conger's threshing stopped. The seal then let it go and it sank out of sight. For a few moments the exhausted and wounded seal rested while the waves gently washed over it and then it, too, disappeared beneath the surface of the blood-stained water.

Our lobster pots, usually in strings of four or six, would be set at the end of the jetty or close into the rocks that abound around the headlines. Going to check the pots was also very exciting but very disappointing when they were found to be empty, with the bait gone. Happily, this did not happen too often. Unlike the situation today, the waters around our coasts teemed with marine life and because of it, catches were generally rewarding.

At first I did not think that I would ever find the courage to plunge my hand into the pot to grasp one of its occupants and at the same time manage to avoid its dangerous claws, whilst manoeuvring its body out through the so narrow neck of the pot. The big lobsters were the most formidable as not only did one have to avoid those vicious claws but the strong flapping tail. However, I was slowly gaining that courage when something happened that put me back quite a time.

It happened one evening when, fortunately, Bob Williams was with us. We were off Caernant headland. I was in charge of the tiller while the two men were busy lifting and emptying the pots. The catch was quite good, with several crabs and a lobster or two in each. In the last one to come up there was only the one lobster but it was an exceptionally large specimen, certainly the largest we had ever caught and at once we became excited, wondering whether its size would break any records. I remember thinking that, being so large, it must have had some difficulty in getting into the pot. As I watched, my Father grasped it firmly across the back and brought it up to the neck opening. The lobster, resisting its removal, fought madly with flailing claws snapping and tail flapping furiously.

After losing his grip several times, my Father once again succeeded in getting it as far as the neck. Suddenly, he let out a piercing cry of pain and we saw that his hand was firmly gripped in the monster's big claw. For a moment we did not know what to do for we knew that the lobster would never relax its grip. Before we had time to think further, my Father, in desperation, raised his foot and brought it crashing down so heavily on the pot that the boat rocked as if it would capsize. At once Bob jumped forward and together they eventually succeeded in smashing the pot to smithereens including, of course, the hapless monster. The injured hand, although not bleeding, was badly crushed and black and blue and obviously needed treatment as quickly as possible. Without bothering to re-bait the pots, Bob threw them overboard and we made for home.

The family were shocked when they heard what had happened and saw the result and did all they could to ease the pain. Whether any bones were broken I do not know but I suspect that some must have been. It was a week or two before the pain subsided and many weeks before the hand was usable again but it never regained its normal shape.

Apart from that fright, I was only once again ever frightened in the boat. On that particular occasion, my Mother made it quite clear that she did not want us to go out fishing that evening because, although it was mainly sunny, there was a stiff breeze and white horses were very much in evidence. My Father, too, although feeling that it was safe enough for himself and Bob Vaughan, tried to dissuade me, telling me that conditions were far too rough and that I might be thrown overboard and drowned. That last possibility only made me all the more determined to go for it if I could drown then so could he and I did not at all like the idea of his drowning and leaving me behind.

We set off from the jetty and at once I realised that it was rougher than usual. However, I expected I would soon get used to it and I settled down to enjoy the trip. My enjoyment was short-lived when the boat began pitching and rolling to such an extent that even holding on to my seat was a major effort. The further we went out the worse it became but by this time the lines were out and the fish biting so well that there was no question of our turning back. On and on we went, with each on-coming wave seeming to be larger and each trough deeper than the last; up, over and down, in endless motion, with spray flying everywhere and the mackerel seemingly hell-bent on being caught. No sooner did the spinner touch the water than they obligingly hooked themselves on. The boat was filling with flapping fish and I could not help but wonder if they, too, had had enough of the sea and were willing to commit suicide to get out of it. I certainly did not want to see any more and so crawled into the bow locker to hide. The men took no notice of me whatsoever. They were far too busily occupied.

The evening wore on and we seemed to have been at sea for hours when I heard my Father say that the wind was coming round so it was time we got out of it. Daring to peep out of my hiding place, I saw through the almost blinding spray, Bob swing the tiller over, heard the surge of power from the engine and felt our change of direction. In what seemed a short time we were back at the jetty and what a relief it was to feel something firm beneath my feet again. I was asked, in a tone of 'Well, you were warned,' whether I had enjoyed the trip and, determined not to let myself down, I mentally begged for forgiveness and replied that it had been super.

Our catch, or rather theirs, amounted to two hundred

and seventy-four fish in what turned out to have been only two and a half hours. As always, having taken what we needed for ourselves, the remainder was shared in the village.

That frightening experience did nothing to dampen my enthusiasm but instead impressed on me the importance of being able to swim. The result was that only a short time afterwards, I had achieved that skill and without embarrassment to anyone else.

Chapter XVI

Never a Dull Moment

November the fifth, Guy Fawkes night, was a very important date in the Nant calendar. Looked forward to with great anticipation, it was one of the occasions in which most of the villagers participated, the children, of course, being the most actively involved. The venue was always Cae Bach which, being in the centre of the village, was an ideal site.

The falling of the autumn leaves and the changing of the ferns to bracken was the signal to start gathering this natural fuel for our giant bonfire. Every evening and at week-ends we children diligently collected this material and as much dead wood as we could find. Filling our sacks to the brim, each load was then taken to a dry place for storage. A popular storage area was, in many cases, the outside toilets and if a good harvest had been gathered, there was little room left to perform the natural functions for which the little buildings had been designed. Nevertheless, parents were most accommodating and no complaints were ever made.

As the great night drew near, empty bottles were collected and the ritual carried out of calling at each house, asking for contributions in the form of paraffin. Rags and pieces of sacking were also much in demand. These, wrapped around the ends of long poles and liberally soaked with paraffin, made excellent torches. Added to these tasks was the making of the guys and, generally, each child made his or her own. For this much searching went on in each household for the most suitable garments for the job. This sometimes caused dissention between parents and children as to what was considered suitable. I know that on one occasion in our house, trouble arose when Garnie and I made a mistake and were seen preparing to dress ours in my Father's and Will's suits, which we then discovered were far from ready to be discarded. Our mistake was the taking for granted that, as they seldom wore them, they probably did not like them.

About the second or third of the month, depending on the weather, the mountain of material was brought out of storage as the children industriously moved back and forth from storage to site, like bees to and from their hives. When all had been delivered to the field, a large circular wall was formed with the bracken, leaves and wood and the bonfire built in the centre. Once this was complete, then all that remained to be done was the placing of the resplendent guys in the circle on the evening of the fifth, immediately after school.

With the guys in position, there was nothing else to be done so we waited excitedly and impatiently for seven o'clock when the great event would begin. Shortly before the hour, everyone gathered in our drive in readiness for the procession and the torches were lit and distributed among the older and more responsible. As the hour struck, Will would emerge from the house carrying his piano accordion and, as though of one accord, an orderly line was formed behind him. Those carrying the torches then took up their positions at the head and on each side of the procession. The music then began and to the strains of 'Men of Harlech' and the sound of many melodious voices, we proceeded along the drive.

On our arrival in the field, the guys were inspected and admired by the adults and then, after liberal soakings with the paraffin, the bonfire was set alight to excited cries of glee. For some time we would watch the flames as they leapt higher and higher, penetrating the surrounding darkness, causing the branches of the nearby trees to quiver in the increasing heat as though dancing in time to the music. Eventually, the guys would be engulfed in the flames and this was always the signal to set off the fireworks. Although every family had their own supply, only one firework would be set off at a time and appreciated to the full before the next one was lit. The bangers were highly effective, as the sounds echoed along the mountains and these were the favourites among the boys, the younger children and girls preferring the sparklers, fountains and Catherine wheels while everyone, of course, loved the rockets.

The little field became a blaze of dancing lights, with the flames and rising sparks from the bonfire, the lights of the torches positioned in the furthest corners of the field and the myriad of colours exploding from the fireworks. When the last firework, usually a rocket, had faded away in the night sky, those that had brought potatoes would place them around the edge of the fire. In no time they would be ready to eat and how delicious they were, even though part of the burnt peel also found its way into one's mouth.

Some hours later, when the bonfire had become just a glowing ring of ashes, everyone gathered around the dying embers and, to the accompaniment of the accordion, sang a few more songs to round off what never failed to be a most wonderful evening. Tired but very happy, we would then make our way home.

Despite the fact that fireworks in those days contained a much larger quantity of explosive, never was there an accident, nor did anyone suffer even a minor injury.

The next important event to look forward to was, of course, Christmas and our second Christmas in the valley set a pattern in many respects for succeeding Christmases during our years there. By this time we knew everyone and had, ourselves, become part of the Nant community. For the children it was a particularly exciting time as so much seemed to happen.

The first event which always took place one evening during our last week of term was the School Concert. It was always taken very seriously and great effort was put into the rehearsals for perfection on the night. The concert was held in the Chapel, with the audience seated in the pews and the children performing in the enclosed area immediately below the pulpit. This area was known as the 'Sêt Fawr', big seat. Raised on a form of dais, with the exception of the pulpit, this was the most important part of the Chapel for here, separated from the congregation and surrounded by a carved, highly polished wood railing, was the long seat where the Elders and dignitaries sat during the services. Immediately behind the 'Sêt Fawr' was the organ where S'miss sat to play and direct us, 'the cast'. The programme consisted of country dancing, French Reels, recitation, singing, both solo and unison, and action songs. The girls were usually more enthusiastic than the boys as this presented the opportunity to dress up in our party dresses and some even had dancing pumps. An added bonus was if one was chosen to take part in the annual action song which told of a Mother's care for her baby and how that care shaped the world's destiny, the bonus being that a doll was required to represent the baby and as one could not possibly be seen to be using the same doll twice, proud parents never failed to respond. Despite her limited resources of casting material, S'miss still produced a good show, which both parents and 'stars' thoroughly enjoyed and talked of for days later. The next was always on the last afternoon of term when my Mother and Ethel came to the school and distributed a bag of sweets to each one of us after which we sang a song in appreciation.

At home, all would be bustle and activity especially in the kitchen where the air was filled with mouth-watering aromas but there I was not particularly welcome despite my offers to help. I was, however, allowed to assist with one enjoyable task, that of decorating the Christmas tree. The arrival of the tree usually caused some commotion as it was always so large but eventually it would be cut down to the right size and would stand, even then reaching almost to the ceiling, in a tub inside the bay of the dining room window. My Father would place the fairy at the very top and the rest of us would decorate the branches with bells, lanterns, baubles of every hue, tinsel and lastly the coloured lights which flashed on and off. Having finished, we would stand and gaze with admiration at our handiwork and, without fail, everyone would remark that it was even better than the year before.

Christmas Eve I always thought was very exciting. Only one more day to go, but what a very long day it always seemed to be. On one occasion, more for something to do rather than to see something I was not supposed to see, I decided to scout around to see if I could discover where the presents were hidden. Having searched several likely places, I suddenly thought of the big Grandfather clock. Making sure that no-one was around, as the clock was a positive 'no go area', I carefully unlocked the door and was just bending down to feel around inside when I heard someone coming. In my panic, I decided to hide inside the clock and so, without delay, climbed in. As I did so I bumped against the pendulum and to quote an expression of my Father's 'All hell was let loose'. The result was not a good one for me but would have been much worse had it not been for the season of goodwill.

On that day, once lunch was over, the dining room was out of bounds for me until seven o'clock, when the children from the village arrived. With us all assembled, my Mother would lead us in and there we would see the tree, laden with presents. There were also presents on the tub and on the floor. Amid gasps of wonder and delight, we would quickly settle ourselves on cushions on the floor, and moments later would come the loud knocking at the door, to be followed by the entry of Santa Claus in his long red cloak and flowing white beard. Calling each child out in turn, he would present the gifts. With the distribution of the gifts over, Santa would ask for volunteers to sing a song, perform a dance or recite a poem for him. The response at first was always very slow with everyone, including myself, too shy to make a move but, eventually, with a little encouragement, a brave volunteers' hand would go up and 'the ice was broken'. Suddenly enthusiasm would grow and several hands would shoot up, all then anxious to perform their party piece. It mattered not that the 'numbers' were always repetitions of the preceding Christmases and that little Robert Gwilym Jones, who only achieved his sixth birthday after we had left Nant, always sang with great feeling and conviction 'I'm twenty-one today'. That the assembled company and, in particular, Santa Claus enjoyed it was all that mattered to us volunteers. By the time we had exhausted our repertoire, the excitement and effort would tell on the younger ones so lemonade and mince pies were brought in and were very quickly disposed of. Soon after this, the children left for home, everyone having wished everyone else a Happy Christmas. For the first few years, I felt so disappointed that my Father, for some reason, could not be present, always coming in just after Santa had left, so missing all the fun and, in particular, the opportunity of seeing Santa Claus.

On some occasions Christmas Day and Boxing Day were spent with friends. On others the compliment would be returned and our friends would come and stay with us. Wherever the venue, Christmas afternoon was the only dull time, due to the fact that all the adults went to sleep and playing had to be carried out in a very restrained way.

One Christmas afternoon I was playing with a particularly large balloon when, suddenly, it seemed to be drawn towards the fireplace and the next moment it had disappeared up the chimney. I thought it was quite funny and would have liked to have woken everyone up to tell them about it but dare not, so turned my attention to something else when, suddenly, a cloud of black smoke came billowing out into the room. This was quickly followed by further dense clouds of smoke which brought the 'sleepers' coughing and spluttering to life, and wondering what on earth was happening. Realising then that the balloon had something to do with it, I told them what had happened. Their reaction was not pleasing but it spurred them into action and they all dashed outside to look up at the chimney. Will then ran indoors and came out again with his binoculars, saying that the lounge was black with smoke. Nothing at all could be seen on the chimney, so my Father sent Garnie to Johnnie Price's to ask him if he would come at once. Within a few minutes Mr Price arrived and after a short discussion, our longest ladder and a long wooden pole with a nail in the end were brought out. The ladder was put in position and up went Mr Price, carrying the pole. Reaching the roof, he crawled along until he had reached the chimney while we all watched nervously from below. Carefully he lowered the pole into the chimney pot and after a little manoeuvring of the pole, we heard a muffled bang and saw smoke come spiralling out.

To Mr Price's eternal credit, not for a moment did he look anything but full of goodwill, despite being called out on such a day. It would have been perfectly understandable had he felt like crowning me which, incidentally, he almost did one morning some time later but by accident rather than design. He was busily fitting new doors and frames to a number of houses in the village when I wandered past and decided to stop and have a chat with him. Whilst talking to him, I leaned against the newly positioned but yet unpinned door frame. The frame moved only slightly but sufficient to dislodge a two-pound mallet resting on the fan-light frame immediately above me. With a dull thud and a blinding pain, I felt the blow as the mallet landed squarely on my head and I fell to the ground. For a moment I felt too stunned to move or even cry out as stars appeared before my eyes and I felt sure I was going to be sick. Mr Price was horrified and looked as if he, too, was going to be sick. Quickly picking me up, he carried me home, where my Mother attended to the rapidly enlarging lump on my head and Lizzie made him a strong cup of tea, liberally laced with what I now realise was brandy. In only a short time my headache had eased and I was eager to go out and show my friends the lump which, by then, was almost as big as a pigeon's egg but the effect on Mr Price was more severe and it took a while longer for him to recover sufficiently to return to his duties.

Forty years were to pass after we left the valley before I met Mr Price again and his first words to me, said with a beaming smile, were 'Good gracious, not you again. I should have finished you off that time with the mallet'. He then recalled the event in detail and told me how terribly shocked and frightened he had been. Sadly, since our meeting, Mr Price has passed away.

With the main Christmas festivities over, there was still New Year's Day to look forward to. On that day we children went from house to house, wishing the occupants a happy new year and in return were offered fruit or sweets or a piece of cake and sometimes were invited in for a warm. The more goodwill encountered, the more the likelihood of tummy aches later in the day but this was accepted philosophically as one of the hazards of giving pleasure to others.

By Christmas time the surrounding mountain tops were usually hidden beneath a deep mantle of snow, transforming the grey starkness to a scene of sheer beauty. On clear days the scene was breathtakingly beautiful, with the peaks silhouetted against a bright blue sky and the snow sparkling and glistening in the winter sunshine, resembling a myriad of jewels set into some massive Christmas cake. Despite the familiarity of the scene, it never failed to impress us.

The arrival of snow on the mountains was no guarantee that it would simultaneously fall in the valley, or arrive in time for the Christmas holiday, at least not in any quantity, but when it did come, understandably it was not welcomed by our parents but to us children it was pure joy and we made the most of it. Snowmen were made and some were fine specimens. Snowball fights were organised with a wall of snow built to separate the teams. This game kept us entertained for hours on end but, best of all, was what we described as sledging, or tobogganing though that description was rather more imaginative than factual in view of our equipment.

The most popular place for this winter sport was one of Tŷ Ucha's fields just below Coed Ellis Bach. Here water from the mountain spread across the meadow grass and froze as it ran down the slope, so providing an excellent slide. For this, necessity was the Mother of invention for few possessed anything resembling a toboggan so, instead, we used, and became quite skilled with, spare bits of board, old pieces of matting and saucepans and frying pans. The latter were highly prized as the handles were ideal for steering. At times it proved difficult for some to find even these commodities but the others willingly shared their equipment. This had one drawback in that one had to wait for one's turn and so frequently led to impatience and, eventually, to bottomless trousers, torn skirts and shredded knickers which later, at home, usually resulted in that part of one's anatomy being well and truly warmed.

I did not know it at the time but learned later that it was a good thing that no-one, that is as far as I know, ever broke off bits of ice to suck it as children are sometimes inclined to do. This water was the overspill from a stream high up in the mountain and contained excessive amounts of chemical property which was an exceedingly powerful laxative.

Whilst we children made the most of all that winter provided, it was no fun for our parents for they had to face the difficulties created by such conditions. For the men working in the quarry, particularly those on the rock face, their task became so much more hazardous in icy conditions and at times impossible which, in turn, resulted in loss of earnings. It was no picnic either, for those in the loading gang, exposed and vulnerable as the jetty was to the North Westerlies from whence the wind came so often in the winter time. The greatest hardship for the women was the getting out of and coming back to the valley. When conditions were particularly wintery, the Screw Hill was treacherous, with every step needing extreme care but there was at least shelter until one reached the top, where the worst part of the journey began. It was there that the icy and often gale force wind bit furiously into every exposed inch of one's person and so fiercly did it blow that keeping one's feet and even being able to get one's breath was a major struggle.

I so vividly remember one particular winter journey when returning home with Garnie from Pwllheli. It had started snowing before we left the town and as the bus trundled along, the snow, already thick on the mountains, began falling fast and furiously and quickly built up on the road surface. By the time we reached Llithfaen there were at least a few inches lying underfoot and a blizzard had developed.

Hand in hand, fighting against the wind and driving snow, we slowly began the long trek home. Slithering and sliding one step backwards for every two forward, we pushed onwards up the hill. Gaining ground and benefitting from the warmth generated by our efforts, we began to enjoy the fight against the elements, imagining that we were pioneers struggling to achieve some vital goal in the face of all odds. Soldiering on, we knew that once we rounded the first bend on the Screw Hill, we would be sheltered but were not prepared for the onslaught that met us as we reached the level ground on top. Here the wind did not just blow but howled and screeched eerily in our ears, with its icy blast whipping into our faces and the snow almost blinding us. Clumps of heather and even pieces of corrugated sheeting, from heaven knows where, sped past us, bowled along like feathers by the unrelenting wind. Suddenly as we stumbled along, I found I could not get my breath and was losing the battle to keep on my feet. I became very frightened but could say nothing as I was so breathless and, in any case, had

I been able, my words would have been carried away the moment they were uttered. Fortunately, although in difficulty himself, Garnie realised the trouble I was in. Still holding on to me, he pushed me firmly behind him and indicated that I should grasp his raincoat belt with both hands and hold on as tightly as I could. Clutching his belt as though my life depended on it and sheltered by his body, I was able to breathe more easily and was no longer in danger of being blown off my feet. Starting off again with our heads bent as low as possible against the wind and snow, we made slightly better progress.

By this time the snow was deep under our feet, completely obliterating the track but as visibility was almost nil and the snow driving into our eyes forcing us to keep them shut most of the time, it did not really matter for we instinctively knew our way home. Above the howling wind, I suddenly heard a loud cracking sound coming from nearby and through narrowed eyes I saw that one of the telephone wires which ran along the mountain to the quarry, had come down and was whipping freely and dangerously along the ground. Keeping well clear of it, we stumbled on, with the blizzard raging around us. Despite the shelter of Garnie's back, my face stung with the cold and my legs ached with the effort to lift my feet clear of the snow.

I began to think that I could not go one step further when I realised that we were going downhill and, opening my eyes as much as I dare, I could just see ahead of us a huge snowdrift, covering what I knew was the Nant boundary wall. The sight was so welcoming that I almost forgot my aches and exhaustion and with renewed energy, I determined to carry on. From that point, conditions seemed to improve a little and the going became easier. At last we reached and rounded that first bend and as we began the descent, the change was immediately noticeable. No longer did I have to crouch behind Garnie but was able once more to walk beside him, holding his hand.

In short time we had rounded the second bend and there the conditions were so calm in comparison, it was as though we had entered another world. True, it was still snowing hard and very cold but now we were protected by the mountains from the unleashed fury still raging above. Taking care, for the track was very slippery, we reached the bottom without mishap. There the snow fell in large flakes, drifting down almost silently and occasionally swirling in the light wind, making it hard to believe that only a short time before, we had been battling for our lives. At least, that was how it had seemed to me. The relief of arriving home defies description but so exhausted were we that whilst sitting by the fire, drinking hot Ovaltine and telling our story, we both fell asleep before we had finished.

The Christmas holidays were always over too soon but, nevertheless, we returned to school glowing with good health and eager to get on with our lessons. There was also the fact that we were keen to see S'miss again and tell her all about our holiday. On reflection, I realise that her regular post-holiday request for essays on 'My Holiday' rather than verbal accounts was good educational strategy and it never failed.

Chapter XVII

A Case of Conceit

Styles and fashions were seldom in evidence in Nant as our environment demanded only the most practical of wear. That is not to say that no-one was interested. On the contrary, when our women folk went to Chapel or to town, their appearance generally compared favourably with most.

Apart from shopping in Pwllheli, a number chose to buy through the mail order catalogues and these catalogues were well and truly thumbed and carefully studied before ordering. Others took advantage of the services of Mr Jones, the proprietor of the little shop in Llithfaen known as the Fron. Mr Jones Fron came to the village regularly, bringing with him samples of his goods and also catalogues from which one could choose. Unlike buying in the town, one did not necessarily have to pay on delivery but could become a member of what was known as the Club and so pay an agreed sum every week.

In such a close community it was not surprising that when giving something new its first airing, everyone would notice and admiring glances were the order of the day but seldom did anyone have the bad manners to comment unless invited to do so. The children, on the other hand, had no such inhibitions. Appearing in something new was an open invitation to close examination of the article, questions as to where one had got it, how much it had cost and finally, the summing up on whether it suited one or not.

Not only were new clothes and shoes subjected to this scrutiny and interest but anything that was different. It, therefore, could have been no surprise to Olwen Tŷ Canol when she arrived at school one morning wearing spectacles for the first time, to find herself the centre of attraction. My interest on this occasion was much greater than any of the other children and I just could not take my eyes off her. In any case, being older than I and much taller, I had always considered her to be someone worthy of respect. Added to that was the fact that only a short time before, she had discovered a new way to sing which intrigued me and for days I had been practising the new sound.

The spectacles made her look so studious and superior and her new image filled me with admiration. I asked her why she was wearing spectacles and where she had got them. She replied that she had been examined by an Optician in Pwllheli and he had advised that she should wear them and so her mother had bought them in this 'shop'. She then took them off so that I could have a good look. They were really something; not the usual steel rimmed type one so often saw. These had tortoiseshell frames and little ivory-like pads to rest on each side of the nose. How I wished I could have a similar pair for I was sure that they would do a great deal for me. Suddenly, it dawned on me that perhaps I could but then I remembered that there was nothing wrong with my eyesight. I then decided that I would have to give the problem some thought. By the end of the morning I had solved it. The answer was simple. I must convince everyone that I was finding difficulty in seeing clearly. The plan was put into operation that afternoon when work was put on the blackboard and I broke the news to S'miss. Not much notice was taken but then I realised that it would take time and a great deal of determination. Day by day I persevered and, slowly but surely, the plan took effect both at home and at school.

Having committed myself, I began to think about what I was doing and felt guilty. My actions were deceitful and would God not punish me for such deceit? Then I reasoned that God only punished people when their actions hurt others. My actions did not hurt anybody so, armed with the protection of this reasoning, I carried on with my plan. At long last my parents questioned me about my new habit of holding books close up to my face and screwing up my eyes when reading and my vague answer convinced them that it was time I had an eye test. Quite soon afterwards, and to my delight, I was told that an appointment had been made for me to see an Optician in Pwllheli.

The day duly arrived and my Mother took me for the examination. After a short wait, the Optician called us in to his surgery and I was told to sit in a large chair. On the wall directly in front of me were a number of white cards with the letters of the alphabet printed on them. The letters at the top of each one were large and bold, becoming smaller as one read down until at the bottom they became very small and faint. It was then that the enormity of my actions hit me and I became very nervous. I wished I had never started the whole business but it was too late; the die was cast.

The Optician pointed to one of the cards and asked me to read out the letters. For a moment I panicked but then, in a flash, inspiration came. I decided that the best policy was to clearly read out the largest letters and falter with the smaller ones, at the same time remembering to read 'E' as 'F', 'O' as 'C', 'H' as 'A', 'R' as 'P' and so on. This part of the test was completed without comment and I felt a little more at ease for I had not expected it to be so simple but I wondered what was to come next. This, too proved to be no problem, being a repeat of the first part except that it was done with first one eye covered and then the other. Next a small, pencil-like light was shone into each eye and finally a most peculiar-looking pair of spectacles were put on and different pieces of glass tried in turn and then taken out. This was repeated several times and each time I was asked to read the letters again. What a palaver it was. I was beginning to think it just was not worth it when the Optician indicated that he had finished and told my Mother that there was no doubt that I needed spectacles for reading.

'Good gracious,' it was over and what was more had been a success. I could hardly believe it. Little pangs of conscience began to nag me but I ignored them and went on to tell him that I would like tortoiseshell frames with little ivory rests for my nose and a red case to keep them in. Smiling down at me, he said he would see what he could do and then began writing something on a card. I waited, thinking that in only a few moments he would give me the glasses but, instead, received quite a shock when I heard him tell my Mother that they would be ready in two weeks. The disappointment was almost unbearable and I could have cried for I had pictured myself wearing them to school on the very next day. I was about to suggest to him that another two weeks might cause irreparable damage to my sight when I remembered my deceit so thought better of it and instead politely thanked him and then left with my Mother.

Two weeks seemed an age to wait but slowly the time passed and we returned to the Optician to collect the spectacles. To my delight, they were exactly like Olwen's and although the case was not red but maroon, it was near enough. Inside, the case was lined with rich velvet which had a lovely smell and attached to the lid was an oval card with my name printed on it. The Optician carefully put them on for me then handed me a mirror so that I could see myself and asked whether I liked them and if they were comfortable. Assuring him that I did and that they were, I gazed at my new image. I could hardly believe that the studious and intelligent-looking little girl in the mirror was really me. Oh, there was no doubt that they were a success.

While I sat admiring myself, my Mother settled the money side of things, which was seven shillings and sixpence and which, to my mind, was a bargain.

Soon afterwards we left the 'shop' and made our way home. Never had I been in more of a hurry to get there, so that I could exhibit my new self. As soon as we got off the bus in Llithfaen, I put them on and as we passed people we know, although they did not stop and say anything, I felt sure they were impressed.

On our arrival home, everyone inspected them and said how smart they were but emphasised that I should wear them only for reading. I explained that I had to keep them on at first so as to get used to them and my excuse was accepted without comment. At school next day everyone crowded around and the general opinion was that they were very nice. Even S'miss passed some complimentary remarks so I was well satisfied and felt that my efforts had been very worthwhile.

For some weeks I proudly wore them every waking hour

but then I began to find them a handicap as one had to be so careful when involved in any activity, not to break them. As time went on they became more and more of a handicap and so much so that I decided that the only thing to do was to tell everyone that they had been so good they had restored perfect vision and that I no longer needed them. Being admired for being studious and intelligent was all very well but when it interfered with one's activities then sacrifices had to be made. Without delay I made my remarkable recovery known and much to my surprise, no one questioned it.

The reason for this became clear many years later when I came across the long-forgotten spectacles in the back of a seldom-used drawer. Seeing them again reminded me to tell my Mother of my scheming and deceit. Having completed my confession, to which she had listened patiently, she smiled and informed me that the Optician had not been fooled for one moment and so had provided me with plain glass lenses.

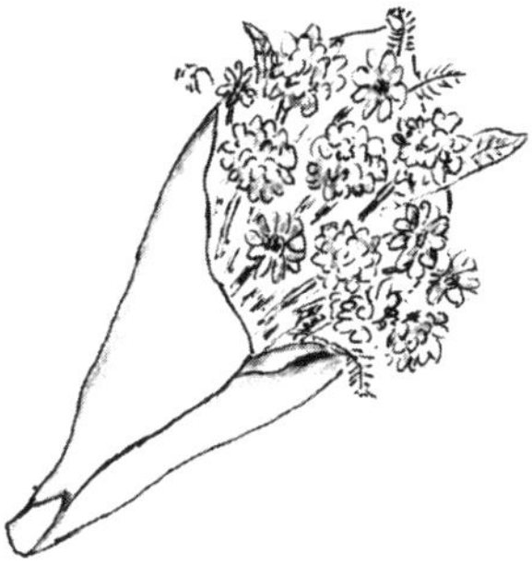

Chapter XVIII

Bessie and Ceridwen

Bessie Owen was a strikingly pretty girl with her long, naturally curly golden hair, a lovely complexion and a happy disposition. She lived at Mountain View with her parents, Mr & Mrs William Owen and her younger brother Gwilym. Mr Owen was a tall, quiet man and his wife a good-looking woman who as well as having a fine singing voice, was also an accomplished pianist. Often when passing their house I would hear Mrs Owen singing and playing and would stop for as long as possible to listen to the lovely music.

Bessie was several years older than I and, having passed her scholarship, was a pupil at Pwllheli County School but Gwilym was still a pupil at Nant. Both children were popular members of the community and the local boys, not only of Nant but Llithfaen too, greatly admired Bessie, for she was not only pretty but also charming.

Among her best friends was Ceridwen Davies of Bay View. Ceridwen was a quiet and a studious girl who was also very pretty and well-liked by everyone. Like Bessie she was a pupil at the County School and so each day the two girls travelled together to Pwllheli and when at home they spent most of their spare time in each other's company.

Bessie was fifteen years old when, in early December 1933, an important event was to take place at one of the Chapels in Llithfaen. The Owen family, like many others, were greatly looking forward to the event. Bessie was particularly excited as she was to wear a new coat that her mother had ordered especially for the occasion from Mr Jones' shop at the Fron in Llithfaen. As the coat was not in stock, Mr Jones had sent away for it and had requested urgent despatch as his customer needed it by a certain date.

One evening, only a few days prior to the event, Bessie, having finished her homework earlier than usual, decided to go to Ceridwen's for an hour or two. As she left the house, she called to her parents, telling them where she was going and saying that she would not be late home.

Within minutes the two girls were enjoying themselves at Bay View. The conversation turned to the coming event and Ceridwen asked Bessie whether Mr Jones had brought her new coat. Bessie replied that he had not and that she was getting a little anxious about it as time was getting short. Still discussing the odds of its delivery time, they began to wonder whether it might not already be at the shop but that Mr Jones had not had the opportunity to bring it to Nant. While mulling over that possibility and on the spur of the moment, they decided to go to the shop to enquire.

It was a bright moonlight night, but bitterly cold and freezing hard as the two girls set out. They reached the Fron, but to their great disappointment found that the coat had still not arrived. Mr Jones told them how sorry he was and that he expected it any day. He promised that as soon as he received it he would bring it to Nant. The girls thanked him and left to begin their journey home.

As they made their way through Llithfaen village, they saw Ceridwen's brother, Guto, and his friend, Philip Glyn Williams of Sea View, coming towards them on their motor bikes. Seeing the girls, the boys stopped to talk to them. During the conversation the girls asked if they could have a ride on the motor bikes, but the boys, not at all keen on the idea, refused, saying that it was too late to go anywhere worthwhile. The girls then began pleading with them, saying that they did not want to go anywhere special, but just for a ride. Unable to resist their pleas any longer, the boys agreed.

Bessie sat on Guto's machine and his sister on Philip's. After a brief discussion, it was decided that they would go as far as Criccieth, nine miles away. Arriving at Criccieth, they immediately turned for home as by that time it was getting really late and Bessie was concerned as her parents were under the impression that she was still at Bay View.

I was fast asleep when I was awakened by the shrill sound of our telephone bell. It rang and rang and I was wondering why someone did not answer it when I heard my Father's voice as he came out of his bedroom. I then heard him hurrying downstairs, to be followed moments later by my mother. I continued listening, holding my breath to enable me to hear more clearly, but apart from faint sounds I could hear nothing else. I must have fallen asleep again quite quickly for the next thing I knew was that I was awakened by the sound of loud and bitter crying. Instantly recalling the incessant ringing of the telephone, I realized that something was wrong and became a little frightened. For a moment or two I got back under the bed-clothes, pulling them over my head to try and drown the sounds, but it was useless, so I decided to get up and go out on to the landing to see what was happening.

Out on the landing I looked down into the hall, but could see no-one. The lights were on all over the house and as well as the crying, I could hear several voices. At that moment Garnie came out of his bedroom and asked me what was going on. I told him that I did not know and asked him to go and find out but he refused, saying that he was afraid of getting into trouble. Just then the dining-room door opened and my father, Will and Mr Owen came out looking extremely upset. As we watched, we saw Will go to the hall-stand, put on his hat and coat and then, almost immediately, he and Mr Owen left the house. My Father shut the door behind them and returned to the dining-room.

Still huddled on the landing, we were desperately trying to guess what it was all about when Lizzie came up the stairs, looking extremely distressed. We asked her what had happened and for a moment she seemed unable to answer. Then in a whisper she told us that Bessie Owen had been hurt in an accident. Mrs Owen was being looked after by our parents while Will and Mr Owen had gone to Llithfaen to find out about it. She then advised us to go back to bed at once before anyone saw us and before we caught our death of cold.

I climbed back into bed, still wondering how the accident had happened and hoping that Bessie was not badly hurt. I could not understand why Will and Mr Owen had gone to Llithfaen for surely it must be terribly late and so Bessie would not be there at that time of night. With these confused thoughts I eventually fell asleep.

When I entered the dining-room the next morning, everyone was very quiet. At once I remembered the events of the night before and asked how Bessie was and what had happened. For a moment there was silence, and then my

Mother told me that Bessie had been killed in a motor bike accident. I was stunned and could not believe it, but then, looking at the faces around the dining-room table, I knew that it must be true and, young as I was, I saw for the first time what shock and sadness did to people. My Mother would say no more except that I was not to play in the village that day.

It was later that I learned of the events leading to that fateful accident. How, as they rounded a sharp bend on the outskirts of the village of Llanystumdwy – the birth place of Lloyd George – the icy conditions of the road caused both machines to skid into one another and then smash into a stone wall. The girls were thrown off by the impact and Bessie was killed instantly. Ceridwen sustained serious injuries but, miraculously, Guto and Philip escaped with little more than shock.

Bessie's body was brought to the vestry of the Chapel where she had planned and looked forward so much to taking part in the celebrations that week-end. Ceridwen was detained in hospital in Porthmadog and the boys, after a check-up, were allowed to go home.

The telephone call to our house was from the Police to ask my Father to break the news to Mr and Mrs Owen. Later I heard him say that it was one of the most heartbreaking tasks that he had ever had to perform and the more so for, when he arrived at their house, everyone was in bed. They had retired early, expecting that Bessie would be returning quite soon.

Our little community was stunned and shocked. Losing Bessie was losing one of the family, for one family we undoubtedly were. Our grief was paramount and the village was silent for days.

The funeral took place a few days later in bitterly cold weather. First a service was held at her home and then the mourners left for Llithfaen for interment at her chapel. With the exception of those of my age and younger, almost the whole population of Nant and Llithfaen, as well as many from miles around, attended the funeral. As the mourners stood around the open grave, it seemed that the heavens, too, were mourning for the sky turned black and it began to snow heavily. Bessie's mother was utterly distraught and wept pitifully as did most of those present.

Ceridwen, broken-hearted, was unable to attend her best friends' funeral as she was still very ill in hospital and was to remain there for some time. Eventually she returned home, but a pale shadow of her former self. As the months went by she appeared to slowly improve, but then, suddenly, in the following June, she suffered a relapse and again had to be rushed to hospital. Tragically she, too, was not to return to us for she died there of a cerebral haemorrhage. Like Bessie, Ceridwen was just fifteen years old.

The accident and their untimely deaths left a deep scar on us all and even to this day it remains, for not one of us has forgotten them.

Chapter XIX

Ways and Means

During my first visit to the shops it did not occur to me to wonder how the stock had arrived there. That it was there was all that mattered. Like so many things about Nant, realization dawned gradually, growing with me, so to speak, and when fully realized, did not seem at all odd. These were my only experiences and so were accepted as the natural order of things, for if that was how it was done in Nant, then there was no other way.

The horses and sledges were our lifeline as far as necessities were concerned, for everything that was beyond human transportation relied upon their power. It was, therefore, in this manner that Evan Wynne, three times a week, and George Matt, once weekly, brought their goods to the village. In these days of supermarkets, where it is a case of cart it yourself or do without, the efforts of these men

Evan Wynne Owen (grocer)

to deliver the goods regardless of weather conditions were highly commendable.

Evan Wynne also owned a grocery shop in Llithfaen where his wife would take charge on his Nant days. Leaving Llithfaen at about ten o'clock in the morning, he would come down to Tŷ Canol to catch the horse. Having caught and then harnessed the animal to the sledge, he would lead it back to the top of the Screw Hill where, at noon, he would rendezvous with the bread van. The van not only brought bread, but also the goods for the shop. With the bread and goods transferred to the sledge, he would set off on the return journey to Nant and on arrival would unload and then return the horse to Tŷ Canol. Only then could he open for business, and more often than not, the shop remained open until late in the evening. Only on occasions, when there had been a particularly high tide, would he shut the shop for an hour or so to go hunting crabs and lobsters under the rocks on the beach.

Evan Wynne was not the only one to follow this pursuit. Those of the village, including we children, enjoyed the hunt, and all that was needed for this was a long, straight, iron rod, with one end bent into the form of a hook. The hooked end was pushed under those rocks which were left exposed after the high tide and then drawn out, sweeping before it anything lurking beneath. Many an enjoyable meal was provided by this method.

The horses were in no danger of becoming redundant, for no vehicle was capable of coping with such gradients and sharp bends. However, there were those who, from time to time, would come and attempt to be the first to conquer the formidable track. An occasional vehicle would achieve some measure of success, only to become stuck part of the way down. News of this would travel fast and on reaching the village, a number of children would race to the scene to help push it back up the hill. If successful, they would be rewarded with pennies. Failure to move the vehicle would necessitate calling out Mr Thomas Tŷ Canol or Mr Hughes Tŷ Ucha with their horses, which was generally the case.

Such was the challenge of this hill that every Easter, motor cycling clubs would come there from as far afield as Liverpool to test their machines. Some of these would achieve the descent, but few would succeed on the return journey, and a number would come to grief.

One vehicle, however, did make it to the valley, but by a most unorthodox route. Its arrival caused not only a great deal of excitement, but a great deal of concern, and when it happened, the news spread like wild-fire.

We children were busily occupied with play, when we heard that there had been an accident. A car had crashed over Graig Ddu. Instinctively we looked towards the mountain, but could see nothing as the lower region was hidden from the village at that point. A number of people were already running towards the area and we, wanting to see exactly what had happened, ran after them. Everyone looked extremely anxious; fearful of what they would find. Even the youngest amongst us realized that anyone having crashed down that sheer rock face would at least be severely injured, if not fatally so.

Breathlessly we arrived on the scene to find a few people already there. All were staring helplessly at the sad sight of the shattered remains of a car, lying at the foot of the rock, with its wreckage strewn over a wide area. It was impossible to get near the car as that particular terrain was mainly bog, being where the mountain streams converged, forming the river which fed our reservoir which was a few yards lower down the valley. Someone asked what had happened to the occupants and we were told that, mercifully, there had been no-one in the car when it crashed. Later we heard the story. It appeared that the car was being driven along the track which ran across the mountain to Caernant when, above Graig Ddu, the steering suddenly snapped and the vehicle careered off the track towards the edge of the precipice. Seconds before it plunged over, the three young men occupants were able to scramble to safety. It had been a miraculous escape and was a great relief to everyone.

With the excitement over, we were about to leave when we spotted something among the ferns. At first we had no idea what it was, but then one of the boys discovered that it was the car's klaxon horn. This piece of equipment was to amuse us for days until it was taken away by our elders who said that they could not stand the noise for one moment longer. As we noisily made our way back to the village with our new toy, little did we know that the crash was to cause a minor crisis in our community.

It was some time later that day that the petrol-tainted

water found its way into our taps. As the reservoir was our only source of drinking water, the situation was very serious, but no-one knew what to do about it. Removal of the wrecked car was discussed, but almost immediately dismissed for its position in the bog made it impossible to reach, let alone get it out. It soon became obvious that there was nothing that anyone could do but wait until the petrol had worked its way through the system. How long that would take no-one knew. In the meantime, all we could do was hope and pray for heavy rain in the next few days. As though in answer to our prayers, the next morning dawned with heavy, black clouds and soon the heavens opened and the so welcome rain poured down for many hours. With every possible container brought into use, plus the few water butts in the village, every drop was saved. Rain came, too, on the following two days and so we survived without too much difficulty until the reservoir was once again clear of petrol.

Some years later, two more cars came plunging down into the valley but, fortunately, did not land in the stream. On neither occasion was anyone in the vehicle when they came toppling over, but the circumstances of the accident led to suspicion that they were caused by design rather than by accident. Eventually one was proved to be the result of a plan to claim insurance, but I am uncertain about the other, as both occurred after my time there.

During the summer months occasional holiday-makers would find their way down to the valley and were invariably spotted by the children. As strangers were rare in Nant, we were always eager to talk to them and they, in return, never failed to show great interest in our isolated existence and would shower us with questions.

These people were mainly town dwellers but, of course, dedicated hikers for had they not been, they would not have ventured down the Screw Hill, particularly as from the top there was no sign of human habitation below. Without exception they would remark on the rugged beauty and tranquility of our surroundings and, hearing of our way of life, would be amazed that a civilised existence in such an isolated, and to them inaccessible place, was not only possible but enjoyable to us. Seeing this, the hardier of them would become almost envious of our position until they realized that this involved living there not only in the summer but also in the long winter months. This realization soon dampened their envy.

Apart from the holiday makers, other occasional visitors were the divers. These men's services were essential to ensure safe clearance for the ships in the jetty area.

While the Screw Hill presented its problems and challenges, particularly to outsiders, so on occasions did our other boundary, the sea. Although the valley was so sheltered by the mountains, our bay was open to the fury of storms and gales, especially when the wind came from the north-west. During these storms and the resultant heavy swells, large and sometimes quite enormous rocks would be dislodged from the beach. These were then bowled over like nine-pins and driven by wind and water into the sea. Rocks off shore would also be disturbed and over a period of time, these would build up on the sea bed, so affecting the depth of water at the end of the jetty and presenting a serious hazard to ships.

To deal with this hazard, divers would have to be called in from Liverpool, and for us children this was a most exciting event. Should it occur during term-time. S'miss would be notified beforehand and on occasions she would take us to the end of the jetty to watch the proceedings. Once there she would warn us not to chatter, get in anyone's way or move from our positions unless otherwise directed.

It says much for her control of us that with so many children of varying ages on an open jetty where misbehaviour could so easily have caused an accident if not a tragedy, never was there a complaint about us or even a minor accident.

There were always two divers to attend to the problem and as there was so much to be done, they would waste no time. Great interest was paid by the children to their every move and especially when they donned their peculiar-looking suits. The suits were made of thick, black rubber, so different from today's lightweight wet suits, and with the exception of hands and feet, completely enveloped the body. The head gear, which resembled a fish bowl, was large and heavy, made of brass with a glass panel protected by wire mesh in the front, through which the diver could see where he was and what he was doing. This head piece was put over the head and screwed down firmly on to a metal yoke on the shoulders of the suit to ensure that it was air-tight. Special footwear was worn in the form of lead-weighted boots which prevented the diver from floating upside-down and helped him to stand his ground on the sea-bed. To enable breathing, a long hose was attached to the head piece with its other end fitted to the pump. The pump resembled a large box with a handle similar to that of a mangle and this handle, when turned, operated the bellows which supplied air to the diver.

When all the equipment was laid out and the divers were ready, one of them would descend into the water while his partner operated the pump. After a short time they would reverse their roles. Eventually the explosives were taken down and when both divers were back on the jetty, the explosives were detonated. This would be the highlight of the proceedings for us as we waited for the bangs. Suddenly there would come a series of muffled explosions and the water would burst up almost to jetty height. Before the excitement had died down, all would be still and silent again. Once more the divers would disappear under the water to inspect the result and, having satisfied themselves that the job was well and truly done, would prepare to leave. It was at this time that we were allowed to see their suits and equipment in more detail, and some were lucky enough to be able to try on the head piece. This was always considered to be a great honour. Having seen all there was to see, S'miss would gather us together and, having expressed our thanks, would lead us back to the school.

Apart from the Screw Hill, there was one other track that led out of the valley. It was not an easy route as it involved passing along the quarry bank which was out of bounds when blasting was imminent, or in progress, and from there it climbed steadily through the wooded area which covered the southern slopes of the mountain directly above the beach. While in dry conditions this walk between the trees was so pleasant and especially so in autumn when blackberries and hazelnuts could be picked along the way, in wet conditions it was most uncomfortable. The narrowness of the track where, in places, the trees almost met, usually meant a good soaking as one brushed against them while struggling along the slippery path. Once out of the trees, the going became easier until the track suddenly ended at a stile in a stone wall. From the other side it continued through a field into a farmyard then up another short but steep incline. Eventually it reached level ground from where it passed through two gates and finally out on to the main Llithfaen to Nefyn road.

The fact of having to face such stiff climbs to get out of the valley meant little or nothing to us children. We were so used to it our legs and lungs grew strong and healthily because of it. The fuss made about it by strangers and visitors never failed to surprise us, and on occasions made us angry when some of them expressed pity for our plight in having to live in what they described as a 'God-forsaken hole'. Their pity, however, fell on stony ground for to us Nant was a mini paradise.

Chapter XX

Well Occupied

With the nearest cinema in Pwllheli, going to the pictures, as we called it, was a rare treat for us in Nant. In those pre-bingo, pre-television days, the town sported two such establishments. One was the Palladium, the other the Town Hall Picture House. The Palladium, in contrast to the Town Hall, was a new, imposing looking building with a wide flight of steps leading up to glass doors at the entrance. Inside was a richly carpeted foyer from where the carpet continued up a sweeping staircase to the balcony seats and the restaurant. The restaurant, with its glass-topped green wicker leg tables and matching chairs, attracted me almost as much as the film shows, for there, one was served with delicious ice-cream and mouth-watering, cream-oozing cakes.

Among the most popular screen heart-throbs and stars of the time were Jean Arthur, Greta Garbo, Carole Lombard,

Clark Gable and Robert Taylor. Should any of these be on the programme, I stood a good chance of being taken by Ethel as she was a keen fan. The main feature seldom interested me and frequently I would be asleep by the end of it, but I adored the cartoons. Mickey Mouse, Popeye and Donald Duck in particular, filled me with wonder and the next day would find me recounting every detail to my friends.

My Father did not at all care for the cinema. In fact, I remember him going on one occasion only and that occasion was many years later as a result of pressure put on him by the family. The film was 'Jamaica Inn', a sea-faring tale of smugglers in the windjammer days which we all thought would interest him. It did do so, but even then only to a degree. Nevertheless, his lack of interest in film-going did not prevent him from thinking that something of that nature would provide fine entertainment for the rest of us in Nant during the long, dark winter evenings. True, there was an occasional magic lantern show in Llithfaen to which some people went but at that distance it was not ideal.

On arrival home one lunch-time, I was surprised to see two parcels in the hall, one very long and thin, the other large and square. Rushing in to my Mother, I excitedly asked what they were and why they had not been opened. She replied that they belonged to my Father. They were a secret and were not to be touched until he came home. She hurriedly added that I could quickly dismiss any thoughts of ringing him up as he had been adamant about it being a secret. I returned to the hall and examined every inch of the parcels but, apart from seeing that they came from some studios in London, I was none the wiser.

Throughout the afternoon, I could not concentrate on my lessons. The thought of what was in those parcels was almost burning a hole in my brain. They must be very special or they would not be a secret, although no-one in the house was due for a birthday and it was nowhere near Christmas. Whatever could they be? Try as I might, I could find no answer. The bell went at last and instead of going home I went straight down to the office but, despite my wiles and pleadings, my Father refused to reveal his secret.

That evening, after what seemed to me to be the longest meal he had ever had, he was ready to unwrap the parcels. From the first parcel he carefully extracted a most odd-looking contraption. Then came a box, out of which he took a flat, round tin, inside which was a reel. As I watched, wide-eyed, he explained that the peculiar-looking object was a cinematograph, on the reel was a film and in the long parcel was a screen, similar to the one at the cinema.

With mounting excitement, we waited while he read the book of instructions and then proceeded to assemble the machine. Next, the screen was put in position over the dining-room window and the lights were switched off. After a few technical hitches, the film came on and we sat back in wonder and amazement to watch one of Charlie Chaplin's films. The fact that it was a silent film and one had to read the sub-titles to follow the story, did nothing to spoil our enjoyment. That it was possible to sit and watch such a thing in our own dining-room, was simply fantastic.

When it was over, I discovered that the cinematograph and screen were ours to keep, but the film was on loan. Should a film be kept longer than the two day hire period, a penalty as well as extra fees would have to be paid, so care had to be taken never to incur a penalty.

Arrangements were made to hire one feature film and one cartoon every two weeks during the winter months and invite anyone and everyone in the village to join us for the showing. For the performance, the dinning-room furniture was moved against the walls, cushions laid out in rows on the floor for the children and chairs at the back for the adults. The films were shown as planned every other week and generally there was a 'full house'. Among the best-remembered films were, 'Marvels of the Amazon', a wonderful production of a journey down that mighty river, 'Tiger Bay', starring the beautiful Chinese actress, Anna May Wong, numerous Charlie Chaplain comedies, and the inimitable Mickey Mouse, Popeye and Donald Duck cartoons. The project proved to be a highlight of those winter evenings and, on occasions, even enticed friends from Llithfaen to join us. The new innovation not only provided great entertainment, but for us children the advantage of notching up yet another mark against the other villages to prove that we in Nant moved with the times.

The success of this venture led to thoughts of providing other forms of pastimes and so the next acquisition was a billiard table. One of our bedrooms was cleared, two or three easy chairs placed in the corners and it became the billiard room. This, too, proved to be a success and reversed the roles of those who had previously gone to Llithfaen to play when, instead, their boys came to Nant for a game. I have since been told that the journey was a small price to pay for the enjoyment of those evenings for, at the end of the evening, there were sandwiches, cakes, biscuits and lemonade which my Mother thought essential for still growing men. As the players became more proficient, so teams were chosen for serious competitions and although friendly, the matches were as keenly played and supported locally as today's national tournaments.

I, too, was very keen on the game and was sometimes allowed to play with one or two friends, usually against Garnie and his friend, Robert Banston, but this was tolerated rather than encouraged. When the other boys came, we would consider ourselves lucky to be allowed to attend to the scoreboard. Failing to be allowed in at all, we would amuse ourselves by knocking on the door and running away, or by pushing urgent messages under the door. This was always short-lived fun, for complaints to my Father would soon put a stop to it.

Quite some time after the arrival of the billiard table, Robert and his parents moved to Llithfaen. With no sign of new tenants for the house my Father, not wishing it to remain empty, decided that we children could use it for games. The bigger boys were given possession of the upstairs, and it became a mini boxing club, while we younger ones had the downstairs. The only furniture was two old, wooden chairs which the boys took possession of, but it was of no concern to us as we made the downstairs quite comfortable with empty gunpowder boxes. These were in plentiful supply from the quarry and were ideal, as they were clean and strong and substituted for chairs and tables and were ideal for storing things. Lighting was provided by candles placed in jam-jars. On rare occasions we were allowed a wood fire in the grate and with some old matting on the floor, the place was warm and cosy.

On reflection, our parents must have had faith in our common sense to allow us to have such things as matches and candles. True, we were loosely kept an eye on, but never once did we betray that faith. Presumably, the answer was that, unlike some of today's young, we were never without something to do although it was generally of our own making; being bored was something totally outside our experience and, of course, we were not faced with the disadvantage of acres of concrete.

There was, however, one unfortunate incident involving the play-house, but not with fire. Little David Roberts, Menna and Sam Roberts' son, had wandered alone upstairs and was happily playing there when a figure, enshrouded in a white sheet appeared in the doorway. Seeing what he thought was a ghost, he became absolutely terrified and jumped straight out through the window. Hearing the crash, neighbours ran out and found him lying on the ground, covered in blood. Immediately, willing hands carried him home where, to everyone's relief and amazement, it was found that his only injury was severely cut head. Having been cleaned up, David was carried to Llithfaen where, at his grandmother's the doctor put five stitches in the cut.

The perpetrator of the accident was never identified, having got away through the back door while everyone was busily engaged at the front. Doubtless, it was meant to be an innocent bit of fun but, as with so many intentional jokes, could have so easily ended in tragedy. Happily, David recovered without any ill effects, and there never was another such incident.

The boxing provided great fun and was taken just as seriously as the billiards, the contestants secretly fancying themselves as budding Tommy Farr's or Joe Louis's. Talk of bantam-weights, feather-weights and heavy-weights became part of our everyday jargon. A contest between one of the Llithfaen boys and one of ours was cause for great excitement and never failed to draw a number of spectators. Not only the boys took part in these contests but also a number of the young married men.

While Will occasionally took part in most sports, his keenest interest was in music and to this end he would invite music-loving friends to share his passion. Three of the regulars came from Llithfaen, Ioan Mai Evans, George (Matt) Williams of our shop and Ifor Owen or Ifor Nest as we knew him as Nest was the name of his home. Will played the guitar, piano accordion and banjo and the others, the fiddle and violin and all were accomplished instrumentalists. Added to this were fine singing voices, Ifor Nest's in particular.

Although I, too, was keenly interested in music, my talents as a two finger pianist were not welcome, but I was permitted to sit in on the sessions on the strict condition that I did not speak or move about. Despite the severity of the conditions I accepted them as I had fallen deeply in love with Ifor Nest. The fact that I was about five at the time and he probably in his late teens, was of no concern to me. My reward would come when they stopped for refreshments and I was then sometimes allowed to sit on his knee.

Of the outdoor sports, football was the most popular. Due to our small numbers and variety of ages, enlisting a full team was difficult but pro-Nant supporters from Llithfaen readily 'signed on' and produced a reasonable team. Cae Bach, the little field between our drive and the village gardens was ideal for the pitch as it was fairly level. The lack of refinements such as goal posts and nets, was no handicap as coats and scarves or piles of stones were adequate. Football boots, too, were non-existent, but as many of the boys wore hob-nail boots – the most suitable footwear for such terrain as ours, these were ideal for the game. The girls, too, played on some occasions, but for us the hazard of those boots was rather off-putting for serious involvement.

With no outside lighting system, playing outside after dark was generally limited to moonlit nights, and then only such games as hide and seek were practical. Nevertheless, at these times we managed to thoroughly enjoy ourselves. The greatest handicap was that of being called in for bed-time. This always seemed to happen when one had found the perfect hiding place and had yet to be discovered. My call frequently came before anyone else's and under the circumstances, was extremely difficult to respond to. In any case, it was never welcome, but my call of, 'Coming in a minute', would reassure that I was near at hand and would sometimes gain me an extension. After this would come a number of calls, each more urgent than the last and to which I would finally have to respond, but the result by that time was seldom one of great pleasure to see me. These circumstances were far from satisfactory so I tried not hearing the first few calls, claiming that I must have been just our of ear-shot. This ruse was a complete failure after the second attempt.

Tiring of the situation and on the verge of putting a stop to my participation in these moonlit games, my Father had what he considered was a brilliant idea. From his sea-faring days, he had kept a Bosun's whistle which he treasured and it was this that was brought out to solve the problem. Being loud and shrill, its sound penetrated almost the length and breadth of the valley, so nowhere could I be and not hear it. The first blow would give me ten minutes notice and the next would be the dead-line. It certainly did solve the problem for my parents but not from my point of view.

Ever conscious of our needs and wishing to see us achieve the best from our childhood, my Father next had what we all considered a first class idea, that of having an electric lamp fitted to the outside wall of our house. The lamp was soon in position and proved to be a great advantage. Not only did it light up the wide area around the front door, but was sufficiently powerful to illuminate as far as the bend halfway up the drive.

No longer were we confined to hide and seek but had a choice. Cowboys and Indians was ideal in these circumstances, the dark shadows perfect for ambushes and observation, and the lower branches of the trees serving as horses from which one could drop on to one's clearly seen but unsuspecting adversaries. Guns were always any piece of wood that bore some resemblance, sometimes regardless of how remote, to the real thing. If chosen carelessly, one ran the risk of brandishing a piece so dead that, on poking one's captive in the chest and demanding that he fall down dead, the muzzle would disintegrate with the result that the captor became the captive. We girls were seldom allowed much of the action, but instead were detailed to look after the camps, dress imaginary wounds and cook the food. Although not entirely happy with our role, we nonetheless enjoyed every moment.

To the reader, particularly in this day and age, our pleasures and pastimes may seem to have been so unsophisticated and simplistic as to have been extremely dull. However, to us they were what dreams are made of and were played out in our little piece of heaven.

Chapter XXI

Caernant

Caernant Quarry, independent of Nant and Carreg-y-Llam, was owned by the Croft Granite Company, a family concern that also owned Tŷ Uchaf farm. Situated high up on the valley's northern boundary, on that part of the mountain that ran sheer to the sea, its galleried workings in such a prominent position bore sad witness to man's destructive powers.

Known commercially as Port Rivals its jetty, a short distance along the beach from ours, was linked to the quarry by a narrow gauge railway. Unlike our quarries, Caernant dealt mainly with one particular shipping company whose ships all carried that company's name. Three I remember were the *Lady Thomas*, the *Doris Thomas* and the *Nancy Thomas*. The *Doris Thomas* I have particular reason to remember. It has been said that there was a family tie-up with the shipping company and the quarry, but I have not been able to prove this.

Above the quarry, not far from the mountain top, stood a lonely looking house. It was, in fact, a bungalow, but for some reason was always referred to by the children as a house. I had often wondered who lived there and on asking was told that it belonged to the quarry and had been built for the manager. The manager at the time being a bachelor and not wishing to live there alone, stayed at the 'Vic' in Llithfaen, so leaving the house unoccupied. Its location in such an isolated spot and the fact that it had been empty for some time, led to rumours among the children that the house was haunted. All sorts of eerie stories were told about it and it was these stories that prompted Garnie and his friends to go there one afternoon to investigate.

Setting off eagerly and full of confidence, they made the long trek up the mountain but, nearing the house, their earlier bravado deserted them. With one nervously pushing the other ahead, they reached the front door and to their great relief found that it was locked and barred. Finding no other means of entry, all they could do was peep through the windows and, seeing nothing of any consequence, they returned home to tell of their great disappointment.

The visit to the house was forgotten until one day a policeman was seen entering the village. So seldom was there reason for a policeman to visit Nant that the sight aroused not a little curiosity. That curiosity turned to utter disbelief when it became known that the boys had been reported to the authorities for breaking, entering and causing wilful damage to the so-called 'Haunted House'. When questioned by the policeman each boy in turn categorically denied the allegations, but despite their denials they and their parents were warned that they would be hearing further on the matter.

Not having taken the warning too seriously, everyone was surprised when, a short time later, the parents received letters informing them that their sons were summoned to appear later that month at the Magistrate's Court to answer charges. The news soon got around the village and even those not directly involved were angry, feeling that to cast a slur on any one of our community was to slander us all. Not for one moment did anyone entertain the thought that the boys were guilty. Mischievous certainly, but wanton little vandals or criminals, never.

The waiting proved to be daunting, but at last the day arrived and the boys accompanied by their fathers left for Pwllheli. Those left waiting in the village felt worried about the outcome, despite their conviction of the boys' innocence. Feelings ran particularly high among the children, who speculated on what would happen should the 'Judge' refuse to believe them. Perhaps they would be thrown into gaol for years and fed on only bread and water! That such a dreadful thing should happen to them was beyond contemplation and so, like everyone else, we uneasily awaited their return.

It was early afternoon when they eventually arrived home and one look at their jubilant faces told us that all must be well and they could hardly wait to tell us what had taken place. On hearing their case called, they nervously went forward and were directed to take the stand. This directive proved to be a mistake for in that position the boys were almost hidden from view, leaving only one pair of eyes, those of the tallest boy, and a number of heads, visible to the court. Seeing the humour of the situation, a number of those present began laughing but the chairman was not at all amused. Instead, looking somewhat annoyed, he asked that a box or something similar be brought for them to stand on. These were quickly provided but even this aid to their height was not totally successful for now, although most of the tallest's face was visible, the rest were represented solely by their eyes.

Some whispering went on at the bench and eventually the hearing began. Statements were made by the police and the company's representative and all were based largely on hear-say. The boys were then asked to answer truthfully and to the best of their ability all questions put to them. Due to the difficulty of seeing the accused, this part of the proceedings became farcial. After struggling for some minutes the chairman, in exasperation, called a halt, saying that it was beyond his comprehension why such little boys, on such scant evidence, had been summoned to the court in the first place. He then turned to his fellow magistrates and after further whispering, announced that he was dismissing the case as the bench had decided that there was no case to answer.

For us in Nant the result meant that justice had triumphed for we had known all along that the boys were innocent. A little later we discovered that the actual damage to the property amounted to broken windows. This need not have been the result of vandalism but could just as easily have been caused by stray stones when blasting was carried out at the quarry.

The beach at Caernant, unlike Nant, was mainly large stones and boulders, so we younger children seldom had any desire to go there. Later this proved to be fortuitous.

It was some two years after the court case that, one day, Garnie and three friends took a stroll along to that beach. The tide was out at the time and whilst playing around at the water's edge, one of the boys caught hold of a wire stay which ran from a post on the jetty to a metal bolt set into a slab of concrete on the beach below. Suddenly, he called out that he could not free himself from the wire. The others looked up and at first thought he was joking until they saw that his whole body was jerking like a puppet on a string. Immediately, they ran forward and the first on the scene, taking hold of his friend's out-stretched hand to pull him away, found to his horror that he, too, was held fast. Instantly the other two boys linked hands and, together grasping the captives, they pulled with all their might, and after some effort finally succeeded in freeing them. For some time afterwards they lay on the ground, still shaking and jerking from the shock. Gradually the effects wore off and the moment they were able, they hurried home to tell my Father what had happened.

Hearing about the incident and their narrow escape, my Father was absolutely furious and at once telephoned Caernant's manager, informing him that the wire was live and demanded that it immediately be made safe. The manager, too, was most upset when he heard about it and assured my Father that it would be attended to at once. Despite this assurance, the boys were warned never to go near that wire again.

The wisdom of that warning was brought home to them one glorious summer afternoon, not long after the incident. It was a Sunday and, being a Sunday, the village was quiet, with the weekday sounds of the quarry stilled. No ships were berthed at either Carreg-y-Llam or at our jetty, but there was one at Caernant and another out in the bay waiting to come in.

In our house, lunch had been over for some time. The grown-ups were resting and I was preparing to go to the beach. Suddenly, the peace of the afternoon was shattered when someone knocked loudly and urgently on our front door. I heard Lizzie answer the door and then rush to summon my Father. The next think I heard was my Father hurrying out of the house and calling to my brother as he

View across Bay to Trwyn y Gorlech and Caernant showing Nant and Caernant Jetties

went, 'There has been an accident. Quickly, get blankets, hot water bottles and some brandy and bring them to Caernant beach.' Immediately Will and Garnie responded and in what seemed only seconds they were on their way.

Wondering what on earth could have happened, I decided to follow them and began running as fast as my legs would carry me. As I ran down the slope, I was joined by many other people. The news spread like wild-fire and half the population seemed to be running to the scene. We reached the grassy mound just above the beach and there, surrounded by men, including my Father, lay a young man. He was wearing bathing trunks and lying perfectly still. I could see no sign of blood or any injury, but then I saw that his face was very blue and his lips an even darker blue. Very quickly, though gently, he was wrapped in the blankets and my Father and another man, a stranger, bent oven him and seemed to be very close to his face. Everyone was very quiet, but as such a crowd had gathered, we were asked by one of the men to move back and everyone immediately obeyed.

I heard someone say that Dr Jack had been sent for and also that a doctor from Nefyn was being sought. I wondered how a doctor from Nefyn could possibly get there before Dr Jack. I then heard that some of the loading gang had gone there by ship in a desperate attempt to get help as quickly as possible. It appeared that the ship awaiting her turn in the bay had been signalled to come in and she, responding immediately, had found just enough room to nose in to the end of the jetty astern of the *Doris* who was in the process of being loaded. The moment she was close enough, the men jumped aboard, told the captain what had happened and asked him to take them to Nefyn to get a doctor. Without a moment's delay, the ship was turned about and made for Nefyn at full speed. They had covered about half the distance when, to their amazement, someone spotted the doctor fishing from a rowing boat only a short distance away. Hardly able to believe their eyes, they informed the captain. The ship immediately hove to and the doctor was hailed. Only minutes later, with the doctor aboard, they were on their way back to the jetty. However, their commendable efforts in what must have been record time proved to have been in vain for on their arrival they found Dr Jack already there.

The moment the doctor appeared, sighs of relief and feelings of hope ran through the anxious onlookers. Automatically everyone, with the exception of my Father and the stranger, moved further back while the doctor immediately got to work on his patient. For some minutes I could not see exactly what he was doing, but I did see that when he rose to his feet he was shaking his head and his expression was one of utter and hopeless despair. He spoke very quietly to the stranger and when he had finished the man, whose face was ashen, looked down at the so still figure of the young man then turned and, burying his face in his hands, began sobbing as though his heart would break.

A whisper went through the crowd, 'He has gone!' and as though unable to move, we stood there, shocked and silent, with heads bowed. In the silence I looked around me and suddenly became aware of all that surrounded us. I saw the sun dancing and sparkling on the sea as it must always have done; the mountains green and lush, silhouetted against the blue August sky, silent and as ageless as ever, but showing no sign of what they had witnessed. Even the grass beneath my feet, with its dry, yellowing patches, meant more to me at that moment than ever before. How could our little world be so beautiful and yet witness, without sign or change, the tragedy that had come among us. Despite all that beauty, for us the sun seemed to have gone out and our grief and despair was as great as if it had happened to one of our own little community. Realizing that there was nothing that anyone could do, the people sadly and dispiritedly made their way home and we children followed them.

On my arrival home I told my Mother and the others all I knew. Some time later my Father and brothers arrived, accompanied by the stranger whom I had seen earlier bending over the young man. It was only then, when I heard that the stranger was the young man's father, that I fully realized why he was so grief-stricken. My Father, too, looked extremely upset and I could also see anger on his face as he made for the telephone. Who he telephoned I do not know for at that moment Ethel ushered me out to play.

Everywhere there was an air of sadness. We children gathered together, talking about the tragedy although at that time we did not know the cause of it. No-one wanted to play. We just hung about. Another friend joined us and told us that the body had been taken to the chapel, so we stood in the square, looking towards the little building, wondering about the young man, with our thoughts in confusion as to why his life had been taken away.

Eventually Garnie came to tell me that it was time for tea and to my surprise told me that we were to have our tea in the kitchen with Lizzie. While we ate he told us the whole, sad story. The stranger, who was a Mr Keill, was a Liverpool man and was chief engineer on the *Doris Thomas.* His twenty year old son, Robert, had begged to be allowed to accompany him on that voyage. At first it had not seemed possible, but then it was finally agreed that he could do so, on the understanding that, although he would take on the duties of a trimmer, he would not be a 'signed on' member of the crew.

The ship was bound from Liverpool to Cornwall, calling en route for stone at Caernant. All went well on the voyage and they berthed at the expected time at the jetty. At dinner-time on the ship the young man asked his father if he could go for a swim. His father was not at all keen on the idea because, although the weather was fine, the sea was a little choppy, so he said he would prefer him not to do so. He then served him with his dinner and did not see his son again until he was called to the beach.

Obviously the young man, like so many young people when given parental advice, thought that his father was being over cautious. Disregarding his parent's wish and confident of his ability, for he was an experienced and powerful swimmer, he dived off the side of the ship into the sea. Those that watched him for a few moments saw how able he was and envied his obvious enjoyment. They then turned away to get on with the job in hand.

Having enjoyed his swim, the young man made for the shore and, on reaching the point where the beach shelved, to aid his climb out of the water, he caught hold of the wire stay. Tragically, the wire was discharging electricity and in his wet condition he stood no chance and was instantaneously electrocuted.

The inquest with a jury was held at the chapel and was attended by representatives of the parties concerned and the parents and brother-in-law of the deceased who had travelled from Liverpool. Several people gave evidence and among them Captain David Evans of Llithfaen, who was employed by the company as a pilot and was also in charge of the electric motor on the jetty. He testified that he was carrying out his duties on the jetty when he looked down towards the beach end and saw something dangling on the wire stay. He got down there as fast as he could and found that it was a young man, hanging by his left arm. He tried to push him off with this shoulder and eventually succeeded in doing so. Immediately he applied artificial respiration and then rushed to phone the doctor. He went on to say that on two previous occasions he had detected a leakage of electricity in the stays and had reported both to the manager. One he had been able to deal with himself; the other had been attended to by an electrical engineer from Pwllheli.

Another witness was the manager. Giving evidence, he said that the company had no qualified electricians, but they had men capable of supervising maintenance of existing plants, and so repairs were carried out without being reported to him. Leakage on that particular stay had not been reported to him, but a previous leakage on another stay on the same pole had been. He had then given certain instructions which he believed had been carried out and that every precaution was taken to protect the quarrymen.

The district electrical engineer for the power company testified that he had examined the h.t. poles and stays and found that every precaution for earthing was good and that all the usual precautions for insulation had been taken by the company. In his opinion the accident had been the result of a breakdown of the cable.

When all the evidence had been heard, the jury returned a verdict of accidental death by electrocution and sympathy was extended to the family. After the inquest the family came to our house for a short time and I shall never forget their grief and how deeply we felt for them.

From time to time and for various reasons, a few men from the village took up employment at Caernant. Some remained there for years but, regardless of this, there were those of us in Nant who felt that the quarry was inferior to ours, both location wise and industrially which, in reality, was utterly ridiculous. Whether this was due to the fact that we as a community were bound up with our two quarries and as such were prejudiced against any competition, is difficult to determine. Certainly relations between Caernant and my father were not always the most cordial and the court case did not do much to help. Added to that was another grievance of which I was not aware until preparing this book. It was then I was told that on occasions when a man left the quarry, having left of his own accord or having been 'fired', he frequently found employment at Trefor quarry.

Trefor was located immediately over the mountain from Caernant. To get there by any orthodox route meant a journey of some four miles which was totally impracticable so a short cut over the top was used. This short cut crossed Caernant land and, on some occasions, when it became known that an ex-employee had been taken on at Trefor, someone in authority ordered that the gate across the path be locked, making it impossible for them to proceed. This then, if factual, would certainly have been reason enough to strain even the best of relationships. However, our questionable feelings of superiority took a sharp dive when Caernant outlived Nant quarry by more than two decades and Carreg-y-Llam by quite a few years, its location proving invaluable when the last war broke out and it was found possible to transport the stone from there by road and so dispense with the shipping. Regrettably today Caernant, too, is a quarry of the past.

Chapter XXII

A Square Peg

I was in my eighth year and was utterly happy and content at Nant school. In fact, my little world was Utopia, so I was absolutely astonished and bewildered when, one day, I heard my parents discussing the possibility of my going to boarding school. I immediately wanted to know what it was all about and why they had thought of such a thing. Surely they must be joking. They could not possibly be serious. But, no, they were not joking; they were only too serious.

I just could not understand it, or the need to change things. In answer to my questions about it they answered that they had been concerned for some time about my rapidly disappearing use of English and my rough and tomboyish behaviour. Hearing this astounded me – good gracious, there was nothing wrong with my English. I always spoke English at home and at school there were English lessons every week and I did not think that I was at all rough or tomboyish.

Ignoring my protestations, they told me that the school was a private boarding school in a town some miles away. A daughter of friends of theirs was a pupil at the school and she was very happy there so they had no doubt that I, too, would be happy and would have the benefit of her companionship. As far as I was concerned, I did not care who went there and I was pretty sure that I would not like it. Besides, the girl they referred to was years older than I, so she would not want to be bothered with me.

The more I thought about it, the more I failed to think of one good reason for going there. Even if I had not minded changing schools, which I most certainly did, the thought of leaving Nant for months at a time was unthinkable. I made my point, but it was quickly dismissed by my Mother, who said that I should not be away for months. She and my Father would call periodically to bring me home for week-ends and, as well, there would be lots of long holidays. Her words did nothing to convince or reassure me for as the conversation, or rather the argument, as it had now become, continued, reasons against the idea kept springing up in my mind. Reasons such as, what about my friends, who would go on errands to the shop, help my Father with the boat and, most important, there was the danger that I might become a sissy. That really was a frightening thought.

As quickly as I put forward each good reason so immediately it was counteracted with answers such as, my friends would still be there when I came home, Garnie would have to do all the errands, my Father would try and do his best to survive in the boat without my help and learning to be a young lady was not going to turn me into a sissy.

At this point, Ethel came into the room and, joining in

the conversation, said that I was a very foolish little girl not realize how lucky I was to have such an opportunity and many children would give their right arms to go in my place. Ethel always seemed to know of so many people who would give their right arms for so many different things, yet I had never seen anyone without one. I could not resist replying that if they were stupid enough to sacrifice an arm to be in my position, then they deserved to do so. The result of this was my being sent upstairs to ponder on my bad manners and remain there until I regretted them and was ready to apologise. The last thing I heard as I left the room was Ethel saying that the decision to send me to boarding school was not one moment too soon.

As the days passed, it became obvious that this was one battle I was going to lose. Had I only my Father to deal with, I was sure that he would have seen reason, but the women were determined and he was swayed by them. Without his support, I stood no chance and so to uphold my dignity, I gave in.

Having surrendered, I was told to think of how smart I would look in the school uniform and how I would enjoy the games there. It appeared that there were tennis courts and I would be able to play with the racquet that Jacqueline had given me. As I did not wish to spend further unnecessary time upstairs, I received this news with apparent pleasure.

Not long after this, the friends called with their daughter. She told me about the school and I did my best to show interest. During their visit it was arranged that my Mother and I would travel with them on the first day.

As the days went by, I began to think that this boarding school business was not going to be so bad after all. I was keen on games of any sort and liked the idea of learning to play tennis on a real court. The uniform had been purchased and was really quite nice. I even fancied myself in the tie and the long, black stockings looked most grown-up. The result was that I was determined to give it a try. Having come to this decision, I looked forward to the new term with some excitement.

The great day arrived and we set off. Arriving at the school, I was introduced to the owners of the establishment, two spinster ladies who were also the senior mistresses. I shall refer to them as Miss Emily and Miss Hilda. My first thought was that they must be very old as they both had grey hair, not lovely dark hair like S'miss, and both looked rather forbidding, not at all kindly and pretty like S'miss and Miss Lewis. The two ladies spoke to my mother and although I was too nervous to take much in, one thing did register and that was that all pocket money was held by Miss Hilda and was handed out in small measures every Friday. I was soon to learn that small was an exaggeration, at least to my mind, as I found it to be minute. Fruit, we were told, was given daily to each girl. That statement, too, proved to be somewhat lacking in accuracy.

My Mother left soon afterwards and I was taken to a room which was full of girls and where morning prayers were about to start. One of the first things I noticed was that there were very few girls of my age. Most were older and the majority of those were much older. As soon as prayers were over, I was escorted by Miss Emily to a classroom and allocated a desk. I did not take part in any of the lessons that morning but, instead, was given two test papers, one arithmetic and the other English. The English paper seemed reasonable, but some of the sums were completely incomprehensible to me. When morning break came, much to Miss Emily's disgust, I had completed only the English paper and with much tut-tutting, I was told that I would have to finish the other by lunch-time.

To my surprise, morning break did not mean playtime outside as I had been used to, but just a fifteen minute cessation of lessons. During that time we were allowed to talk quietly to each other and eat the apple or orange that we were given. If absolutely necessary, we were allowed to visit the toilet. It was at the first break that a girl of my age came and spoke to me. She was a very nice girl and became my best friend at the school. Unfortunately for me, she lived in the town so had no need to board.

By lunch-time I had completed the arithmetic paper but felt that half of it must be wrong. Miss Emily took the paper, looked at it and with a stony face said that she could not imagine what sort of school I had come from. Her comments made me feel very hurt and angry. I should like to have told her that it was the best and that I never achieved less than eight out of ten for arithmetic but decided that it would not go down well so said nothing.

Lunch over and still we did not go out, even though it was a fine day. The afternoon was taken up mainly with spelling and reading out aloud in turn. This pleased me as I enjoyed reading and spelling had never been a problem. In time my name was called out and I began where the last girl had left off. I had not reached the end of my first paragraph when Miss Emily rapped her ruler hard on the desk and in a pained voice, begged me to stop. The whole class turned to look at me whilst Miss Emily upbraided me for my speech which, it seemed, utterly horrified and appalled her. She then called me to the front of the class. Telling the others to concentrate on their spelling, she explained to me with obvious enforced patience, that young ladies did not pronounce the 'a' in such words as 'pass', 'last', 'father', and the like with a hard 'a', as in 'man', 'pan', etc., but softly to sound like 'parss', 'larst', 'farther' and so on. Allowing no quarter for my Welsh intonations, she informed me that I was to keep repeating the words to myself until my pronounciation was acceptable to her.

Eventually lessons ended and it was tea-time. I thought that we were sure to be going out to play after tea, but, no, some chatting went on for a short time and then it was 'prep.' time. 'Prep.' meant nothing to me, but I soon discovered that it was study time, homework as I would have called it. When this was over, the younger girls, of which I was one, were each given a glass of milk and a biscuit and as soon as we had finished, we were told it was bedtime.

Until now I had no idea where my bedroom was and was looking forward to seeing it. I had read so many stories about the fun had in school dormitories, the pillow fights, midnight picnics and lots of talk and so on. Miss Emily took me upstairs. Up and up we went to the very top of the building where she led me into a small, sparsely furnished, single bedroom. I was so terribly disappointed but obviously said nothing. I was then shown where the bathroom was and told that I would be called in the morning and on hearing the call, I must rise immediately. Miss Emily then left me.

Shut in that little room by myself, I felt very unhappy and lonely. I crossed to the window and looked out. It was still daylight and I saw that my room was at the back of the building, from where I could see the tennis court. That, at least, did exist, which cheered me up a little. Once in bed, I could not sleep so I decided that the best thing to do was to practice my pronounciation. I was determined that I was not going to be made to feel silly again so set about it with fervour. Repeating 'larst' and 'parst' and the other words over and over again, I fell asleep. Little did I know that my 'a's were only the beginning and that almost every word containing the letter 'o', as well as many others, were incorrectly pronounced and that I would be called out to the front every reading lesson for weeks to come.

I was beginning to think that we would never be going out when, on the first Friday morning, we were given some spending money. My allocation was tuppence and at break-time we were taken under escort to a tuck shop only a few doors away. Having spent our allowance, we were told that we could eat our purchases that evening and at the week-end.

During lunch-time, I overheard talk of an outing that evening and on asking one of the girls, I discovered that every Friday evening, weather permitting, the girls were taken for a walk. This was more like it and I began to feel excited. The day seemed very long but eventually the final bell rang and it was tea-time. As soon as we had finished, after a shorter than usual prep., we were told to prepare ourselves for the outing. Within minutes we were all assembled and set off in crocodile fashion with Miss Emily at the front and Miss Hilda bringing up the rear.

We marched along, swinging our arms and stopping for nothing until we had covered about half a mile in the form of a square, around the block and back to the school. I could hardly believe that that was it and, disappointedly, returned to my room.

Well, I had survived my first week, but I did not like any of it. I began on my sweets and savoured each one with more pleasure that I had ever done before. To my dismay, I found that I had finished them and, having nothing to read, had no alternative but to go to bed and work on my pronounciation. How I longed to be back in Nant, but it was no use thinking about it. I just had to stick this out and the thought made me determined not to be beaten and, besides, coming from Nant, I was supposed to be tough, so I would show them that at least I was no sissy.

The weeks passed and as far as lessons were concerned, my biggest bug-bear apart from my speech was arithmetic.

This really upsets me as I had previously enjoyed the subject and gained good marks. The trouble was that I still could not cope with the decimals, fractions and percentages, which I had not come up against before and because of it I was denied my fruit at break, one of the school rules being that no pupil would be given her fruit when her work was unsatisfactory.

At last my week-end at home came around and my parents came to collect me. They wanted to know everything about the school and how I had liked it. I thought of those first few days and how I had longed to see them and tell them how much I hated it all, but having promised myself not to give in, I concentrated on putting their minds at ease. Within minutes of my arrival home I rushed to the village to see my friends and was pleased to see how they admired my uniform. Some even seemed to envy my being away at school. Little did they know.

The week-end was over quickly and it was back to 'prison', for that is what it was for me. The pattern continued much the same at the school except that, as time passed, my Welsh accent diminished and in a few months was even acceptable to Miss Emily. The plum in the mouth was growing well. Some understanding of the arithmetic was gained, but became a subject that I disliked intensely. Strangely, I do not remember very much about any of the other subjects taught at the school.

The only thing I looked forward to was tennis and one lovely day I was told that I was to be included in the tennis party that afternoon. I hurried upstairs to get ready and then we set off with our rackets. I was very proud of my racket and extremely pleased when some of the girls admired it. Arriving at the court, Miss Emily took one look at me and then with a look of horror, she pointed to my feet, saying that Clarks sandals were not allowed on the court as they had heels which would mark the turf. She added that she would contact my parents regarding the provision of tennis shoes. In the meantime, this was a good opportunity for me to catch up on my arithmetic. She then detailed one of the older girls to escort me back to the classroom.

Sitting there alone with my exercise book, I fought hard not to cry. Miss Emily obviously did not like me and was jumping at any opportunity to pick on me. But then I reasoned that she had said that I could play, and if I did not have the correct footwear, then it was not her fault. With this in mind, I determined not to cry for, should I do so, I certainly would be ridiculed when everyone returned and found me with red-rimmed eyes.

The weeks went by and the pattern remained the same. My 'a's and 'o's and the rest had become acceptable which made life much easier and the family felt that their money was well spent. Even the arithmetic problem was lessening by a small degree.

One day, one of my small circle of friends came upstairs crying. She was a year older than I and so would not cry unless something very serious had occurred. Asking her what had happened, I was amazed to hear that she was crying because she had been told that she had to leave the school. For a moment, I could only think of how lucky she was and that had it been me, I should have rejoiced. However, I wanted to know why she had to leave, and she told me that she did not really understand the reason herself. It was something to do with her father owning a greengrocery shop. It did not make sense to me either but, nevertheless, leave she did.

By this time, I had enjoyed a number of tennis lessons and, apart from going home, these lessons were the highlight of my life. One fine summer day, tennis was scheduled for three o'clock and, as always on these occasions, the other lessons seemed to drag on. My efforts with arithmetic that morning had not been too successful, so I knew that Miss Emily would be displeased, but I did not dream that her displeasure would stretch as far as depriving me of playing that afternoon. At a quarter to three, everyone, with the exception of myself, was told to put their books away and get ready, and I was told to get on with the sums I had earlier failed to get right. I could hardly believe my ears but one look at Miss Emily's face left me in no doubt.

The classroom was so quiet with everyone gone and I felt so disappointed that once again I was near to tears. I began on the beastly sums, but could not concentrate, no matter how hard I tried. Giving up, I crossed to the window and looked out. As I stood there, thinking of home and of Nant, I suddenly felt very angry. Whatever was I doing in this place? I hated everything about it and it seemed I always would. That was it. My mind was made up. I would not stay a moment longer. I picked up my exercise book and text book and without going to my bedroom to collect even a cardigan, I walked out in my gym-slip.

Reaching the road, I knew the general direction of the bus terminus, but felt very nervous as I had seldom travelled on buses and never without my Mother. As I walked on, doubts of being able to get home began worrying me such as, would I know which was the right bus, how would I manage without money and would the conductor turn me off in the middle of nowhere. Oh well, I would just have to worry about that when the time came. I knew that with a bit of luck I would not be missed until some time after half-past four and by that time I hoped to be well on my way.

I reached the terminus and saw a number of buses standing there empty. Among them was a familiar-looking one so I went to the front and to my great relief saw

'Llithfaen' in big letters in the glass piece above the driver's cab. As it was empty, I was uncertain whether to board it then or to wait when, suddenly, a crowd of schoolchildren arrived and began piling into the bus. This was my cue so, mingling with them, I got on. A few minutes later the driver arrived and, to my surprise, with no sign of a conductor, we were off. I breathed a sigh of relief for, with any luck, the driver would not know that I had no money until we reached the other end. Nevertheless, I felt a little sick with the worry of it.

We reached a small village and two boys got off. I did not think that they had paid, but then realized that they probably had return tickets. The journey continued, with stops here and there for other children to get off. After what seemed hours, I saw the welcoming sight of Llithfaen come into view and minutes later, the bus pulled up outside the Post Office. Now came the next hurdle, but I need not have worried because, to my amazement, the children at the back pulled up a large handle at the rear of the bus which opened the emergency door and out they jumped. Seeing this as my chance, I ran along the aisle and followed suit.

I literally skipped down the Screw Hill and my heart sang although the final hurdle was yet to be overcome; that of my parents' reaction to what I had done. Well, I had crossed several bridges since three o'clock so would cross the next one when I came to it.

How beautiful the mountains looked that day. The streams, usually cascading over Graig Ddu, reduced to faint white lines by a series of fine weeks, were still music to my ears. The sheep dotted around grazed unconcernedly and even the stones on the track were so familiar, I felt I knew them, every single one. At last the village came into sight. I was home. Although having been away only weeks at a time, this time I felt I was really home and for the first time in my seven years, I knew the true feeling of joy. Savouring the wonderful feeling, I made it last until I reached our drive.

At the front door I stopped, took a deep breath and knocked. My Mother opened the door and, seeing me there, was for a moment speechless with surprise. Regaining her composure, she ushered me in and asked me so many questions that I did not know which to answer first. However, I eventually managed to tell her my reason for being there and then rushed to telephone my Father. He, too, was extremely surprised and between the excitement in my voice, got the gist of the story. My call had to be short as my Mother was anxious to inform the school of my whereabouts. What was said I did not know but when my Father came home, my Mother voiced the opinion that I ought to return to the school until at least the end of term. I begged them not to send me back and to my great relief my Father answered that as I had been so unhappy and, because of it, did not seem to have gained very much, he thought it best that I stay home and resume my lessons at Nant school.

The next day my Mother informed the school that I would not be returning and arranged to collect my belongings. The result was that my belongings could not be found and never were found. The loss of my racquet was that which grieved me most. Many years later, when discussing the school with my parents, I was utterly shocked to hear that after leaving I had been accused of stealing some pencils from there. A more ridiculous accusation would be hard to imagine as pencils were never in short supply at home, there being boxes of them at the office. The text book I had been working from and which I did take with me, I still have today and clearly printed on the cover are the words, 'Suitable for pupils of 11½ to 13 years.'

I should now say that these were my impressions and my own personal feelings whilst at the school. The other girls seemed to accept the rules and form of education with less difficulty than I and I believe that some were even happy there. Whether my misery was due to my own failure and inadequacy or to the system, is not for me to say. What I am certain of is that, having previously had such freedom of movement and expression, added to the fact that I was not happy anywhere away from the valley, my chances of settling to another way of life were remote from the start.

Chapter XXIII

The Quarry

The demand for granite was becoming greater and greater, not only for the network of roads being built throughout the nation but for tunnels and many other civil engineering projects, so that work in the quarries was in full swing. All that mattered in the industry was output and more output to ensure that no ship left the little jetties with one chipping less than her holds would carry. The ever-deepening scars on our beautiful mountains bore witness to the tremendous efforts to fulfil this need. Ironically, the end product of these efforts, which revolutionised travel and communication in the kingdom, did nothing for us in the valley. Our means of travel was still the long trek up the mountain track, no doubt wider but otherwise unaltered since man first found his way down there, a factor that, later, was to cause much anger and even heartache.

With so much need and urgency, unemployment was greatly reduced. Apart from the workforce resident in the village, there were many who came from outside and so, yet again, men travelled several miles each day to their work. Those travellers, on reaching Llithfaen, would join their colleagues from that village and take the short cut across the mountain which descended immediately above the quarry. Those with bicycles and the few more fortunate motor-bike owners left their machines along the way until their return at the end of the day. Never was concern felt about leaving their machines unattended for no-one on principle would dream of touching them.

At the height of its activity, Nant Quarry employed approximately fifty men and Carreg-y-Llam in the region of sixty. The work force was divided into a number of trades and categories. The man in charge of Nant was my Father. Then came the foreman who was responsible to him for all work carried out. Next would come the rock men. These were highly skilled and particularly the head rock man, who would lead a team of three or four men. His task was to examine the rock face, recognise the flaws, the cracks and the veins and from his survey choose the most suitable area for blasting. Under his direction the team would move in to drill the holes required for the explosive.

The explosive was always gunpowder as, unlike others such as gelignite, it did not shatter, so ruining the rock face and throwing stones in all directions. Instead, it produced a deeper and more controlled explosion. The drilling of the holes with mechanical drills would take the best part of a day to reach the required depth of twenty to twenty-two feet and on occasions would take even longer. This was often carried out high up on the rock face and so necessitated the use of ropes.

The preparation to drill, in itself, was no easy task and it depended on the drilling site and the type of drilling equipment available at the time. In the early days before mechanisation, the equipment was simply a can of water for cooling the drill, a hammer and a series of drills of varying lengths. The drills were hand-held and driven into the rock by hammering and turning so for this method very little preparation was needed. In the early thirties the pneumatic drill was introduced to the quarry. This obviously brought great advantages but also disadvantages in that not only was it a heavy piece of equipment weighing over a hundred pounds but also, due to its vibratory motion, had to be securely anchored. This, therefore, did require a great deal of preparation in that it had to be mounted on a tripod which, in turn, had to be firmly secured to the rock face. This was done by drilling three holes, approximately four feet apart in the rock to receive the tripod legs and to counteract the vibration, fifty-six pound weights were attached to each leg. To operate both types, all the rock man required was a small rock ledge to hold his drills and provide a foothold. His weight would be taken up by a one and a half inch diameter rope which was looped around his thigh, with the long tail end brought up to waist level and then tucked into itself.

A few year later, a lighter drill was designed which could be held by hand and made the operation much easier but this, too, needed preparation in that the operator required a substantial rock ledge or platform to stand on. The fixing of the platform meant drilling holes into the solid rock and then driving iron bars into the holes to support a number of wooden planks. Only when all was secure could drilling commence. The compressed air drills were hollow, allowing blasts of air to pass through to remove dust and sludge from the drilled hole and as with the manually-operated, water was used for cooling.

Group of quarrymen standing in front of what is believed to have been the largest rock brought down in one piece in Nant quarry

Demonstration of a pressing problem, another view of the largest rock

Once the depth was achieved, the head rock man would place the explosive in the hole, initially about five pounds, by shaking the powder along a copper tube. Copper, being non-ferrous, eliminated the danger of sparks igniting the powder. The detonator fuse was then fed into the hole and finally sufficient granite dust to contain the subsequent explosion. This was then fired and allowed to cool, during which time the resulting cracks were examined. The extent of these would determine the amount of powder required for the next blast and this procedure was then repeated three or four times.

The purpose of these preliminary explosions was to open up the seams behind the rock face, known in quarrying terms as 'springing the rock'. This springing ensured a clean fall of stone in the final blast. For this final blast, from fifty to one hundred and fifty pounds of gunpowder would be used and on rare occasions as much as two hundred and fifty pounds to bring down hundreds of tons of granite. So accurate was the blast that the rock face would slide cleanly away and slowly descend to the rock shelf below. Only on rare occasions was any damage caused by these enormous falls to such things as rails and waggons but never to life or limb.

The shelves, banks or galleries were known as 'Boncs', of which there were eight in Nant but only three were in operation in my time there. Each gallery bore a name and among the original ones was Bonc Buenos Aires and Bonc Palestine, so named, it was said, because one of the men who opened them up had been to those parts of the world. Another reason given was that as the two were situated some distance from the mill such titles would be apt. Less colourful but descriptive names were given to the last three, Bonc Isa meaning the lower bank, Bonc Bach as it was the smallest and Bonc Sir Fôn as Anglesey was in view to the north.

Once the rock was on the shelf, the next in the chain of order moved in. These were the pop-drillers. These, too, were skilled craftsmen. Theirs was the task of drilling what were termed as pop-holes in the massive boulders produced by the fall to reduce them to a manageable size. Drilling complete, again the head rock-man would be needed to place the explosive but this time using gelignite.

With blasting over, it was then the turn of the gang of breakers to come into action. As their title suggests, their task was that of breaking up the rocks to a size which the crusher could accommodate. For this, special hammers would be used, pointed at one end and blunt at the other. The sharp end only was hardened and tempered while the other was soft in order to eliminate the risk of injury by flying splinters of stone. Frequently, the points blunted and the soft ends became worn and burred over. These were re-sharpened and reshaped by the blacksmith, each gallery having its own smithy. When one remembers that this was granite, it is easy to understand the muscle and effort needed by the breakers to make an impression on this so hard mineral, and why the blacksmith was never idle.

In the early days, there were two other categories of tradesmen who, in order, came between the rock-man and the breakers. These were blockers and settsmen, a breed on their own with a skill that has sadly almost died out. The blockers would handle the fall and by merely looking at the massive boulders, often as large as a house, could make a fair assessment of how many small sections known as cubes could be produced from each one. The settsmen, with just the one tool of their trade, a dressing hammer known as a triffler, would take the cubes and with the deftness of a sculptor would shape the rocks into perfectly formed brick-like setts.

Holding the cube while working on it was not easy. Some

solved the problem by placing it on an eighteen inch block and holding it with the inside edge of their shoe. For this method, the blacksmith fitted a piece of steel on to the shoe but even the steel did not last long. These setts were in great demand for road building and today can still be seen in a number of towns and cities. To achieve the skill of a settsman demanded a two-year apprenticeship and while serving out the time, no wages were received, the opportunity of such training being considered by the employer to be ample reward.

The last link on the quarry shelf were the labourers, trammers, brakesmen and one plate layer. To the labourers fell the task of clearing all rubble and from it picking out the good stones and loading them into waggons. A waggon held approximately two and a quarter tons and when loaded was pushed by a trammer along a narrow-gauge railway line to the top of a steep incline. Here it was hooked on to a wire hawser which ran from a drum above and from there it descended to a lower level, its weight being utilised to draw up on a parallel line a returning empty waggon. At the lower level it was unhooked and pushed on to the weighbridge where its load was recorded and from there to the tipping table where its contents were tipped down a shute leading to the crushing mill below. On rare occasions a waggon would become derailed and at once willing hands would hurry to assist even though it meant losing time and therefore loosing money.

The spirit of comradeship among the men was strong, as was their belief in upholding the old traditions. One of these traditions was carried out whenever a man was about to be married. The prospective bridegroom, accompanied by his oldest colleague, would be put into one of the waggons and while being pushed along by their workmates, the older man would offer him words of wisdom and advice. On their return the young man would then have to make a speech. This ritual always took place at lunch time and on as near a day as possible to the wedding day.

The galleries were divided up into sections known as bargains and to every bargain ran a branch line from the main railway. Each man was allocated a bargain and could load only from this section until it was cleared. Should the amount of stone be less in his bargain than in that of his neighbour's, it was deemed to be the luck of the draw and he would hope for better luck after the next fall. A number of metal tallies were allocated to each man with his number stamped on them. These he would attach, one to each loaded waggon, so that when weighed the load would be recorded against his name. In the summertime, when orders were usually plentiful and ships were not hampered by the weather, this piece-work system often allowed these men's earnings to be above that of the craftsman's set wage. Added to that were two shifts per day and some of the men took advantage of this and worked a double shift. Wintertime had the reverse effect with its short daylight hours, bad weather and slackening off of orders. In the early thirties quarry labourers earned, on average, something in the region of twenty-five shillings a week as opposed to the fifteen shillings earned by farm labourers, so men were easily wooed away from the land.

The weighbridge office was a neat little hut, perched on a ledge at the bottom of the incline and normally accommodated one clerk. On one occasion during my time in the valley, one of the employees on the piece-work system, an extremely conscientious young man, was mystified by the fact that suddenly his wages dropped to a level no higher than those that would not or could not put as much effort into their work as he did. The following week the same thing happened so he spoke to others whose work output was similar to his own. They confirmed that their money was also down and they were as concerned and mystified as he. He then discovered that those of lower output were well pleased with what seemed to be an increase in wages. It was at this point that he realised that a new clerk had taken up employment at the weighbridge. Feeling that this may have some bearing on the matter, he went to the little hut to try and sort things out. The clerk intimated that he was very busy and told him to come another time. This reception aroused his suspicions and he, determined to get satisfaction on his next visit. Despite his determination that next visit was a complete failure as the clerk refused even to open the door. Feeling helpless and angry, he decided to go and discuss the situation and his elder brother who also worked in the quarry. His brother, a tall, well-built man, listened patiently to the story and then, without a word, he downed tools and strode off determinedly to the little hut.

As he approached, the inmate, who at the time was looking out of the window, saw him coming and recognised that here came a man who was in no mood to mince matters. Rushing to the door, he locked and barred it. The big man, unable to gain entry and with mounting fury, went to the window and demanded to be let in immediately. The inmate signalled that he should go away and shouted that if he did not do so, he would get him 'fired'.

Bandying words no further, the big man walked back a few paces and then, turning, he ran straight for the office. With power borne of speed and strength, he jumped into the air, coming down with both feet crashing into the little hut, sending it toppling over the edge, with the clerk rolling about inside, screaming for mercy. Glancing over the edge, the assailant watched as it rolled over and over down the incline. As it came to rest he calmly walked away to tell his brother that he was sure that there would be no further discrepancies with wages. His prediction proved to be correct and his suspicions justified for it transpired that the clerk, not wishing to bother with the trouble of individually recording weights with tallies, simply recorded total output and divided that by the number of men.

My Father appeared ignorant of the event and for obvious reasons did not enquire into the matter, the problem, as he put it, having been settled on the spot. What did concern him was when men who were obviously unfit reported for work. One such case was that of a man who was suffering from severe toothache due to several tooth abcesses which were causing considerable swelling of his face. My Father, seeing that he was in great pain, immediately ordered him home, not only because he was unfit for work but because in that state, he was a danger to himself and to those around him.

As earnings ceased when a man stopped work, no-one welcomed being ordered home and in this case there were those who considered my Father's order to be unjust. What they did not appreciate was that the man's life at work was my Father's responsibility and his order was in the employee's best interest. What they could not know was that in the event of a conscientious worker being sent home due to illness, records for the lost time did not always show the absence at the end of a fortnight when pay day came around.

The heart of the quarry was the crushing mill, noisy and dust-laden caused by the constant grinding of the great steel jaws of the crusher and the inevitable dust that this produced. No effort was spared by those men whose task it was to ensure that the machinery ran smoothly and in the event of a breakdown, speedily get things going again, for if the crusher stopped then the whole quarry system was in danger of grinding to a halt.

Once through the crusher, the stones, broken into various sizes of chippings, were fed on to the screens for grading and from there into large storage bins. A day's output was in the region of two hundred and fifty to three hundred tons. The moment a ship came in, the chippings were released on to a conveyor belt which took them along the jetty to the ship.

Ships did not call at regular intervals. Notice of one coming was by telephone on the day of her arrival, giving sailing time from her port of departure. Her berthing time at Nant would then be calculated according to the distance she had to steam and the state of the tide on her arrival.

Once a ship arrived in the bay, she stood off until she received the signal to come in. The signalling was carried out with flags. A white flag instructed her to come in and a red flag informed her that it was too rough to load. For messages such as 'a doctor is required' or 'come in at a specific time', the Maritime Code was used. In cases where a number of ships waited in the bay at one and the same time the name of the next on the list would be spelt out. After dark, lights were used, green signifying clearance and red the reverse. For other messages, morse code was practised. Carreg-y-Llam had the advantage of a tall mast on which international flags were hoisted to instruct the captains whether to berth at that jetty or first go to Nant, the decision always being made at Nant.

The moment the time of the arrival of a ship was known the quarry foreman chose his gang of loaders. Only one man was automatically called for his duty, he being the loading ganger, the others dependent on who could best be spared. Being chosen for the loading gang was usually welcomed when it was out of normal working hours as it gave the opportunity to earn a little extra money, time and a quarter being paid for the first two hours and thereafter time and a half. Sunday loading would rate double time. However, it was not so welcome when having to crawl out of a warm bed on a wild winter's night with gale-force winds blowing and rain lashing down. Despite the slim chance of a ship berthing in such conditions, the loaders still had to turn out to cover that chance. Should she not do so then they would receive no payment. Often when turning out in the early hours of the morning in such weather, the men returning home, soaked to the skin, would have time only to change their clothing and snatch a quick bite before going out again to start another day's work.

An example of the hazards of this night loading was an incident that took place at Carreg-y-Llam. It was a bitterly cold and dark January night, with a strong wind blowing and a heavy sea running. Every man was heavily clad in an attempt to combat the penetrating and biting cold. The S.S. *Kylefirth* was bucking away at the jetty and half loaded when the foreman, Mr Griff Williams, stepped aboard to get the necessary papers signed by the captain. Having completed his errand, he was stepping back from the ship to the jetty when the vessel gave an enormous lurch, throwing him between the vessel and the jetty into the almost freezing water below. Being high tide, there was twenty-five feet of water and, weighed down by his heavy clothing, he went straight to the bottom. As the buoyancy brought him back to the surface, he was in imminent danger of being sucked into the ship's propeller but with great presence of mind and despite his diminishing strength, he managed to grab hold of one of the jetty piles and from there struggle underneath the jetty.

Above him, everyone was fully occupied with the job in hand and in such conditions intent on getting it done as quickly as possible. By an amazing stroke of good fortune, one of the ship's crew happened to look up as the ship lurched and saw the foreman disappear. Without thought for his own safety he dived into the water. Finding Mr Williams clinging to the piles, he grabbed the back of his overcoat and with seemingly super-human strength, dragged him back up on to the jetty.

The captain was so shocked by the night's event that he did not wish to continue loading but the foreman, surprisingly calm and unconcerned, made light of the incident and urged everyone to carry on. He was then taken home, where he took a hot bath and retired to bed.

The next morning he suffered such pains in his chest that his wife insisted that the doctor be called in. It was then discovered that he had sustained three broken ribs, the result of hitting the ship's fender as he went down. His rescuer, for his act of selflessness and bravery, was awarded a gold watch, a reward that he richly deserved.

The quarry employed one carpenter and shared another with Carreg-y-Llam. The carpenters were not only responsible for repairs and maintenance in the quarry but also for the houses in the village.

The last link, or the pulse, was the office where my Father spent the largest part of his time and where the shipping clerk worked away like a beaver aided by an office trainee. This, then, completed the quarry chain and made for a small and efficient industry.

Chapter XXIV

Distribution

The breed of men that go down to the sea in ships, and their vessels, were essential to us. Although we children were so used to seeing the ships coming and going, we thought their role and that of the sailor a most exciting way of life, a life of pleasure sailing the seas to all sorts of romantic places. Their names, the S.S. *Colin, Wythburn, Kyle Prince, Glenmaroon, Carrickmore, Stanley Force* and *Greta Force,* to name but a few, were as familiar to us as our own but that familiarity did nothing to blunt our joy at seeing them steaming in. Neither did it spoil the dreams of some that one day they, too, would sail with them. How little we knew of the circumstances, the privations and hardship. How could we have known that to the sailors, the stone trade was a nightmare, that the name of the game was distribution and that nothing else mattered.

To the sailor, our bay was not exactly the location he

SS Wythburn *loading at Nant Jetty*

A Steam Coaster arriving at Carreg-y-Llam

Loading the Point of Ayr

SS Dalegarth Force *of W. S. Kennagh & Co.*

would have chosen to bring his ship. Its setting, framed by the mountains so beautiful to behold but so treacherous was the Irish Sea that no sailor would dare take liberties with it. In the twenties the two ports were not even marked on the charts so location was purely by word of mouth from already initiated captains, their method dependent entirely on the sighting of the twin peaks of the Rivals, always easier when coming from a westerly direction or in clear moonlight. Making for further difficulties was the presence of loadstone in the mountains which interfered with compasses.

The jetty at Nant, constructed of wooden piles, was two hundred and fifty feet long and loading, ideally, was carried out two hours before and one hour after high tide. The water here did not achieve the depth of Carreg-y-Llam and had the additional hazard of a sunken rock in the vicinity of the jetty. Most ships' masters knew of this and so were wary of going alongside too soon or remaining too long after high water. The regulars, recognising tidal marks on the beach and on the jetty, knew exactly the right time to go alongside. Due to this, the larger ships part loaded only at Portnant and completed at Carreg-y-Llam.

The ruling factor at all times was wind direction. Wind from the East, when at force eight, had little or no effect at the jetties as the mountains provided shelter from this quarter, whereas even a moderate force six from anywhere between South-west through West to North-west caused a heavy sea and made berthing impossible. Even having berthed in comfortable conditions, keeping a constant weather eye was essential as by half loading time such deterioration could occur as to necessitate full steam out to a safe anchorage. This was usually Porthdinllaen or Holyhead. In the words of one of the masters, 'a good place to get out of in a hurry if the wind came round whilst loading'. It has been told that when a newly promoted shipmaster enquired from an old shellback about our quarries area, he was advised that if he had to go there in the wintertime to be sure to pick a summer's day.

As on all rock-bound and precipitous coasts such as ours, these conditions were due mainly to there being no long shelving beach for the water to 'spill on' and so break its momentum. Instead, it crashed against the rock face, especially at high water, having a rebounding effect on the incoming water, so causing further turbulence. This was accentuated at Carreg-y-Llam because of its short projecting headland. This constant movement caused a heavy ranging to and fro of the vessels, so powerful that mooring ropes and wires often broke. A Shipmaster, arriving with his vessel with anything less than good condition, faced the constant threat of ropes and wires parting, so causing damage to the jetties as well as his command. Because of it, steam was never shut off from the main engines throughout the entire loading period and an engineer stood by the controls at the ready.

Due to the short length of the jetty, constant heaving and slackening for positioning was the task of those on deck. Orders had to be bellowed to be heard above the deafening noise of the granite gravitating down the chute and in bad weather there was competition from the elements.

In addition to the ship's usual mooring ropes, two coir springs with wire pennants ran out from the jetty and were fastened fore and aft on the ship. These springs helped a great deal to combat the heavy swell and surge of the sea. In such conditions ordinary fenders were of no value to protect the ship's hull so, instead, a belting was fitted on all vessels. This belting was a continuous wooden fender some six or seven inches in width and of similar thickness, fastened between angle irons riveted to the hull and forming a channel along the side of the vessel. The wood itself was

The Dutch M. V. Maraboe *aground near Carreg-y-Llam*

The M. V. Maraboe *again with the rescue tug* Ranger

protected by a continuous iron strap of approximately five eighth gauge and about four inches wide. The strap, in addition to being riveted to the hull at its extreme ends, was also held by 'iron dubs' which were driven through countersunk holes into the wood, thus binding all externally. Largely the construction was fitted at loaded water-line level except that it bore relationship to the vessel's sheer and accordingly rose considerably towards the forward end which was in the vicinity of the vertical of the break of the forecastle-head. The after end of the belting finished at the 'run'. That is, where the stern commenced to fine away to shape smooth delivery of the water towards the propeller and rudder. Since the upper part of the stern continued as per the width of the decks, so a short 'after' belting was fitted at quarter-deck level. This continued the permanent fendering where damaging contact with jetty pilings was most likely to occur.

Despite all the care and precautions, trouble still arose from time to time. Such was the case of the S.S. *Comber,* a six-hundred ton vessel with no double bottom. While loading at Carreg-y-Llam in heavy weather, she broke adrift and struck the rocks immediately beneath the cliff face. Badly holed, she stuck fast on the rocks, the crew fortunately managing to scramble to safety.

The owners decided it was possible to salvage her so sent along on another of their ships, the S.S. *Oranmore,* an old bosun from their boat-yard to effect the repairs. For the operation, the bosun was provided with a portable shed which was to be placed in the *Comber*'s forehatch, a little donkey boiler, forty tons of coal and some hoses. To get alongside the *Comber* in her position under those cliffs was, in itself, a dangerous and difficult feat apart from the problem of transferring the equipment from one ship to the other. However, the transfer was achieved and the bosun got on with the job of patching the hole. It was no easy task but was eventually accomplished satisfactorily. He then pumped her out and finally got a rope off to the *Oranmore* who towed her back to her home port. A successful mission and all in a day's work for those involved.

Among a number of others suffering the same plight but, regrettably, beyond rescue, was the S.S. *Edith,* a two-hundred and forty ton vessel. Her mooring ropes had fouled her propellor as she was about to leave and she sank in a matter of minutes. A salutory warning to all those who called at the jetties.

A Dutch ship, the M.V. *Maraboe,* had a somewhat different experience which was born of the captain's fool-hardiness. A heavy swell was running when she came into the bay a full two hours before berthing time. Ignoring the absence of any 'come in' signals, the made straight for the jetty. The foreman, looking out from the quarry, was amazed to see her come alongside and immediately ran down to the jetty. By the time he reached the ship, he saw that she was beginning to drift and, recognising the danger she was in, he jumped aboard to help with the ropes. Despite everyone's frantic efforts to hold her, she continued to drift and in no time was driven aground.

The heavy swell of the in-coming tide lifted her, with each following surge, further and further up the beach. The now fearful captain ordered all hands to abandon ship, to which the anxious crew readily responded. Gathering up their belongings, they threw them on to the beach and, without delay, proceeded to follow them. With the crew gone, the captain made to leave, when he realised that the foreman was making no move to go with him. Turning to him he asked, 'Aren't you coming?' The foreman, shaking his head, replied firmly, 'No, I am not. If you are leaving I intend to stay aboard.'

The captain, for a moment uncertain what to do,

suddenly realised that should he abandon the ship, the foreman would then be in a position to claim salvage. Without further hesitation, he called down to the crew, ordering all hands back on deck and another mad scramble ensued to get everything back on board.

The ship was in a sorry plight, with a large hole in her bottom and one propellor missing. She lay there, a pathetic sight, her stern low down in the water when the high tide came and her bow high up on the beach, looking for all the world like a stranded whale.

The following day a tug, the S.S. *Ranger,* arrived to effect temporary repairs and to pull her off. After some difficulty this was achieved and the tow to Holyhead began, where it was planned to carry out more positive patching. Unfortunately, she had covered very little distance when she began leaking so badly that they had to turn back and make for the nearer port of Porthdinllaen. Further patching was effected and once again they made for Holyhead, reaching there only just in time. Some days were spent in Holyhead where more extensive repairs were carried out and, finally, she was successfully towed to the lough in Belfast. Sadly, before she could receive further attention, she sank in the lough and remains there to this day. Another victim of the hazards of the stone trade.

Yet another event was that told to me by a retired captain of that which took place when, as a young mariner, he was at the wheel of a ship coming in to the little port of Trefor. Trefor was a neighbour of ours, being just around the north headland of the bay. The ship and crew, newcomers to the port, arrived at dusk and began looking for the place. Whilst cautiously sounding their way in, the captain went below to consult Brown's Almanac. There he found reference to there being a white light exhibited on the quay at night when ships were expected, and a white flag in the daytime.

SS Wythburn *of Monroe Brothers Shipping Co. In 1940 she was blown up by an acoustic mine in Barry Roads whilst weighing anchor preparatory to entering the dock. All hands were lost with the exception of the mate.*

SS Donaghmore *in foreground on her way in to Carreg-y-Llam with SS* Carnalea *in right background approaching Nant jetty, both ships of John Kelly Ltd., with SS* Colin *of Monroe Brothers in left background.*

Moving in under the mountains and exercising every possible care, they kept peering ahead but could see no sign of any light. Concern was growing with every passing moment. Suddenly, they saw a small vessel coming towards them. As she sidled by, the captain, out of keeping with custom, called down to her, 'We're bound for Trefor – Where is it?'

'In there,' came the answer. 'Just keep going. They are expecting you.'

By this time it was dark but they moved forward with a little more confidence and the next moment spotted a light ahead. At once the decision was made to go in and the ship's whistle was blown.

Still carefully sounding, they prowled along with one man trying to penetrate the darkness through binoculars. Seeing a sudden flash of light, he called out, 'Is someone waving that light or not?' Everyone strained to see but no-one answered for no-one was sure and so did not want to be committed. As they crept further forward, the light moved positively and only as it swung away were they able to see clearly that it was not a signal intended for them but, instead, was a car coming out of a garage. Instantly recognising their immediate danger, the captain ordered full astern and, eventually finding different soundings, they made their way out to a safe anchorage where they stayed the night.

The next morning the quay could clearly be seen and they went in without further trouble. On the quay stood a very tall, old quarryman who watched them come alongside. As they made fast, he looked the ship up and down and then in an aggrieved tone said, 'We expected you to come in last night.'

The captain replied, 'We couldn't come in because we couldn't see your light.'

'Well, it was there, it was there; I have only just taken it away,' answered the quarryman.

'Where is it then?' asked the captain.

'There it is over there,' answered the quarryman, pointing to a battered old hurricane lamp, so blackened by smoke that it was no wonder that it had been impossible to see its light. The captain, understandably a little irritated, then said, 'I couldn't see your flag up either and it says in the Almanac that a white flag will be exhibited during daylight hours.'

'Yes, that's right,' agreed the quarryman. 'I'm just going to take it in now.'

The captain, looking around and still unable to see any flag, asked, 'Where?'

'Out there,' replied the quarryman and repeated, 'I'm just going to take it in now.'

The captain, by this time feeling thoroughly exasperated, asked again, 'Well, where is it then?'

'There it is. Look!' said the unperturbed quarryman and re-pointed to a stone-breaker's hammer standing on the capping of the quay. Following the direction of his pointing finger, the captain then saw the hammer and saw that, attached to its handle by two corners and hanging limply, was a handkerchief or something very similar which, many moons before, may have been white. Uncertain whether to smile or shout, the captain and crew looked at each other, shrugged their shoulders and proceeded to get down to the job in hand.

In its early days, Carreg-y-Llam was the proud possessor of two jetties but some ships, holding on too long in bad weather conditions, strained its west jetty to such an extent that it became unusable. At that time loading from both jetties was by fixed chute from a light railway with tipping tubs. When, later, a conveyor belt was installed, it was a distinct advantage but, nevertheless, it posed a new problem, that of assessing the load en-rout to the ship. The

SS Chasmoor *of John Kelly Ltd. steaming out of Carreg-y-Llam.*
This vessel foundered in 1936 on voyage from Dubln to Newport while in ballast.

only method being guesswork but this guesswork was developed into fine art by the foreman who, using his stop-watch, knew by experience, depending on the thickness on the belt, that every fifteen minutes represented a hundred tons of chippings. On occasions such as Saturday afternoons, the men in charge of the bins, when wishing to get away early, would release more stone than usual on to the belt and as a result, completely throw the calculations.

At one time the bins at Carreg-y-Llam, having no levers to operate the doors, presented an even greater problem, the known capacity of the bins when full being the only means of calculating the weight supplied. Once opened, there was no means of closing the doors, leaving the ship no alternative but to receive 'the lot'. This, in turn, added to the mariners' difficulties as the ranging in the ever-moving waters rendered it impossible to read draughts or obtain a true mean reading of the plimsoll. Seldom in those days did a vessel receive just her load but generally finished up deeply overloaded to commence her passage. Had it been possible to level off the cargo, such levelling would have rendered the vessel too stiff in her sea movements. To counteract this, the cargo in each hold was teemed to an apex so that when rolling, the vessel was steadier and had less tendency to strain. This state of affairs was very well in fine weather, but should the weather change, it brought another danger, a danger that all on board were acutely aware of, that of the vessel's reaction to heavy seas which could cause the stones to shift. Once shifting started, each following roll made easier further shifting, causing the ship to list and so creating the possibility of turning turtle.

Having arrived safely at their destination, should this be in daylight, still left one gauntlet to run, that of the Board of Trade's Load Line Inspector, with his plumb bob and rule book. He was a man to be reckoned with, as his eagle eye would immediately spot an overloaded vessel. Even without a heavy list to attract his attention, he was forever on the look-out for some mate or master of whom he could make his victim. At some ports, cranes were ever ready to swoop into the holds the moment the vessel came alongside, thus giving the chance of lessening the load and so bringing the plimsoll out of the water before the B.O.T. Inspector arrived. Should luck be on their side, then master and mate could breathe more easily.

At small and out of the way ports, discharge was a much more lengthy and tedious manoeuvre involving the ship's own derricks and winches for off-loading into railway waggons. These smaller ports did, however, have one great advantage; being so out of the way, the official's visit was less likely.

The master and mate were in the unenviable position of being between the devil and the deep blue sea regarding the weight they carried. On the one hand, if a vessel was found to be over-loaded, the Board of Trade imposed a heavy penalty which the owners were forced to pay. In the event, this reflected on the master and mate, with repercussions which could well jeopardise their employment and even affect their career. On the other hand, should they carry anything less than a full cargo, then the owners would be displeased.

A case in point was that of an intrepid master who asked one of his crew members who was about to go ashore, if he would post a letter for him, adding that he would know when they reached the next port whether the letter had been posted. The sailor asked why that was so. The master explained that if he saw a man waiting on the quay with a suitcase, he would know that is was the man that had come to take over his command and that in his pocket would be a letter of dismissal. He further explained that he had just received a nasty, three-foolscap page letter from the owners, tearing him to pieces for a passage some days earlier. On that passage, he had been a few tons short in cargo, whilst carrying a number of tons of bunkers which they considered unnecessary. His letter was in reply, reminding them that a few trips earlier he had loaded at the quarries and was approximately two truck-loads over-weight. For that they had not even written him a line so why had he now received this lengthy three-page letter?

Under such circumstances, it is easy to understand the awful dilemma which constantly faced the masters and mates. Not only was the master responsible for the ship but for the welfare of his crew and many of these captains took this responsibility very seriously. Though many have long since gone, they are still remembered with great respect and affection by those that serve under them. During the shipping slump and depression of the early thirties, these men were sadly exploited. Some, having been in command of the big sailing ships and Atlantic liners, were reduced to taking any job on the Coasters. There were many occasions when every man on board was a certificated master or officer and the firemen were qualified engineers.

Apart from the constant hazards and dangers faced daily by the mariners, their working conditions were dominated by the one ruling factor, that of distribution and distribution at all costs. From the smallest two hundred and forty ton vessels to the larger twelve hundred tonners, nothing could be allowed to interfere with the speediest possible collection, passage and delivery of their cargoes, the sailors being the mere instruments to keep this system running smoothly.

The smaller vessels carried a complement of five or six men composed of master, mate, engineer-cum-fireman and two or three seamen, the larger vessels up to twelve men, which included a first and second engineer, a cook/steward to look after the officers and the remainder were additional hands.

Wages for the crew were paid weekly and were very low. To quote one of the masters, who summed it up in modern jargon, 'One week in peanuts and the next in liquorice allsorts.' The master's wage, too, was very low. In the late thirties his pay would hardly reach the grand sum of eight pounds a week even when this included his bonus. Bonus was paid at the rate of three farthings per every ton of cargo carried in one month, plus an extra ten pounds if he managed to keep his ship out of trouble for a period of twelve months. Each man was responsible for providing his own bed and bedding and the purchasing and cooking of his own food, the only cooking utensils provided by the owners being one frying-pan and a kettle. All cooking was done in the galley and the meals then carried forward to the accommodation by which time they were well-cooled.

The smaller vessels had no washing facilities but the larger did provide wash hand-basins in the cabins, for the masters, mates and engineers. Running water was not laid on so filling and emptying was by bucket. Again quoting one of the masters, 'Crews' W.C. discharge was by the bucket and chuck it system!' The crews worked a twelve-hour day for seven days a week in watches of four hours on and four hours off. In theory, this did not seem unreasonable as conditions were in those days. In practice, it was more a dream than reality for often they were required to be on duty for long hours beyond their watches for which no overtime was paid, the agreement being that time off in lieu would be granted. Unfortunately this, too, was only in theory for it proved that time off was possible only when there were no cargoes and that being so, then crews were then paid off.

At the start of a passage, preparations for sailing kept all occupied. Only when under way would the watch system come into operation. Having been on duty for the first four hours, a sailor would not exactly be resting for the next four as in this so-called off-duty period he had to prepare and cook his food, attend to his ablutions, repair any torn clothing; write necessary letters and those wishing to further their careers would hope for time to study. Any time left over could be used to rest. Should bad weather be encountered then this off-duty would be forfeited. In the event of reaching port at the end of a watch, again the time would be lost as no man could be spared during berthing and loading. It was, therefore, not uncommon that a man could be on duty for as long as eighteen hours without a break and this situation could continue for many days. The master, too, was as much caught up in this system as his men and in fact the more conscientious he was, the more his involvement. Should things go wrong, his was the sole responsibility and his whole career rested on his actions and decisions.

High days and holiday meant little or nothing to the mariners for distribution must continue. It was usual for arrangements to be such that the ships would be on passage on days such as Christmas Day and Boxing Day and other public holidays, ensuring that no time at all was lost. Christmas Day would find the ships heading for the Scottish ports where work was normally carried out on that day but New Year's Day being widely celebrated in Scotland found them back on this side of the border. On one rare occasion a ship did arrive at Carreg-y-Llam on Christmas Day. The sailors, pretending to be angry at loading being carried out at such a time, accused the loaders of not being Christians, to which the loaders replied that they did not work on Christmas Day; they only loaded boats.

In the quarries' heyday a large number of shipping companies were involved in the stone trade. Many were commendable in that they cared for the men who served them so well and prided themselves on providing the best ships possible for the job and some of those have survived and are thriving today.

These companies kept their crews for long periods of time. Others left much to be desired and crews stayed on only as long as absolutely necessary.

While the owners may seem to have been the villains in the scheme of things, one has to bear in mind that working conditions, accepted as normal in those days, were vastly different from those tolerated today. Not only did they have the expenses of building the ships, maintaining and running them, paying the crews, but also had to face continuous competition for the cargoes. The greatest competition came from Continental ships who were famous for their undercutting tactics. These were under charter to British Agents.

The 'foreigners', as they were known in the trade, had the advantage of there being a somewhat lower standard of living in their home countries which allowed them to hire their crews cheaply. Added to this was the fact that some carried their wives and families on board, so cutting their over-all costs. The undercutting was seen so often at the Agency offices when calling for orders. Whatever sum was quoted by the company's representative, would be counteracted by the foreigners with offers of sixpence or so less per ton. A further advantage was that the majority of their ships were fitted with diesel engines as opposed to our steam-driven vessels and as far as our sailors were concerned, these 'foreigners' contributed nothing except a constant threat to their livelihood.

The Continental ships were regular callers at our two ports and as they came alongside, the Customs Officer, whose unenviable task it was to travel from Llithfaen at all hours and in all weathers, would be waiting on the jetty to go aboard to clear them. The Dutch ships, in particular, were never short of bottles of gin and many of these bottles found their way along the jetty and up the hills from the two quarries when the Customs Officer happened to be looking the other way. At our house there was seldom a shortage of this spirit.

As well as stone, the Coasters carried a varied cargo including coal and grain. The dust and dirt created by these commodities settled over the vessels like a mantle and penetrated into everything on board. Keeping everything clean and shipshape was considered essential by most crews and owners but under such circumstances was no easy task. There were a few odd ships whose employees and owners did not contribute to this code of practice and because of it were in an appalling state but the majority were a credit to the flags they flew.

One of the owners was so fastidious that he paid regular visits to ensure that his fleet was literally spotless. On one of his visits, having carried out his usual inspection, he stood proudly on the quay to watch his vessel steam away. At the time a severe gale was blowing the ship against the quay and because of it the captain was experiencing great difficulty in getting her away. Decisively stepping within reach of her, the owner placed the point of his umbrella against her hull and proceeded to push. Moments later the vessel moved away, leaving the gentleman with a highly satisfied smile on his face, his wonders having been performed.

On another occasion, the same owner had one of his captains on the mat regarding his expenses. Looking very put out, he said, 'This portage bill of yours, Captain, I can't have it. This sixpennyworth of nails – one shilling.' To which the captain replied, 'Well, Sir, you surely do not expect me to pay for them out of my own pocket.' The captain was certainly no fool and undoubtedly this owner was an eccentric character but, in comparison with some of the mavericks in business at that time, he was a good employer.

Change of cargo involved sweeping the holds clean before taking on the next load. In cases where a cargo such as maize had been discharged before arrival at Nant, the crew, in the process of sweeping, would often collect a hundred-weight and sometimes as much as two hundred-weight of the grain. This was then exchanged with the loading gang for potatoes fresh from the ground and buttermilk which made for a very tasty meal. Not only potatoes and buttermilk were enjoyed after loading at Nant but at times many a crab and lobster found their way on board. These were acquired from the lobster-pots that my Father so carefully baited and set so hopefully at the end of the jetty but frequently provided such a poor catch. On the other hand, the foreman, Mr Griff Williams, who set his pots off Carreg-y-Llam jetty, had much greater success. Unable to understand this, my Father finally came to the conclusion that Mr Williams was regularly helping himself to our catch. Believing in this case in an eye for an eye, my Father felt fully justified in returning the compliment.

Only now, over forty years later, has the full story been revealed when one of the captains told me of how, when no-one was looking, they would pull up the pots and relieve them of their contents. Mr Williams in turn, unknown to my Father, was well aware that it was my Father that was raiding his pots but until now had no idea of the reason for his actions. Recently, when discussing it with him, in answer to my question of why he did or said nothing about it he replied that as he did not care for crab or lobster, he really did not mind. In view of what has now come to light, I cannot help but wonder whether my Father was the only pot-raider at Carreg-y-Llam.

The 'foreigners' were keen to supplement their supplies with fresh fare but some adopted more positive methods of acquisition and chose to eat things that to us would be totally unpalatable. Whether this was due to their wretched conditions or opportunism is difficult to tell.

An example of this was witnessed by the foreman when one morning, a Belgian ship – her captain a newcomer to our ports – having been delayed by misty conditions, came late into the bay. It was very damp and misty, with a flat, calm sea when she same alongside. Immediately mooring was completed, seven or eight sailors left the ship, each carrying a frying-pan. The foreman and loading gang stood, open-mouthed, watching them as they proceeded along the jetty until they disappeared up the bank behind the office. Some half an hour later they re-appeared, looking very pleased with themselves and with their frying-pans full of snails. Losing no further time, they hurried back on board.

By half loading time it became obvious that should the ship remain at the jetty any longer, she would be grounded. The foreman, not wishing to see the ship in trouble, went aboard to advise the captain to cease loading and to move out into the bay until the next high water. As he left the ship, he looked into the galley and there saw the crew greedily tucking into a massive plateful of snails, with juice and grease running freely out of the corners of their mouths. The sight so sickened him that he rushed back on to the jetty, fearing that at any moment he would be violently sick. Having recovered, he began to walk to Carreg-y-Llam where further duties awaited him. As he walked along the beach, he glanced seawards and saw that the ship was safely anchored in the bay and with a feeling of satisfaction, he continued on his way. Suddenly, his attention was caught by the sight of a boat with a number of men on board, being lowered from the ship. Intrigued, he stopped to watch and saw the boat head for the shore where, on gaining the beach, it was quickly pulled up and the men disappeared into the trees above the shore-line. Finding it difficult to believe that they were on another snail hunt, he decided to hurry to his destination and keep a look-out from there. His vigil was not for long for a short time later he saw the men re-appear carrying something bulky. Using his binoculars, he saw to his amazement that their burden was a fully-grown sheep which they bundled into the boat and hastily rowed to the ship.

Later in the day the ship came back alongside to complete her loading. The foreman, having had the necessary papers signed, was returning from the captain's cabin when, once again, he looked into the galley. This time he was not so surprised to see, hanging from the ceiling, joints of mutton so professionally cut and jointed that even a master butcher would have been proud to have accomplished.

These drastic measures adopted by some of the 'foreigners' to obtain food disgusted our own ships' crew who felt, and rightly so, that this only added fuel to the arguments of those always ready to condemn the sailor. In truth, however, the public were generally ignorant, or did not wish to know of the sailor's life and work, his image for centuries having been tarnished by those who knew little or nothing about the subject or the men, labelling them as drunkards, as dirty and lacking in morals.

Even John Masefield, the Poet Laureate, having sailed the seas in his youth and travelled widely, wrote so well on the subject but, nevertheless, referred to the ships that traded around these islands in his famous poem 'Cargoes' as dirty British coasters, such generalisation doing nothing for the men who worked so hard to confound this image.

A perfect example of the general disregard for these sailors was the way in which an event regarding one of the steam coasters was reported. The event occurred when the ship was running before heavy weather into the Shannon at dead of night. While negotiating the stretch near Kilcradaun Head, the on-coming sea broke over her with such force that it washed away her lifeboats. It happened at the change of the watch and at the same moment as the fireman was up on deck emptying the ash bucket. Tragically, the fireman was swept overboard and was drowned. The press reported that the ship had lost her boats, her ash bucket and also a fireman – in that order, the fireman qualifying only as an 'also'.

True, these little coasters did not excite the imagination or conjure up romantic pictures such as those of sailing the seven seas, of rounding Cape Horn, battling in the roaring forties or fighting to make way in the Southern Ocean but, nevertheless, faced other just as real perils which deep sea sailors readily acknowledged. These were the men who were not afraid of the land and did not need the stars to steer by. Strewn along their path were the wrecks which bore witness to the ever-present dangers which allowed for no error. The stout little vessels, like the men who sailed them, loved them and cursed them, played their part valiantly throughout the last war. Sadly, so many were lost as a result of enemy action and so many of those were the ships that we in Nant had known so well and to this day remember with affection.

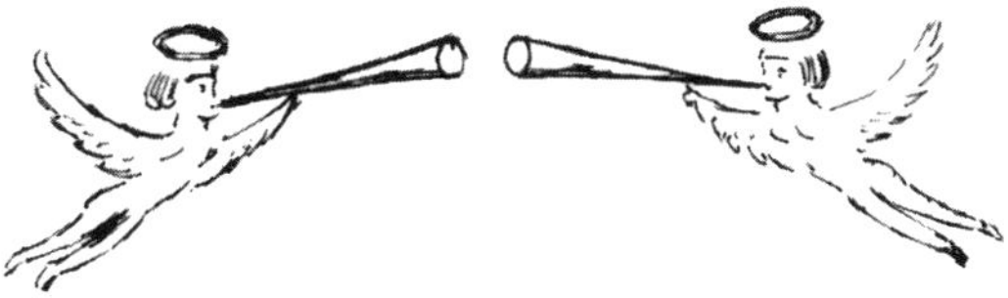

Chapter XXV

Little Saints and Little Sinners

In Nant, as in all Welsh villages, the Chapel held a prominent place and our little Presbyterian Chapel was no exception. Providing not only spiritual guidance on Sundays, it was also a form of Community Centre where meetings, singing practices, Band of Hope and concerts were held. Whilst not every family were members, the majority were, but no distinctions were made and all were welcome to participate in everything that went on. Being such a small congregation, we did not warrant a full time Minister so shared with Llithfaen their resident Minister, the Reverend Idris Owen.

The Reverend Owen was a man of deep religious beliefs and dedication to his calling. He was also a kindly man whom, I believe, held great affection for us and particularly the children who, in turn, had affection and respect for him.

School / Chapel

Should any of his flock stray, it cast no reflection on his efforts to make good God-fearing Christians of us for he left no stone unturned. His strength of oratory and preaching was so powerful that few could have been his equal.

Every fourth Sunday he made his journey to Nant to conduct services for us and between times, lay preachers and visiting Ministers would deputise for him. He also came to lead our Band of Hope meetings and took a keen interest in Ysgolion Sul Eisteddfods. These were Sunday School Festivals in which we children competed. Coming shortly before the great day to hear us going though our paces, he gave advice and made corrections where necessary.

Although our family were members of the Church of Wales, which meant going to Llithfaen to worship, only my mother regularly attended that Church. The only other members in the village were the Jones family at number seven Mountain View. Mr Jones was a sidesman and the family were devout churchgoers so my Mother seldom had to make the journey alone. At such times as Christmas, Easter and Harvest Thanksgiving I looked forward to going with them but otherwise went reluctantly and only when forced to do so.

Attending Chapel was no hardship for me. In fact, it was enjoyable as one felt directly involved in the proceedings which were always lively and easy to relate to. The Chapel itself was welcoming and warm, especially on winter evenings when the lamps were lit, their light shining out into the surrounding darkness like a welcoming beacon. Although daily passing through to the schoolroom, on Sundays the building had a completely different air about it. Everyone wore their best clothes, the ladies wearing smart hats, many adorned with flowers, and the men in dark suits. The smell of the oil-lamps, of mothballs, of the hymn books and the pinewood pews blending to produce an aroma that one found only on Sundays in that little Chapel.

A number of children endeavoured to arrive early in order to get the back pews. There we could whisper amongst ourselves, eat sweets and giggle together, usually about nothing but once having started giggling, it was extremely difficult to stop. Sitting in that position, one could lean well forward and so stand less chance of being noticed. 'Being noticed' was to be avoided at all costs as for succeeding weeks, those caught would be put to sit in a position where a stern eye could be kept on them. Also, the disgrace of behaviour leading to 'being noticed' was not easy to live down.

Another 'early bird' was Menna Roberts, Menna was our resident organist and came early to sort out the hymns and settle herself at the organ. Soon afterwards the rest of the congregation would arrive and to the sounds of hushed voices, shuffling feet, clearing of throats and the occasional cough, we eventually settled down. The moment the

Reverend Owen climbed up to the pulpit, all sound and movement ceased.

The service always began quietly and in low tempo, with hymns in between which were sung with fervence and sincerity, filling the building with melody and harmony such as only Welsh voices can produce. Finally, the high spot of the proceedings, the Sermon. Beginning as calmly and gentle as the still waters of the sea on a windless summer's day, our Minister led us and cajoled us and took us with him into the theme. As he proceeded, so the tempo and tone of his voice increased and the text became clear. Should he have cause to question or chastise, the message would be so cleverly woven into the sermon that no-one could misunderstand. As a result those even remotely guilty of some deed or thought could not fail to recognise their weakness, whether of flesh or spirit, the others exercising if not feeling of guilt then at least some heart searching, all the while the Elders at the front in the 'big seat' nodding in agreement to almost every word, at every pause expressingly loudly and as of one voice 'Ie'n wir'. '*Yes indeed*'.

By this time we at the back were well-primed and the nodding heads never failed to produce the fuel for a good giggle as one or two aped the Elders' movements. Reaching a crescendo and giving his all, the Minister, with perspiration streaming down his face and his hand pounding the pulpit as emphasis, would warn us of the perils of evil and the penalties of hell-fire and damnation that would surely be ours should we stray from the path of righteousness. Such was the effect that even we children paid full attention, feeling a little guilty and afraid, too, for our irreligious behaviour and easy subjection to earthly distractions. With these sober thoughts, the final hymn would be sung and the Service ended. Never did anyone leave with disappointment, but elated and fulfilled and with much to think about. That we children tried his long-suffering patience was a fact and many a man would have given us up in despair, but not our Minister.

The Ysgolion Sul Eisteddfod each year was a great event in our lives and the honour of winning the competitions was highly prized. The event took place at the Madryn Hall in the little town of Nefyn some seven miles distant. Sunday schools from far and wide took part and competition was keen. Added to the competitive and festive atmosphere was the fact that the proceedings took all day. This meant having lunch out, and for us from Nant, this was really a treat.

There were several competitions such as recitation, hand-writing, singing solo and also in unison. Having so few entrants meant that we had to practise much harder than most other schools to stand any change of gaining the necessary points. Every point was vital, for those achieving the highest would be awarded a shield. Thus it was that for weeks before the event S'miss would work tirelessly with us, holding practise sessions after school in her attempt to perfect our efforts. These practises were taken very seriously and S'miss's directions and advice followed to the n'th degree.

It was during one of the final practises that, as usual, the Reverend Owen came to hear us. After listening patiently, he expressed the view that our emphasis in one of the pieces was wrongly placed and explained where he thought it should be. This did not go down at all well as we were practising it as S'miss had directed and, in our opinion, S'miss was never wrong about anything so, although we said nothing, we had no intention of making a change. We were then asked to go through it again, but putting the emphasis where the Minister had suggested. Dutifully we went through the piece, but with the emphasis exactly as before. Thinking that we had not understood, he gave us a voluble demonstration and then asked us to try again. Again we repeated the performance as S'miss had taught us. S'miss, now rather perturbed and giving us dark looks, instructed us to do as we had been asked by Mr Owen. Pretending not to notice her dark looks, we proceeded and like a pack of mules, stubbornly ignored her request.

By this time our Minister was thoroughly exasperated and struggling to keep calm when, suddenly, a stone hit the window with such force that it was a wonder that the glass did not shatter. It was not really as much of a surprise to us as it was to S'miss and Mr Owen, as we had been aware for some time that a few of the boys had been jumping up to peer in through the window, and had been doing their best to distract us and make us giggle by pulling faces at us. Unable to contain ourselves a moment longer, we burst out laughing. For Mr Owen it was the last straw. Flinging down the book he held and raising his hands in the air, he shouted angrily, 'That's it, no more, finish'. He then stormed out of the chapel. For us, the rest of the session was spent in hearing S'miss berate us for our disgraceful behaviour, adding that she was utterly ashamed of us. We were a little ashamed ourselves, but were also confused as to where our loyalties lay. If my memory serves me correctly, I believe that we gained maximum points for that recitation.

Having to withdraw from the competitions because someone had fallen ill at the last minute was always a hazard. This did happen to us once or twice, so S'miss decided to train a reserve for each child. It seemed to have been an excellent idea until the last moment when we were called to go on and do our piece in the 'Unison Party of Eight' section. Whilst the audience and judges awaited our appearance S'miss was desperately trying to sort out the 'stand-ins' from the 'stars'. It was an impossible task as no-one would admit to being a reserve and the audience were becoming restive. Finally, in despair and to everyone's amazement, she led the sixteen of us out on to the stage. As soon as we had finished the audience applauded loudly, but the judges, in no mood to dally, promptly and justifiably disqualified us.

One Sunday, before the service began, Mr Owen announced that Menna was unable to attend and asked if someone would volunteer to take her place at the organ. Everyone turned and looked hopefully at everyone else, but no-one responded. The chances of finding a volunteer were slim as the congregation on that occasion was rather small. Possibly feeling that anyone able to play was too shy to come forward and so needed a little encouragement, he asked again, emphasising that we did not need a virtuoso, just someone capable of playing a few simple notes.

Suddenly it occurred to me that I could play. True, I had only a three finger ability, two on the right hand and one on the left, but I thought it would be acceptable and before I had the chance to lose my nerve, I put up my hand. Mr Owen did not jump at my offer as I had expected but, instead, saying nothing, he studied me thoughtfully with raised eyebrows. I, now a little red in the face, realized that although I was all of seven years old, he was probably hoping for someone older. However, quickly composing himself, he asked me to go forward and as I joined him at the organ, I explained that although I could not play from music I was able to play most tunes. He looked a little surprised but, seemingly satisfied, told me what the number of the hymn was and said that I could find it in the book while he began the Service.

I quickly found the hymn but, on reading the words, I realized to my discomfort that, although they were familiar, I could not remember the tune. By this time the Service was in progress so I could do nothing but wait. Feeling rather worried, I busied myself trying to look as professional as Menna and S'miss by pulling out and pushing in the black knobs above the keyboard and making sure that my feet reached the pedals. Quite soon Mr Owen announced the number of the hymn, but before he could read out the first line as he usually did, I called out that I did not know the tune. Looking down at me kindly, he indicated that it did not matter and from his book chose another hymn. To my extreme embarrassment I had to say that I did not know that one either. He tried again and again the result was the same. Visibly swallowing hard and then loudly clearing his throat, he asked me to tell him what hymns I could play. For a moment I could not think then, suddenly, I remembered the children's hymn 'Iesu Tirion', '*Gentle Jesus*', and I hurriedly told him. With obvious relief but also a smile, he recited the first line and I proceeded very nervously to play.

Surprisingly, I managed the first verse with only a few wrong notes and by the time we had reached the third, I had got the hand of the pedals and felt more confident. The hymn ended and I immediately began looking through the book for another familiar hymn in readiness for the next time. Leafing through, I was beginning to despair when I came across 'Sanctaidd, Sanctaidd, Sanctaidd', '*Holy, Holy, Holy*', which I knew quite well, and so I happily settled on that one.

The moment came and Mr Owen looked questioningly down at me. I made my suggestion which seemed to please him, and away we went. Feeling more at ease, I managed a fairly reasonable rendering and at the end of it felt well satisfied. Unfortunately, this satisfaction proved to be my undoing, for I completely forgot to look for the next hymn until it was too late.

The break for the hymn came and, as before, Mr Owen looked down at me. Unable to offer anything, I looked helplessly back at him while desperately trying to think of a hymn. My mind was a complete blank and, try as I might, I could offer nothing. I did not want to search in the book while everyone was waiting as it had not been easy to find the last one. By this time I was going hot and cold with embarrassment.

The Minister, well aware of my plight, again tried to help me with suggestions, but none were familiar enough to play at a moment's notice. With desperation gripping me and fighting back tears, I remembered something I could play and without a thought blurted out, 'Coming Round the Mountain'. Immediately there were gasps and giggles all around and the Elders turned to look at me with undisguised horror. Mr Owen, with a look of utter disbelief, for a moment remained silent and then, quietly but firmly, said that such a song was never sung in God's house. Realizing my utter foolishness and deeply embarrassed, in blind panic, to redeem myself, I made the situation even worse when, in a weak and trembling voice I suggested the 'Isle of Capri'. Mr Owen, almost choking and struggling to control himself, this time ignored my offer and said that we would again have 'Iesu Tirion'.

Burning with shame, I produced a far from perfect rendition of the tune. As soon as it was over, I wished I could have run away, but had no choice but to sit there and reflect on my folly and determine never again to volunteer for anything.

The Service, after what seemed hours, came to an end and to my utter amazement, Mr Owen thanked me for my efforts. Despite his kindness I was never so glad to get away from anywhere in my life as I was to get away from the chapel that Sunday.

One event shows clearly how confident we were of our Minister's support in times of trouble. One of the boys, in this case a Llithfaen boy, was busily stealing apples from Mr Owen's garden when he was disturbed by the Minister's dog. In his haste to get away over the barbed wire fence, he caught and badly tore his trousers. Terrified of what his mother would say about it, especially when she found out the circumstances, he was reluctant to go home to face the music. Suddenly, an idea occurred to him and without a second thought, he confidently marched up the Minister's path, knocked on the door and then began crying.

Mr Owen opened the door and was most surprised to see the little boy in such a state. At once he asked him what had upset him. Between the most heart-rending sobs the boy told him that as he was passing the gate, the Minister's dog had rushed out and tried to bite him and in so doing had torn his trousers. He then turned so that Mr Owen could see the damage and quickly added that he was afraid to go home as his mother would be furious.

The Minister, at once full of concern, ushered him in and took him to his wife. Mrs Owen, hearing the story and as concerned as her husband about it, at once set about repairing the trousers. In the meantime, the little boy sat happily tucking into a large slice of home-made cake.

Such faith can doubtless move mountains and although one cannot condone such actions, one must at least recognise the initiative, the excellence of our Minister and accept the fact that we children, each and every one of us, were a mixture of little saints and little sinners.

Chapter XXVI

In Sickness and in Health

Epidemics and serious illnesses were uncommon in the valley. Our isolation, the small size of our population, together with the outdoor life we led, were no doubt contributing factors to this. In those pre-multiple vaccination days only on rare occasions did even the childhood ailments spread like wild-fire, but rather choosing one or two at a time.

Our local doctor, Dr Jack Rowlands, known to us all as Dr Jack, must have been eternally grateful for these circumstances for every visit meant a three mile journey from his home and surgery at Llanaelhaearn, followed by the inescapable trek down the Screw Hill. Having received an urgent call to visit, he would arrive breathlessly, often in a remarkably short time, carrying his little black bag and without pausing for breath, would attend to his patient.

Only when satisfied that he had done all that he could would he ask for his usual glass of milk before facing the journey home. For a man short in stature and inclined towards roundness, that journey must have been a struggle. Nevertheless, in fair or foul weather, day or night, not once did he shirk his duty and we in turn did not take advantage of his care of us. Instead, we endeavoured to contain our medical complaints until able to consult him at his once weekly surgeries held at the 'Vic' Hotel in Llithfaen.

A few people in the village preferred to consult a partnership in Pwllheli for medical treatment and so these doctors, too, were no strangers to Nant.

As today's National Health Service was then unborn, his services were generally paid for through an insurance scheme. Contributors to the scheme were known as Panel Patients. The contributions were deducted from the men's wages at the rate of sixpence (2½p) per week for the doctor and hospitalisation and three pence (1.25p) per fortnight for nursing care. Our District Nurse was based at her home in Llithfaen and was also on call to us day or night. Her devotion to duty even Florence Nightingale would have found difficult to criticize.

A medical event greatly looked forward to by the children was that of the Medical Officer of Health's two annual visits to the school. In advance of his coming S'miss would notify our parents and request that our mothers be present at our examination. On the appointed morning, we would arrive at school looking as well turned out as any brigade of guards. Boots and shoes shone to perfection with socks uniformly pulled up as opposed to the usual half mast or 'acey ducey' position and hair gleamed as a result of the more rigorous than usual brushing, the boys' hair looking decidedly wet, having been plastered down with what must have been large quantities of water to keep it in the slicked back position.

Some were fortunate enough to have brilliantine which they liberally used, but which we girls thought made them a bit sissy as we did not think that boys should smell fancy.

The girls wore their brightest ribbons and slides to hold back their plaits and curls with the exception of those like myself who had the disadvantage of the fringe style which did not allow for adornment. I did, however, on one occasion, attempt to improve the natural shine by using brilliantine, or what I thought was brilliantine. I knew that Garnie had a tin of it which was kept in the cabinet fixed to the bathroom wall. The cabinet was well out of my reach, but by standing on top of the lavatory pan lid, I could just manage to open the door with the tips of my fingers and feel inside. Despite the fullness of the cabinet, I managed to feel the round tin and remove it without mishap. Jumping down, I ran to the door to ensure that no-one was coming whilst at the same time I struggled to remove the lid. After several attempts, causing very sore fingers, I eventually succeeded.

The brilliantine seemed rather darker than I thought it should be, but as I might be disturbed at any moment I spent no time thinking about it and proceeded to extract what I thought would be sufficient. Having rubbed it well between my hands to get an even spread of the grease, as I had so often seen the men do, I began smearing it on my hair. It did feel very sticky, but I supposed that was how it should be.

The bathroom mirror, like the cabinet, was too high up for me to be able to see what I was doing, but it did not matter. I would see the result in my dressing table mirror when I had finished. Satisfied that I had supplied enough, I carefully washed my hands. I was more than a little surprised to see the water turn a dark green in colour and to find that the smell was not at all scented but rather strong and very like something else that was familiar but I could not remember what.

The job done, I climbed back again to replace the tin and it was then that I caught a glimpse of myself in the mirror, and the sight was horrific. What had before been a head of blonde hair was now a mass of dark green, greasy streaks. The shock and panic I felt was too much to worry about being discovered using other peope's belongings, and I ran along the landing, screaming for my Mother. My Mother came at once and she, too, was horrified by the sight of me. Between sobs, I told her what I had been doing. Immediately she went to the cabinet and found the tin. At this moment Ethel joined us to find out what all the commotion was about. My Mother, looking absolutely furious, informed her that this silly, stupid, idiotic and very naughty girl had covered her hair with Zambuk ointment and would be going to bed with a smacked bottom and not to school, were it not for the fact that the doctor was coming. With threats of dealing with me later that day and repeated warnings of the dangers of going anywhere near ointment and medicines, they proceeded none too gently to shampoo away my folly. Thanks to their efforts I did arrive in school on time and with my crowning glory in gleaming condition. It was later that day that I discovered that Zambuk was to cure spots and blemishes.

S'miss never failed to comment on our smart appearance and say that she was proud of us, but sometimes added that it was a pity that the doctor did not come every day. As soon as the register had been called we were sent out to the playground to await the doctor's arrival with dire warnings ringing in our ears of what would happen if we should spoil our appearance.

The play would not be the quality of on ordinary day, everyone being afraid to move too freely for fear of getting dirty, displacing a shiny hair or even worse, falling down and ruining everything. We, therefore, stood stiffly in little groups, talking and preening ourselves, S'miss comments having gone down well. However, the duration of our immaculate appearance depended entirely on how long we had to wait before being called in. Generally, we managed to retain our spotless image until the medicals were at an end though those at the end of the queue had lost a little of their lustre by the time their turn came around. The one thing that did irritate me was that, having dressed so carefully and groomed myself so thoroughly purely to impress the doctor, the first thing I had to do in his presence was undress and stand before him, clad only in my knickers. I do not recall any cause for concern brought to light by the examinations but, instead, his praise for our mothers' care of our health. This kindly man, out of his hearing, was affectionately known to us all as 'Mami bach', 'Little mother', as never did he refer to or address any of the mothers by their name but, instead, referred to one and all as 'Mami bach'.

Often the doctor would be accompanied my Mr Sam Owen, the Schools' Attendance Officer, who came to check the register for absenteeism. Unlike the doctor, Mr Owen was unjustly considered to be a man to be feared for we believed that he had the power to send any absentee, or anyone that had been naughty, away to the 'Llong Fawr', the 'Big Ship'. This was a fate to be avoided at all costs as there one could be detained, undergoing hard labour for years and years and years. This power earned him the nickname of 'Y Dyn Llong Fawr', the 'Big Ship Man'. Added to the fact that we cared so much for our school and our teacher, the threat of such a penalty ensured that bad behaviour and truancy were never a problem.

Another annual visitor was Mr Parry, the dentist. News of his coming was always greeted with a great deal of chatter and excitement as much thought had to be given to how many teeth we could encourage him to extract. This was highly important as one's courage rating among one's peers rested on the number of extractions, the amount of blood lost, the size of the cavity and above all, the way one stoically bore up during the treatment.

Playtime found us examining each other's mouths and great delight was shown when a decayed tooth was discovered. Most of those that lacked this essential ingredient were terribly disappointed and on the first occasion I found myself in this unenviable position. I felt almost desperate. I determined that I had to do something about it but had no idea what I could do. I supposed I could try complaining of toothache for the next few days, but was not really keen on the idea and this the more so because it would most likely bring a ban on sweets on the following Tuesday when the shops opened. No, that was out of the question as there was too much to lose.

The answer came when one of the girls came to me looking pleased, saying that she had a very loose front tooth which she was sure the dentist would take out. Well, of course, that was it. Why ever hadn't I thought of it. Still, there were five days to go and I should be able to achieve something by the end of that time, so I set to with a will.

It took a great deal of concentration, but by the day before the visit the feat was accomplished, so much so that the tooth was in danger of falling out without any help from the dentist. Care was then essential when eating and, woe of woe's even sweets had to be denied until after the extraction.

At last the day came and everyone waited. Excitement and trepidation were in the air. Eventually Mr Parry arrived, carrying his little case. As he entered the schoolroom, we got to our feet and politely bade him 'Bore da', 'Good morning'. S'miss then told us to go out to the playground and wait until we were called. Little pangs of fear were now creeping in, but bravely these were kept under control.

After what seemed quite a long time, but was probably only a few minutes S'miss appeared at the door and called in the first patient. At once one of the bigger boys stepped forward and went in like a gladiator into the arena. Only a short time later he was back, a little pale of face, smiling and sporting two first class cavities as well as proudly spitting blood. He had triumphed and set the example for the rest of us to follow.

My turn was not too long in coming and in I went. There was Mr Parry in his white coat, and S'miss's chair waiting for me. I sat down and after a brief inspection, the dentist said that he was going to remove the wobbly tooth. In a moment it was done. Unfortunately there was very little blood with which to impress the others, but when I returned to the playground there were sufficient bloody handkerchiefs to satisfy everyone, so my lack of it went without notice.

When the weather permitted, Mr Parry would make the journey by boat and once treatment was over, he would hurry away to get in a little fishing on his way home. Once he had gone we were free to compare notes. It was then that the horrifying and grizzly tales were exchanged of the suffering borne with dignity and in silence. Before our imaginations ran complete riot, the bell would ring and we had to file back into school. There S'miss would tell us that we had behaved very well, sympathise with those that seemed to be in pain, for now all pretences could be dropped and finally would dismiss us for lunch.

When childhood ailments did trespass into our healthy environment, so unusual was it that the sufferers became almost celebrities. Everyone called to enquire about their progress. Some brought gifts and always S'miss would send her good wishes for a rapid recovery. Quarantine was the worst part as, having recovered, one still had to remain apart from one's friends. It was, therefore, essential that at least one other child had succumbed to ensure companionship during that period.

Scarlet Fever, being a more serious illness, was one that we did not wish to 'fall foul of', not so much for its seriousness, but because it meant being taken away to an isolation hospital some sixteen miles away. To be taken away in itself was unacceptable, but to an isolation hospital was to be dreaded. We had heard that parents could visit only once a week and even then not enter the ward, but have to stand outside and look in through specially designed windows. It seemed the nurses were covered from head to foot in white gowns which made them look like ghosts and no-one knew exactly what they did to you or if they did know, it was certainly a well-kept secret. This I was convinced was because it was so horrible it did not bear talking about. When the disease did strike, for some strange reason it struck only the one or two at the same time and seldom was it two in the same family.

My first memory of Scarlet Fever was when Annie Mair was taken ill and was rushed off to that place. Not only did she have to suffer but also her younger brother, John who, because of it, was not allowed out to play with the rest of us. Another reason for fear was that we had heard that as the patients recovered, their skin peeled off. This sounded dreadful but, despite the horror of such a thing, I had a secret desire to see what a skinless person would look like. Two years later I fell victim to it myself, but felt so ill that I even forgot about becoming skinless though not the fear of being taken away to that place. However, the very severity of my illness was my salvation for Dr Jack felt that I was far too ill for the move and as facilities at home were adequate, it would be better for my Mother to take on the nursing.

Immediately, precautions were taken to ensure that my mother and I were isolated from everyone else in the household. Her bed was moved into my room and a large, white sheet, well soaked in disinfectant, was hung over the outside of the bedroom door and re-soaked every morning. Only the doctor entered the room. Our meals and other necessities were left outside the door by Lizzie and taken inside when she had gone. I clearly remember feeling very ill and on one occasion experiencing some delirium. Not until three or four weeks later when my skin began peeling did I really feel as if I was going to recover. The dreaded peeling proved to be nothing more than like that of an overdose of sunburn and, in fact, was therapeutically ideal as it gave one something to do. Being a lone sufferer, convalescence was more like penal servitude but was well compensated for when freedom was finally gained, by the pleasure of being able to mix with one's friends again and the interest shown by everyone.

One of the most serious cases of contagious illnesses during my time was when June Roberts was taken ill. June was six years old at the time and was one of twin girls. She lived at Mountain View with her devoted grandparents, Mr & Mrs Bob Roberts and her two uncles, John James and Bob. Her illness began, as do so many of the minor ailments, with a sore throat and general malaise, which naturally was thought would quickly clear up with normal home nursing.

Despite every care and attention, June's condition suddenly became worse and so the District Nurse was summoned. Although the nurse responded at once, by the time she arrived June had deteriorated further and as well as running a high fever, she was experiencing great difficulty in breathing. As the nurse hurried up the stairs, she could hear the sounds of the little patient's desperate attempts to breathe. A short examination was all that was needed to confirm her fears that June's life was in danger and that the doctor must be sent for urgently. In response, Uncle Bob immediately rushed out of the house to telephone from his sister's in Sea View. The family, desperate with worry and gripped with fear by the horrifying sounds of their loved one fighting for breath, felt utterly helpless. They were no strangers to grief, having tragically lost a son and daughter, both of whom had been in their early twenties and now they were faced with the possibility of losing yet another loved one. News of illness soon spread throughout the valley and June's illness was no exception. At such times, we children were asked not to worry those afflicted as our parents made the enquiries and gave help when necessary. Hearing about June, we took it for granted that, being winter time, she probably had a bad cold. It, therefore, came as a shock when we were warned by our parents that we must not play anywhere near her home and keep very quiet when passing the house as she was very ill. Being very ill was not something we were accustomed to and we wondered with concern what sort of illness it could possibly be.

Being Sunday and therefore not at school, we gathered in the little square and in low voices talked about it, not only from curiosity but also from fear for June. Whilst gathered there, we saw the nurse arrive and with only a nod to us she hurried in to number four. Trying to imagine what could be happening, we stood watching the house, our concern and curiosity denying our sense of knowing that at such a time we should make ourselves scarce. Annie Mair then joined us and told us that her mother was at June's helping the family but other than that she knew no more than we did.

Soon after the nurse had gone in, the door opened and Uncle Bob rushed out and ran to his sister's house in Sea View. We guessed that he had gone there to telephone as, apart from our house, Mrs Parry-Jones had the only other telephone in the village. Only a few minutes passed before he re-appeared and hurriedly returned home. This development caused us to wonder whom he had telephoned. Perhaps the call was to June's parents far away in Llandudno where they and June's twin sister lived. We all knew that June's mother had not been well since the birth of the twins and was the reason for June being cared for by her maternal grandparents. Then we wondered whether the call was to the doctor and speculation on this went on for some time.

The best part of an hour went by as we quietly continued our observation of the house. Suddenly, we heard footsteps coming along the path and saw Dr Jones from Pwllheli breathlessly hurrying along. As he reached the house, the door opened and he disappeared inside. His coming and the grim expression on his face brought the realisation of how serious the situation must be and that gathered there as we were, observing every movement, showed no respect for those in such trouble. Without another word we left the little square and made our way home.

In our house, as no doubt in all the others, everyone looked anxious. I told them that the nurse and the doctor had arrived and asked them what they thought was happening. My question was not answered. Everyone seemed too pre-occupied but I was told that June was in good hands and that the best thing that I could do was to stay indoors.

At Mr & Mrs Roberts' the doctor found his little patient in a desperate state, fighting a losing battle to get air into her lungs. Immediately recognising the symptoms and making only the briefest examination to confirm his diagnosis, he informed the family that she was suffering from diptheria. Their distress can be imagined as in those days, diptheria was a dreaded disease with a high mortality rate, and added to that the fact that they were so far away from the necessary medical facilities. Wasting not one moment, the doctor explained that although he was not a surgeon, he had no alternative but to operate immediately if he was to save her life. Without further delay, June was gently laid on a table directly in front of the bedroom window and the doctor, using a local anaesthetic, proceeded to operate. Having cut into her throat and thence into the trachea, he fitted the life-saving tube which allowed air to pass unhindered into her lungs.

As though by a miracle, the stentorious and laboured sounds of her gasps for breath diminished and quickly a more natural colour returned to her face, replacing the bluish tinge of only seconds earlier. The relief felt by everyone was immense and almost audible. With the immediate grave danger eliminated, the patient's condition was still nonetheless serious and together with the highly contagious nature of the disease demanded urgent hospitalisation.

Nevertheless, the risk of moving her under those circumstances and the arduous journey involved being an even greater risk, it was decided that the move be delayed for one day. Having satisfied themselves that they had done everything possible, the nurse and doctor then left the village to arrange transportation and hospital admission for the next day.

June meanwhile, though extremely weak and exhausted, not only could breathe freely but was able to make it known that all she wanted was that her Aunt Menna would stay with her. Menna, who had been at her side most of the time, was Mr & Mrs Roberts' daughter-in-law. She lived only a few doors away at number eight with her husband, Sam, and their young son, David. With no thought for herself Menna readily agreed and not wishing to expose her family to infection, sent word of the arrangements to Sam. For the rest of that day and throughout the night she did not move from her little niece's bedside, while she comforted her and attended to her every need.

Early the next morning, the stretcher party arrived to carry June up the Screw Hill to the waiting ambulance. As she was being carried out of the house, her Uncle Bob collapsed in a faint, the result of all the worry and tension which finally had been more than he could bear. While members of the family attended to him the stretcher party set off, accompanied by Menna and a neighbour, Mrs Jenny Owen, who had volunteered to go with them. Mercifully, the weather was good considering that it was the middle of January and they reached the ambulance in good time.

At the hospital they were met by June's parents and, when satisfied that the patient was settled, the two ladies left to make their way home. It was only then that they had time to think of their own predicament, that as contacts, they could so easily pass on the disease to their own families. The nearer they got to home the more worried they became. It seemed that there was nothing they could do when, suddenly, they remembered that alcohol was something used as a sterilising agent and so on their arrival at Llithfaen, they went straight to the 'Vic' and purchased a large bottle of whisky. On their arrival home they immediately prepared a bath of strong disinfected water and, having thoroughly bathed themselves, they each drank a large glass of whisky.

Naturally, great concern was felt by everyone in the village for many days afterwards, not only for June but also for fear of further outbreaks of diptheria which could so quickly become of epidemic proportions. Due partly to the good sense of those two ladies, to everyone's relief no further cases did occur and six weeks later, to our delight, June was considered fit enough to return home.

* * *

In country districts in those days, the art of self-healing with the aid of folk medicines and cures was still widely practised and Nant was no exception. Our reluctance to worry the doctor and nurse for anything less than serious encouraged the awareness that prevention was better than cure and so led us to keeping as fit and healthy as possible. When ailments did strike, the so-called natural medicines or cures were brought in to do the trick and whether psychological or not, on most occasions did just that.

Psychosomatic disorders did not occur. Had they done so they would not have been recognised as such as very few, if any, had heard the word 'psychosomatic', let alone know its meaning. Perhaps that was the very reason that we were not plagued with its disorders coupled with the fact that we were all so busy living our lives and in so doing endeavouring to count our blessings, that there was no need of placebos.

The onset of a sore throat was treated, not by lozenges or unheard of antibiotics, but by goose grease, of which an ample supply was generally kept in every household. The grease, having first been warmed, would be spread on a length of flannel and then applied to the neck where it was wound around and secured with a safety pin. The flannel would then remain in position until all soreness had ceased and cease it invariably did.

Signs of children being out of sorts or looking pale was often diagnosed as the blood being too thin, or in need of purifying. These symptoms were almost expected in spring and autumn when the budding and falling of the leaves were believed to have a related weakening effect on growing children. Some mothers automatically took curative precautions purely because of these seasons. The most popular pick-me-up and guard against such a condition was a course of brimstone and treacle. This was usually made by half filling a jar – an empty jam jar was ideal for this – with black treacle or golden syrup, adding to it a small quantity of flowers of sulphur powder and mixing them as thoroughly as possible. It was not at all unpleasant and looked somewhat attractive with the bright yellow streaks of sulphur which, try as one might, and with today's liquidisers unheard of, never really blended with the treacle. It was doled out a teaspoonful or two at a time, twice a day, until the child had regained his or her vitality.

Another tonic and cure-all favoured by many but, fortunately, not my parents was asafoetida and known locally as 'Assee Fetta'. This was believed to cure such varied ailments as stomach trouble, worms, whooping cough, rheumaticky pains and even given to horses and cows when they were in trouble. When administered to children, two or three drops were carefully placed on a cube of sugar but adults merely added the drops to water then quickly swallowed the milky-looking mixture. Its efficacy may have been without doubt but had I been forced to choose between those ailments and the cure, I should have chosen the former and risked the consequences as the smell of it was utterly nauseating. So atrociously pungent was it that even to go near any of its 'victims' needed some courage. Those treated with what to my mind was a form of violation of taste and nasal senses stoically bore up and gained the respect of the more fortunate.

When symptoms of the common cold appeared, these were treated at once with a concoction known as 'Brwas Menyn', menyn being the Welsh word for butter but translation of brwas defies me. Brwas Menyn was prepared quite simply by placing small cubes of bread in a breakfast cup, liberally sprinkling it with pepper, adding a knob of butter and covering the whole with boiling water. This was then eaten while as hot as one could bear. Its value in relation to the cold was difficult to determine but as it was prepared only on those occasions, its very appearance had therapeutic qualities in nurturing the warm feeling of being cosseted when feeling sorry for one's self.

Another favoured medicament was something known as 'Dutch Drops'. Obtainable only in Holland, these drops were acquired by asking the ships' masters to bring them and this they did whenever possible. The 'drops' came in very small bottles and were not all that cheap, which suggested that they were highly potent. They had the odour of a mixture of Friars Balsam and Stockholm Tar. What they were used for I have no idea for I do not recall them ever being administered to anyone in our house but they were highly prized by those who did take them.

Warts were as offensive and painful then as they are today and local remedies for these unsightly growths knew no bounds. A number of those worked miraculously for some but failed dismally for others. Although not at any time afflicted myself, some of my friends were plagued by them. Among the most popular remedies practised by the children was painting them with the milk of the dandelion stalk and for some it did work, faith in the remedy no doubt playing the biggest part. Harmless as warts generally were, when they grew on the face or mouth, they were totally unacceptable. In an effort to prevent them developing on the mouth many clay pipe smokers painted the mouthpieces of their pipes with bright red paint. Whether the clay was suspected as a contributory cause of the warts or the paint and its colour believed to be inhospitable to the virus, I do not know. Nevertheless, it was for warts in these areas that help was more commonly sought.

Help was available from two particular sources but both were outside the valley. One, who was locally famous, was an aunt of our Mrs Jenny Owen, a lady reputed to have miraculous powers. It was said that her method was simply to blow on the offending wart for a few seconds, after which it would shrivel and die.

The other source was a Mr Owen Griffiths of Llangwnadl, a village some fourteen miles west of Pwllheli. His powers were not only locally renowned but internationally so. People travelled to consult him from as far away as the United States, Australia and New Zealand and they returned home minus their warts. The remedy had been passed on to him by Irish Tinkers who came over on the Coasters. Throughout his life he kept it a closely guarded secret, revealing it to only one member of his family and to this day that secrecy is still respected as the remedy is known only to his direct descendants.

With the lack of any form of indoor plumbing, other than that in our house, the practice of hygiene required much more effort than it does for us today in our all mod. con. dwellings. All water had to be carried from taps which were located across the communal back-yard. There was one tap for every two houses. The lavatories, too, were across the yard but at least there was one to each house and these were situated back to back, in pairs. They were the bucket in a box type and did not have the advantage of later models which incorporated an attached seat and also chemicals to neutralise the contents.

Emptying the lavatories was the regular job of one of the quarrymen and was carried out every Monday evening after dark. At lease it was in my time. The contents were emptied into a metal wheelbarrow which was kept especially for the purpose and when full it was transported to a small field behind Sea View where it was tipped. Several journeys were necessary to complete the job and when finished, a large quantity of quick-lime was spread over the whole. This service was speedily carried out and the quick-lime was nothing if not quick and efficient for no-one could have found the tipping area by following their nose.

Bathing, having laboriously carried and heated on coal fires the gallons of water necessary, was usually carried out in large zinc baths in front of the fire. When not in use, the baths hung on nails in the walls just outside the back doors. Despite all these difficulties, the standard of hygiene was often infinitely better than some areas where many more modern facilities were at hand and would even have compared favourably with some of today's standards.

In recent years an article about Nant was published in one of the popular monthlies and those of us who read it were amazed and angered by the totally inaccurate description of our life there. It described us as a simple, tightly-knit community in our sombre valley, the grubby little children running out to meet their fathers while the haggard, over-worked wives sweated over their primitive stoves. Yet another article in a newspaper referred to the children as ragged-trousered, pale faced and bare-foot, the mothers as grey-faced, prematurely aged, wearily struggling up the mountain to seek what meagre sustenance they could afford from the village above. One can only suppose that the writers must have failed, perhaps unknown to them, to meet the people that could have told them the truth, for the truth was that, agreed, it was a simple way of life, but in a happy and healthy environment. With such caring medics and our own efforts to ward off ailments and diseases, small wonder that we were seldom in sickness but more often in good health.

Chapter XXVII

Uncle Bob

It was January 1936 and the New Year began in our house with a great deal of serious talk between my Father and Will. So pre-occupied were they that any interruptions by me were decidedly unwelcome. The reason for it all was the imminent arrival of a new swing jaw for the crusher. This was an extremely large piece of machinery, weighing over five tons and when in position, would crush granite of up to forty inches in diameter. It was being transported by road from London with a police escort but before it arrived, plans had to be finalised for its method of transportation down the Screw Hill.

The monster arrived on a cold and cloudy Tuesday morning. So heavy was it that the transporting lorry's forward gear lacked sufficient power to bring it up the hill from Llithfaen. This difficulty was finally overcome by putting the lorry into reverse gear and travelling backwards. Once it had reached the top, the mammoth operation began to manoeuvre it down the mountain track on the final stage of its journey. Eight men, including my Father, were involved in the operation, plus one horse. Among the men was forty-one year old Robert Roberts, a senior and experienced rock-man who was my Father's nephew-in-law and so known to me as Uncle Bob.

To assist movement the track surface was planked for yards ahead of the machine and the machine, fitted with skids, was mounted on to a purpose-built sledge beneath which were rollers. For maximum safety new steel wire was used for the block and tackle equipment, the purpose of this equipment being to control the movement of the machine. As soon as the horse was harnessed to the sledge, a number of men took up their positions at the front to assist the animal in pulling the enormous load. Other men with ropes positioned themselves at the rear to check the downward movement and one man was charged with the operating of the lowering tackle.

Despite the difficult conditions, slowly but surely the massive machine moved successfully down the track and on that first day a hundred yards were covered. The morning of the next day was also successful when, by lunch-time, over thirty yards were gained and everyone was well pleased with the progress achieved.

At home, tea was just over and I was sitting quietly on a stool, reading. My Mother, sitting opposite, was busy with some needlework when Lizzie came into the room to say that one of the quarrymen was at the door and wanted to speak to my Mother. She added that he looked extremely upset. My Mother at once hurried out and I moved to follow her, I was told to stay where I was. I wondered why the man was so upset and wished that I had been allowed to go to the door. For a moment I listened but could hear nothing, so decided that it could not be anything serious or I would have heard someone go to the telephone. I thought no more about it and returned to my book.

It was quite some time later when my Mother, accompanied by Ethel, came back into the dining-room. I looked up and could tell by their faces that they were upset so I knew that something serious had happened. Immediately, I asked what was wrong but I received no reply. They did not even seem to notice me. I decided that it would be best to keep quiet and just listen when, suddenly, a horrific thought struck me.

Perhaps something had happened to my Father. Perhaps he had been taken ill or had an accident. Oh no! That was inconceivable. My Father was indestructible so such a thought was ridiculous. I sighed with relief but then another thought struck me. Perhaps it was Will. Fear gripped me and I just could not contain it. I had to know. I asked several times until eventually Ethel answered me, saying that of course Will was all right and would I please get on with my book or find something else to do. She and my Mother then left the room and went into the breakfast room, the 'holy of holies', as my Father referred to it on the occasions when I was not welcome there. I knew better than to follow and so remained where I was, feeling rather worried and trying desperately to guess what could have happened.

Soon afterwards, the telephone rang and I heard both Ethel and my Mother rush along the hall. I listened and gathered that it was my Father on the other end and so at least this confirmed my thoughts that nothing had happened to him. I could glean nothing further other than that he would not be home until late and that my Mother sounded as though she was trying to comfort him.

Garnie came in a few minutes later and at once I asked

him if he knew what was wrong but he knew nothing at all and wanted to know what I was talking about. I asked him to go and find out but he was not keen and thought that we should wait.

Moments later my Mother came into the room again and Garnie asked her what had happened. In a trembling voice she told us that there had been an accident on the Screw Hill, involving the Crusher, and that Uncle Bob had been killed.

Although we had expected bad news, when it came it was more than we could take in. It seemed impossible to believe. Only a few evenings before, Uncle Bob had called to see us. I had sat on his knee and he had sung to me, which was always a treat as he had such a fine tenor voice. His visits had always been a joy, for, as well as singing, he told me exciting stories and many of them were true. He was a born countryman, with the countryman's ability to turn his hand to most things. He would walk miles along the Rivals, hunting foxes with his old dog; later curing the skins to produce beautiful fox fur ties for the ladies. From what to many were just hawthorn branches, he would produce walking sticks and turn them into works of art. Some would have asps curling up the side. Others would have handles shaped into the form of animals' heads and all would be highly polished. These were never sold but generously given, his reward being the pleasure of the work and in the giving.

Often on summer evenings, he would walk over the Rivals from his home in Llanaelhaearn to bring us baskets full of mushrooms. 'Oh, no!' I could not believe that he was dead and yet, despite my failure to imagine never seeing him again, there was that horrible feeling inside that I had experienced when I heard of Bessis's and Ceridwen's fatal accident. These were my first experiences of the conflict of refusing to accept the truth when the truth was too painful.

Suddenly, I remembered Aunt Mary and their son, Hedd Wyn, and my own feelings faded into insignificance. Whatever was it like for them and what would happen to them? Hedd Wyn was a year younger than I and to my mind the most terrible thing in the world had happened to him. I could not begin to imagine his feelings.

Not long afterwards, Will arrived home and it was obvious that he had heard the dreadful news. My Mother asked him if he knew how the accident had happened but he knew no more than she did. He said that he was in a hurry to join Father at Llanaelhaearn as he did not want him to come back down the Screw Hill and pass 'that infernal machine' on his own. Minutes later, he rushed off. I did not see either Will or my Father again that day as I was in bed when they returned late that night.

It was some time later when I learned and was able to understand what had happened. The machine had successfully negotiated Butler's Bend, the most difficult bend, when it reached a part of the track where a large slab of rock protruded for some yards above the mean surface. At that point everyone was ordered to work only on the right of the machine. As the sledge passed over the rock, it began crawling to the left so my Father, who was standing on top of the bank, turned for a brief moment to give the stop signal to the man on the lowering tackle. The moment he turned his head, Uncle Bob and another man, contrary to the order, rushed between the machine and the bank. Both were intent on helping and thought that they could adjust the rollers and so correct the movement. As my Father turned back, he saw to his horror the position of the two men and saw the machine canting towards them as the ground gave way beneath it. Frantically, he shouted to them to get clear and Uncle Bob, responding immediately, leaned towards him and gave him his hand. My Father gripped his out-stretched hand but Uncle Bob's overcoat had caught in a protruding stone and he was held fast. Before he could free himself and in spite of my Father's desperate efforts, the machine toppled on to him.

Without a moment's delay, one of the men rushed away to summon a doctor while the rest worked frantically to free him. In what seemed an impossibly short time, the doctor arrived and confirmed what the men already knew; that Uncle Bob was dead. His spine had been fractured and he had been killed instantly. For some moments the men stood in silence, hardly able to believe that such a thing could have happened and some of them wept openly. Mercifully, there were not two fatalities. The other man involved had been higher up the bank and so had been able to jump clear just in time.

When everyone felt sufficiently recovered, the body was carried to the top of the hill while one of the men went on to arrange its transportation to the church at Llanaelhaearn. My Father's task was more difficult for he had to hurry ahead of them to break the tragic news to Aunty Mary. Several of the men volunteered to go in his place but, shocked and heartbroken as he was, he insisted that it was his responsibility and duty and the more so as she was his late brother's daughter.

For the following few days, the machine was left exactly where it was and only essential work was attended to in the quarry. On the day of the funeral, the quarry was shut down completely and everyone who could do so attended the funeral.

The machine eventually reached the mill and was installed above the old crusher but the advantages that it brought were never fully appreciated for the cost of its transportation had been too high.

Chapter XXVIII

A Sense of Belonging

Many children in the valley became members of the Welsh youth movement, the 'Urdd Gobaith Cymru', commonly known as the 'Urdd'. To be a member of this movement was considered to be something very special and made one feel highly important. S'miss was in charge of enrolment and the ordering of our membership badges. These badges, which cost a shilling, were most attractive, in the form of a gold circle with an inner green circle and in the centre a red dragon on a white shield. They were highly prized and although made of a non-precious metal, were thought by some of us to be pure gold.

Membership meetings took place once a month in the school-room when lessons were over. S'miss presided and read out the news of events at other branches, notices of official decisions and what to us was the highlight, handed out our copies of the movements' magazine, *Cymru'r Plant* (The Children's Wales). In a situation where comic papers were a rarity, this magazine, a tuppence a copy, was the tops. As well as the reports of happenings at other branches and photographs of members or groups who had achieved some noteworthy success, there were short stories, serials and comic strips. These were followed with avid interest, particularly the comic strips which during my time as a member dealt with the escapades of *Twdls a Thwm y Gath* (Tiddles and the Tom-cat). Also at the meetings we were informed of competitive events in the offing and S'miss would decide which, if any, we should enter. As far as we were concerned, we were capable of competing with any branch, but S'miss, aware of our limitations and being responsible for training us, was more realistic. The meetings ended with the Urdd's song. 'Plant Sir Fôn a Plant Sir Fynwy, Plant Cymru Fu'.

The Urdd's annual National Eisteddfod was the movement's greatest event. It was held under canvas and in a different town every year. To take part in the Eisteddfod was a great achievement and to win was out of this world. Regrettably, during my membership the venue was always too far away for it to be practical for us to attend.

Another goal to aim for was that of being able to go to one of the Urdd's holiday camping sites. This, too, did not happen for us during my time, but we did have the pleasure of competing in regional Eisteddfods. Although I cannot remember us winning anything spectacular, the excitement of the competitions and the feeling of belonging when seeing those hundreds of badges were awarded in themselves.

Our isolation in no way caused us to be insular for not only were we involved in local and Welsh activities but whole-heartedly supported and in our own way celebrated the larger national events. The Silver Jubilee in 1935 was one of these and celebrate we did. The Schoolroom became our banqueting hall and for days beforehand the ladies of the village prepared and planned the festive fare while the men looked after the entertainment side of things. Even the children were busily involved, searching for anything red, white and blue to serve as bunting. Several families owned union Jacks and these were brought out of their moth-balls and carefully ironed.

The great day, to which every family contributed financially, finally arrived and we crowded into the schoolroom for the celebration tea. There seemed to be mountains of food, sandwiches with mouth-watering fillings, honey and homemade jams; such a variety of cakes that made choosing almost impossible; jellies and trifles topped with delicious, fresh, farm cream. What a feast it turned out to be and so heartily did we tuck in that afterwards some of us had to rest awhile. When everyone had eaten to full capacity, each child was presented with a Jubilee mug to commemorate the occasion.

With the presentation over, everyone made their way to Cae Mawr where sporting competitions had been arranged. These were not only for the children but for the adults too. There were 'Bite the Apple' competitions, sack races, egg and spoon, three legged, as well as the conventional races, with prizes for the winners and the runners-up. For the ladies there was a Prettiest Ankle competition. My Father and Rowland Davies were the judges and for this the ladies stood behind a long screen of sacking which allowed only their ankles to be seen. Although we children did not compete, it was still great fun, rushing back and forth trying to identify the ankles. Added to all this was a bran tub for lucky dip, each child being allowed one dip, thus ensuring that every child found a present.

The celebrations continued late into the evening and such was our enjoyment that people from Llithfaen, hearing about it, came crowding on top of the mountain to watch our merrymaking. When the sun finally dipped out of sight into the Irish Sea, taking the light from what had been a wonderful day, the gathering broke up and we made our way home, exhausted but so very happy.

As the Jubilee fund had been so generously contributed to there was still a fair surplus left over from expenses. It was, therefore, decided that the money be used to take the children on the next day to the cinema in Pwllheli to see Paul Robeson in the film 'Song of Freedom'. This extra treat was so enjoyed that every detail of the film was remembered for a long time afterwards.

That outing to see a film was not the only organized visit to the cinema. The other was in the interest of our education and it came about as the result of one of Miss Bishop's visits. Miss Bishop was the Area Inspector for Physical Training and came periodically to see us going through our paces and to give lectures on the importance of health and hygiene. Much to our pleasure, she often brought with her a number of large, coloured posters, illustrating aspects of the subject. These were pinned on to the partition and they helped to brighten the school-room. On this particular visit and much to our disappointment, she brought only one poster. However, that disappointment turned to delight when she informed us that a special film on the subject was being shown at Pwllheli Town Hall and pupils above a certain age were being invited to attend. She went on to say that schools were being allocated particular days and our visit was arranged for one day in the following week.

Excitedly, we waited for the appointed day and with only one day to go disaster struck. All those eligible, with the exception of Annie Mair Jones and myself, had been struck down with some sort of 'tummy bug'. With only the two of us eligible pupils well enough to attend school that morning, S'miss offered us her regret, saying that the visit would have to be cancelled. For a moment we were dumfounded. Surely we were not going to be penalised for something that was not our fault. Suddenly, it occurred to us that having escaped the 'bug', did it not prove that we had got the 'hang of' this keeping healthy business and having achieved that, surely we deserved to be allowed to go. Ignoring our reasoning, she repeated that she did not consider it sensible to take just two pupils and urged us to get on with some work.

In those days one did not dream of arguing with a teacher and certainly not with S'miss, but on this occasion we felt justified in trying to get her to alter her decision. Taking our courage in both hands and as politely as we could, we proceeded to plead our case. She listened in silence until we had exhausted our good reasons and then, after a moment's thought and much to our surprise, smilingly agreed to take us. What was more, she asked me to ask my Mother if she would like to accompany us. My Mother accepted the invitation and the four of us enjoyed the film although I cannot remember one detail of it now. What I do remember is that when it was over we went to a little café for tea. There we two children consumed a fair quantity of chocolate eclairs and as a result, spent the journey home feeling mighty sick.

Much as we loved school, like children the world over, any breaks from daily routine were always welcome. The calendar, of course, dictated many of these and those which were not official holidays were celebrated at school. St David's Day on 1st March was one of these. There were no lessons that morning. Instead, we listened to stories about our patron saint, recited appropriate poems and sang Welsh songs and hymns.

John and his dog, his sister Annie Mair (Eileen's best friend) and Eileen

Another event, but quite different and rather sad, was Remembrance Day, when nearly everyone arrived at school wearing a red poppy. That morning we spent remembering those who had given their lives in the first world war. S'miss always carried this out sensitively and touchingly, endeavouring to instil in us the evils and suffering of war and reminding us of the sacrifices made by those brave men for our freedom. As the hour of eleven struck, we arose from our desks and, in keeping with everyone in the kingdom, we stood with head bowed for the two minutes' silence. A prayer was then offered and, finally, we sang the hymn 'Oh God, our help in ages past'.

Harvest Thanksgiving, too, did not pass unnoticed and was celebrated by learning to appreciate how important the harvest was. This always ended with the hymn 'We plough the fields and scatter'.

When it came to outings, Annie Mair, her brother, John,

and I considered ourselves more fortunate than the other children. Being members of the Church of Wales, we were allowed time off school to attend special events organized by that 'body'. One such day off was given to attend a singing festival at a little church in Llangian, a village some distance away and to which we had never been before. As no-one from my family was going, it looked as if I was going to miss out on it until Mr and Mrs Jones offered to take me with them.

The thought of the festival did not particularly excite us, but rather that we wanted to take advantage of the chance of a day off and the opportunity to see pastures new. As it turned out it was just as well that we had not become too excited about the festival for we found it to be extremely boring. Added to that was the problem of trying to keep the music scores clean and uncreased and which was no easy task when we had to carry them around with us in the heat of what turned out to be a scorching summer's day. Besides, we thought that the scores were a complete waste of time. We did not understand the music and could see no sense whatsoever in the layout of the worlds which had lots of long gaps between most of them. We came to the conclusion that they were badly done and therefore a waste of quite good quality paper. However, between the two sessions we were provided with a sumptious tea and Mr and Mrs Jones bought us some sweets, so we felt that we had not fared so badly after all.

Among the most enjoyable school outings were the nature rambles and the end of summer term picnics. The picnics always took place on the beach and what great fun they were. Everyone brought sandwiches and for our tea S'miss provided a large cast-iron kettle which the bigger boys took it in turn to carry. On our arrival, the first task was to collect driftwood for our fire and so at once the beach became a hive of activity, with children hurrying and scurrying to and fro, each striving to impress S'miss with the amount that he or she had collected. Next a tripod was made and with the kettle suspended from it, the fire was lit. Collection of driftwood continued until the kettle had boiled and this was the signal to start the picnic. Bathing was not allowed, so after tea we would play games until our energies waned. After a short rest, we would then search for unusual shells and anything of interest we could find on the beach. It was expected that notice would be taken of all that was done and all that was found for, on the following day, essays on the outing would be required.

Nature study was one of the most popular lessons of all and particularly on the occasions when field study was considered necessary. These field studies were known as nature study rambles and news that one was in the offing filled us with excited anticipation and fervent hopes for good weather on the day. The first of these that I remember took place one spring afternoon. Excitement about it had been building up for days and the evening before found me anxious listening to the weather forecast. The announcer's voice droned on and on about places with strange names: Rockall, Mallin, Hebrides, Minches, Plymouth Sound. Wasn't he ever going to mention us? I was about to despair when at last came Irish Sea. With heart pounding, I heard him say, 'Warm and sunny with light southerly winds.'

'Yipee!' That was all I wanted to hear. The following news of the activities of some man called Hitler, which held so much interest for the rest of the family, held none for me, so I hurried out to tell my friends the good news.

The next morning dawned fine and warm, just as the forecaster had promised and I set off excitedly and happily for school. Settling down to lessons was most difficult for we could think of nothing but the ramble. After what seemed an eternity the bell rang and it was lunch-time.

At one o'clock everyone was back at school and keen to get going on the outing, but we discovered that we were not leaving immediately. There was still another lesson to get through. After much wriggling in our desks, scuffling of feet and very little work, we were told to put our slates away and this was achieved in record time. Brand new note-books were then handed out on which, with newly-sharpened pencils, we each wrote our name and in neat, bold letters across the middle 'Nature Study'. When all was ready, we were told that we were to walk in an orderly fashion and that any wandering away or misbehaviour would be severely dealt with. We were also reminded that the object of the ramble was to study plants and any other things that would add to our understanding of the wonders of nature. Having digested this information, we at last set off, the girls jostling each other to walk next to S'miss and the boys pushing to be at the front. A stern word from S'miss had immediate effect and the desired orderly file was achieved.

At first, several ridiculous objects were seized as possible items for study, our enthusiasm much greater than our common sense but, eventually, we calmed down. Reaching Tŷ Uchaf's farm gate, we filed through into the field. The first discoveries were cowslips and the majority of us rushed forward to pick them, each one calling out in excitement, 'Look, S'miss, what I have found!' S'miss agreed that they were suitable subjects, but warned that only a few should be collected. The chosen specimens were carefully picked and notes on location, etc., entered in our note-books. As we moved on, butterflies were observed and noted, a number of us claiming to have spotted a red admiral, only to be told by S'miss that it was the more common small tortoiseshell. Clover, violets, speedwell and forget-me-nots were recorded as well as certain varieties of grasses. Our notes began to look quite impressive.

Reaching Coed Ellis Bach and the ruins of his cottage, we noticed the change in the plants from those of the open pasture, for here under the trees it was shady. There were pennyworts, anemones, cuckoo pint and several other species. Samples of the leaves from the trees were taken and then S'miss pointed out what was known as Ellis Bach's bowl. This aroused great interest. A number of the children had seen it before and those that had not had most certainly heard about it. Made of granite, it rested on two granite supports and had been shaped by some unknown but highly skilled craftsman into the form of a large, amazingly smooth and perfect round bowl. We tried to lift it but it was too heavy even to move. Regrettably, nothing is known of its history other than that it had been there for many generations. On reflection, I realize that it was very similar to the bowls used in the past for grinding cereal crops and could well have been used for that purpose. While preparing this book I was told that a number of young men students had been to the valley only a short time before to attempt to take the bowl away by boat. Fortunately, its size and weight defied them and they managed only to move it a few yards. Hopefully it will remain there to interest future generations.

The afternoon was drawing to a close and it was time to return to school. We gathered up our specimens and notes and in orderly fashion began to walk back. Above Tŷ Canol, where the track bends sharply downhill towards the house, there was a short cut over rougher ground which met the main footpath some seventy yards on. A number of us took this route, planning to arrive at the junction ahead of S'miss and the others. We were running as fast as we could when, suddenly, I tripped and fell and my forehead struck a sharp, protruding rock. For a moment I was too stunned to cry out or to move, but I instantly felt the pain and the warm blood cascading into my eyes and running down my face. At once, willing hands helped me to my feet and above the horrified cries of 'Ooh!' and 'Ah!' I heard voices calling S'miss. Immediately S'miss and the others came running up to us and I saw the words of admonishment freeze on her lips as she saw the result of my fall. Without a word she took my arm and hurried me to Tŷ Canol.

Mrs Thomas looked quite shocked when she saw the state I was in, but without hesitation ushered us in to the house. A chair was brought forward, bandages and cotton wool brought out and a kettle of water put on the fire. The pain, by this time, was severe and it was all I could do not to cry. Gazing around the kitchen in the hope of seeing something to take my mind off it, I saw that the doorway was crammed with children, those at the front being pushed forward by those at the back, all eager to see what was happening. S'miss, seeing them, sternly ordered them out, with instructions to wait quietly outside.

It was at that moment that I realized that had someone else had the misfortune to be injured then I, too, would have been just as keen to see what was going on and would not have liked being sent out. For the first time I appreciated my injury and, painful as it was, it was some comfort to feel that S'miss would not now have the heart to punish me for deliberately wandering off the recognized route.

A short time later I emerged from Tŷ Canol with a gleaming, white bandage wound around my head. The children's reaction to the bandage, with its fast reddening stain, left nothing to be desired, while I did my best to behave in a way worthy of such an injury. Slowly and somewhat subdued, we returned to school. There, the specimens were put into jars of water, note-books carefully put away and finally school was dismissed.

On my arrival home, my Mother's reaction was one of shock as by then the blood stain on the bandage had spread, but when I assured her that the wound had been well attended to and that I was perfectly all right, she calmed down. However, her concern did not prevent her from letting me know that she hoped I had learned something from the result of my disobedience. When my Father arrived soon afterwards the wound was examined, bathed in permanganate of potash, painted with iodine which was extremely painful, and re-dressed with a new bandage. There then only remained my parade through the village where I hoped most of the people would see me and be suitably impressed. I was not disappointed for those that I did meet were most sympathetic. The fact that my parents were concerned about the possibility of a fair sized scar on my forehead did not worry me in the least for I felt that in all, it had been a most satisfactory day.

Chapter XXIX

A Time of Sorrow

The men of our community were a good, God-fearing and hard-working breed. My Father had great respect for them and I believe they, in turn, had faith in him and would not hesitate to discuss their problems with him. One of these men, for whom he not only had respect but affection too, and who so often came boating with us, was Mr Robert Williams, Mr Williams, or rather Robin Llongau as he was known to everyone in the quarry, Llongau being the Welsh word for ships and so relating to his job as loading ganger, was a man of kindly disposition and utter reliability.

When he first came to Nant, he lived at Sea View with his wife and two daughters, but later moved to Bay View where his son was born. At thirty-six he was in the prime of his life, a strong and healthy man and all was well with his world until one Saturday night in October 1936.

It had been a particularly damp and humid day and by dusk became misty with intermittent drizzle, making for a dirty and unhealthy night. The Greta Force was due in late that night and as usual the loading gang would be turning out. My Father, aware that Mr Williams was suffering from a heavy cold and as a result was far from well, advised him not to turn out, adding that someone else would willingly stand in for him. Mr Williams, unwilling to think of what he considered would have been shirking his duty, made light of his cold and insisted that he was perfectly all right. Unable to demand that he stay at home, as that meant loss of earnings, My Father begged him to reconsider his decision.

Disregarding his condition and believing, as do so many conscientious people, that his presence on the job was vital. Mr Williams turned out as usual. By berthing time the weather had not improved. The clinging, sticky dampness seemed to penetrate into everything, making the workers hot and uncomfortable. As the work proceeded in the heavy humidity, the men noticed that their ganger was shivering and so hurried to complete the loading as quickly as possible.

On Monday morning, Mr Williams was unable to report for work as he was confined to bed with a severe chill and it soon became evident that medical help was needed. Dr Jack was sent for and he came at once. Having examined his patient, he gravely informed Mrs Williams that her husband had developed pneumonia. This was serious news as at that time pneumonia was still so often a killer disease and with little more than such things as linseed poultices, aconite, phosphorous and antimony to combat the disease, one's life literally hung in the balance. In those days not even the medical men could be optimistic about a patient's chances of recovery until what was know as the crises was over.

Day by bay friends and neighbours called at Bay View in

the hope of hearing that the crises had passed and that the patient was showing signs of recovery, but as each day went by, no such news came and gloom and anxiety spread throughout the valley.

One afternoon, much to my surprise, I was told that Mrs Williams had said that I could accompany my Father to see Mr Williams. The visit proved to be one of the saddest moments of my young life. We entered the bedroom and I saw, not our Mr Williams, but a pale shadow of him lying propped up by pillows on the bed. Although I had never before seen anyone seriously ill, I recognized that he was desperately so and saw that he was having great difficulty in breathing and was in obvious pain. In spite of his condition, he weakly raised his hand and did his utmost to smile at us. After only a few moments my Father indicated that I should go downstairs and said that he would join me quite soon. I immediately left the room and as I went down the stairs, I found it difficult not to cry, but I knew that I must not dare do such a thing as it would upset the family when they themselves were being so brave.

Minutes later, my Father came down and after a few words with Mrs Williams we left. As we made our way home, I asked him if Mr Williams was going to die. For a moment or two he seemed unable to answer me, but then said that he was sure he would be better once the crises was over. He then went on to explain to me that the crises was the turning point of the illness and that it occurred any time from the third day to the eleventh day, but more commonly at the end of the first week. The crises came, but instead of improving, Mr Williams' condition became critical. Despair now settled over the valley like a heavy black cloud and all we could do was hope and pray that by some miracle he would recover.

I do not positively remember being told that Mr

Williams had died. I think that this is because at the time I did not wish to accept the fact. I do, however, recall quite clearly how terribly sad everyone was and no-one more than my Father. Again, the feeling of one-ness was evident, drawn even closer in our sorrow for, yet again, we had lost not just a friend but another member of our Nant family.

In the majority of places in those days when a death took place at home, the body was not taken away to a Chapel of Rest as is done today but, instead, was 'laid out' by one or two able neighbours. The undertakers would then place it in the coffin and the open coffin would remain in the front room or parlour, where family and friends would come to pay their last respects. As there was no consecrated ground in the valley, interments had to take place elsewhere, usually in Llithfaen, but as Mr Williams had been born and bred in Rhiw, a village some twenty miles or so distant, it had been his wish to be taken there for burial.

The funeral took place three or four days later. It was the first I had experienced and as did the tragic deaths of Bessie and Ceridwen, it was to leave a lasting impression upon me. That day the quarries were deserted and silent, their very silence bearing witness to the grief felt in our little community. School, too, was closed for the day, but no children played in the little square; they, too, were silent.

At the appointed time, the people gathered by Bay View where the Minister conducted a short service. With the service over, the coffin bearers led the mourners out of the house for the heartbreaking and difficult journey up the mountain. The coffin was secured by ropes to a bier and carried on the shoulders of four men, one at each corner, with stand-ins walking alongside ready to take over their positions as they tired. Further ropes were tied to the front ends of the bier and these ran out ahead to six men who also had stand-ins, the bearers supporting the weight of the

Funeral Cortege beginning the climb up the screw hill

coffin and bier and the six forward men providing the power to pull them up the mountain. The mourners followed behind as they slowly and laboriously made their sorrowful journey. At the top, the hearse and funeral cars awaited them and gathered there, too, were large number of mourners from Llithfaen as well as from further afield. Not everyone was able to make the journey to Rhiw so when the coffin had finally been placed in the hearse, a prayer was offered and then a hymn was sung as a final farewell to their departing friend. The quality and sincerity of that singing was so beautiful as it echoed among the mountains, yet so poignant that it was heart-rending. As the singing died away, the cortege slowly moved off and those unable to follow stood watching in silence until it had disappeared from view.

Not long afterwards, Mrs Williams and the children left Nant, so leaving yet another gap in our little community. For me, this, too, was a sad time for Eirlys and Rhiannon Williams had been among my best friends and I knew how much I would miss them.

Over forty years later, while holidaying in North Wales and prior to contemplating this book, I felt an inexplicable and compelling urge to visit the grave I had never seen. After a number of enquiries and some difficulty, I found the little church-yard, tucked away on a hillside overlooking the treacherous but so very beautiful Hell's Mouth Bay. I climbed over the stile and there, almost opposite the gate, I found what I was looking for.

As I stood there, gazing at the granite headstone in the absolute peace of that sunny June day I noticed that, lying on the grave, and still almost intact, was the glass-covered wreath which I had seen on the day of the funeral. Inside were the china arum lilies and resting on them the now faded memoriam card placed there by his family so long ago.

The sight brought memories flooding back so clearly that I was sure that I heard again the sound of those voices singing on that funeral day. As I walked away I felt sad but felt, too, the strength of those bonds which not only in life but in death, too, it seems, the valley has bound us.

Chapter XXX

The Beginning of the End

Well over a thousand years had passed since the Monks laid their curses on the valley, but as 1937 drew to a close no-one gave thought to the fact that two of those curses had not been denied. There still was no consecrated ground in the valley and as far as was known, no native born boy had married a native born girl. However, it seemed that the third curse had been thwarted for, although ours was the third community and industry it was in no danger of dying. Instead, it was very much alive. The quarry was in full production and such was our confidence that despite an earlier failure, our thoughts turned again to acquiring a classified road.

The earlier request for a road had been made on our behalf by the Lleyn Rural District Council to the Caernarfonshire County Council who were responsible for the maintenance of the Screw Hill. On that occasion the request was turned down on the grounds that the track served only the quarry and was, therefore, in the nature of an occupation. This second attempt by the R.D.C. seemed more hopeful when we were informed that a County Council Inspector was coming to inspect the Screw Hill with a view to building a road on the existing track or constructing a new road on an alternative site.

Feeling sure that the Inspector's findings would be in our favour, we excitedly awaited the result of his report. When it came we were not only bitterly disappointed but astonished and angry. His report stated that it would be impracticable to build on the existing one and a quarter mile track with its one in three gradient as the cost would run to at least twenty thousand pounds and an alternative road would be impossible due to the ruggedness of the coast. He, therefore, felt that the only solution would be for the inhabitants to move to Llithfaen where they could benefit from the facilities in that village. He concluded with the suggestion that the Housing Authority be asked to provide the necessary dwellings.

The County Council readily accepted the Inspector's report, but we certainly did not. The suggestion that we should leave the valley was received with total abhorrence and served only to make us more determined to fight for what we believe was our right. From our point of view the situation was ludicrous. We were the people who helped to produce the stone for the rest of the country to enjoy first class roads, yet ourselves were denied the end product of our efforts.

The R.D.C. then appealed against the findings, pointing out that the land owner was willing to sell any land involved and that the quarry owners were prepared to contribute to the cost of construction. The appeal fell of deaf ears. Instead, we were informed that improvements were shortly to be made to the Screw Hill. This information was received with some scepticism until, to our surprise, only a few days later, two men arrived and carried out some work. The result of their efforts were appreciated to the full when, after the first shower, the surface became a quagmire with the resultant mud blocking the drainage and in turn causing huge ruts to form in the centre of the track. Where before the surface had presented only a few problems, it now became a hazard.

My Father, feeling extremely annoyed about it, decided that something further must be done and to that end a meeting was held at the school. There it was agreed that an appeal in the form of a petition be sent to the Ministry of Transport, together with a request for a visit by them with a view to gaining their approval and a support grant. In addition, it was agreed to enlist the support of the National Press. The latter proved to be worthwhile for the Daily Mirror responded by sending a reporter and a photographer to the valley, and as a result our cause was given sympathetic coverage.

Among those interviewed was my Father, who stated that with some re-routing, the surfacing of the Screw Hill would be a perfectly viable proposition. He disputed the estimated cost of the project as there was abundant material which could be bought cheaply on the spot. He went on to say that he knew of a road in Dorsetshire which was comparable in gradient to the Screw Hill and on which twelve ton lorries travelled daily. In his opinion, the County Council's attitude was absurd and he was prepared to meet any civil engineer in the United Kingdom to submit the reasonableness of our proposition. In conclusion he said that he thought that such an historic and select spot was worthy of attention.

The Ministry of Transport's response was also

favourable, informing us that the Divisional Road Engineer for Wales, together with the County Surveyor, would be visiting the site. Once again our hopes were raised but, again, in vain, for the engineer's findings were little more than a carbon copy of the earlier findings, even to the point of suggesting that we move to Llithfaen. So that was that, there was nothing more we could do other than to treat their suggestion with what we considered was the contempt it deserved.

Despite our disappointment, we soon settled down again and by the summer had something much more exciting to think about. That something was the great, new ocean liner, the S.S. *Mauretania,* which was being built for the Cunard Line at Cammell Laird's shipyard in Birkenhead. It came about when my Father heard that she was nearing completion and would soon be undergoing her sea trials. Wondering whether she may be passing along our coast, he decided to write to the company, asking for her course and date of trials, explaining that should she be anywhere in our vicinity we in the village would make every effort to catch a glimpse of her.

The company's reply came a few days later, with the information that her course was set off the 'Stack' outwards towards the 'Smalls', giving the date of her trials and her expected time off Nant. The writer continued that in view of our interest, the ship would acknowledge us by blowing her siren and reminded us that although she would be some distance out, given reasonable visibility we should be able to see her quite clearly.

As the great day drew near, everyone was fearful that the good weather we were having would break or, even worse, that a sea mist would develop and blot out everything at the crucial moment. However, we need not have worried for dawn broke with clear skies and the promise of yet another fine summer's day. In late morning my Father telephoned the company and was assured that everything was going according to plan and that the liner was under way.

She was due off our bay shortly after two o'clock, but we children started gathering in Cae Mawr long before as, should she be early, we did not want to risk missing her. In any case, we could not concentrate on anything else, so thought it just as well to claim our vantage point early. The fact that the field was sufficiently large to easily accommodate over twenty times our whole population, was totally ignored.

As the time so slowly crept up to two o'clock, a crowd gathered and the air was filled with excited anticipation. After several false sightings of such things as any small craft, or even seagulls, between us and the horizon, the cry went up, 'There she is!' And there she really was. As she steamed across the bay, her bow cutting a foaming white swathe through the so still, blue water, she seemed nearer than we had dared to hope and not a wisp of cloud or mist came to mar our view. She was so beautiful, a vessel of absolute perfection and majesty, her white superstructure dazzling us as it glistened like a fairy castle in the sunshine. Suddenly, she blew her siren, not just once but three times and the knowledge that it was solely for our benefit was the ultimate. We jumped up and down, waving frantically with anything and everything we could lay our hands on and cheered until we were hoarse. All too soon she became just a speck in the distance, but we kept on watching until she had completely disappeared. The thought that we in our isolated little valley, cut off from so many things, were among the first in the world to see the great liner, was simply wonderful and the experience was one we savoured for long after the event.

Little did we know that day that she would make only two round trips to America before her beauty would be

The cottage where Mr William Owen and his sister lived, the last official residence of Nant Gwrtheyrn

hidden by hideous camouflage and that her role for six long years would be that of a troopship. Less did we children dream that the ominous war clouds gathering over Europe would drastically affect our lives. Our parents, of course, were well aware of what war meant and fully realized that should our country be involved then at once the quarry with its total dependence on shipping would be doomed.

As 1938 wore on, the political situation deteriorated even further and the grown-ups seemed to talk of nothing but their fears of a possible war. In our house the radio news bulletins were listed to with grim faces. Even the news of our Prime Minister's euphoric return from his talks with the German Chancellor did very little to convince them that there would be peace in our time. As the weeks went by, the situation became even more worrying and as had been feared, its effects began telling on our industry. Orders which generally slackened off a little in the autumn now fell off drastically. Day after day the piles of chippings grew, in the vain hope that orders would pick up again but, instead, they became so scarce that they were barely enough to keep one quarry going, let alone two. Obviously, one had to be sacrificed and which one was a foregone conclusion. It had to be ours as with war seemingly inevitable, Carreg-y-Llam in that event, could at very little cost be reached by road.

For me, the news that we would be leaving Nant came like a bombshell. I could not and would not believe it. Such a thing was just not possible. How could I leave the valley and leave my friends? Patiently, my parents tried to explain to me that although we would be the first to leave, it was only a matter of time before the others had to do the same as there would be no work for them. Despite their efforts to soften the blow, I refused to accept it as inevitable. I prayed as I had never prayed before that something, I knew not what, would happen to prevent our leaving, but my prayers went unanswered.

One cold and dull February day, the horses arrived in our drive and I watched again, but this time broken-hearted, as our furniture was loaded on to the sledges. I had tried every way I knew, even pretending to be ill, to prevent the move, but failed. Following behind the last load up the Screw Hill, with Puss at my heels, I could not look back. I felt utterly sick at heart. When I reached the top, I once again begged my Father to let us go back, but it was no use. I then noticed that he, too, was upset and realized that, had I not been so selfishly concerned with myself, I would have noticed it earlier. Somehow, this realization eased my feelings and I began to see what it must be like for him and the rest of the family.

We were just getting into the car when I remembered

Puss and I ran back to pick her up from where I had seen her sitting only minutes earlier, but she was no longer there. I looked around and called, but there was no sign of her. The others then joined me and began searching and calling but despite our efforts, it was in vain. Puss was nowhere to be seen. Strangely, our last sight of her had been only a few yards away from the spot where she had joined us on that first day.

The other inhabitants were more fortunate in that they did not have to leave immediately as Carreg-y-Llam absorbed a few of the men and others were taken on at Caernant and Trefor. When, on September 3rd, war broke out, a number of the younger men left to join the armed forces, while others moved away to find employment in more vital industries. Slowly but surely the exodus from the valley began. By the time peace was declared, only a few families remained and one by one they, too, left until, apart from two temporary residents, there remained only Mr William Owen and his sister, who had come from Liverpool to look after him. Unwilling to consider leaving, he stayed on until finally he was forced for health reasons to move away. His going marked the end of the valley's third life.

For a short time during the sixties, the valley became the haunt of vandals as well as host to further temporary residents. These temporary residents, with no seeming purpose in life other than to drift, took up unofficial residence there, living in just a few of the cottages while, it is reputed, using the timber in the others as means for cooking and heating. Should some of the blame be theirs, then together with the efforts of the vandals, their stay, despite its short duration, was sufficiently long to 'disembowel' the little dwellings, leaving only the granite shells.

It was as well that I did not know, as we drove away on that last day that, apart from a short visit of a few hours some

Ex-Nantites, a family reunited (S'miss – front row 4th from left)

months later, long years would pass before I would meet again those friends I was leaving behind. Now, forty years later, I was on my way back and our car journey, that had been dogged with such bad weather for so many miles, ended in brilliant sunshine. On the next evening, Easter Saturday evening, I walked with my family into the Tower Hotel in Pwllheli in a state of great excitement and with not a little trepidation. Would I recognise those friends of so long ago? Would they recognise me or, what was more to the point, would they even remember me?

A number of people walked ahead of us and, as directed, we followed them into what was already a crowded room. For a moment I wondered whether there had been a mistake for among the sea of faces I recognized not one. As I hesitated, out of the crowd came one that I recognized immediately and before I had further time to think, I found myself greeting, and being greeted by, several friends. One of them took me to meet our guest of honour and to my

Eileen meeting her dearly beloved teacher S'miss

delight, there before me was our dearly beloved S'miss, a little smaller than I remembered her and now silver-haired, but otherwise unchanged, even to the old familiar twinkle in her eye. We were at once surrounded by several other people and among them were a number who I was sure I had never met before. Someone introduced us and I then discovered that they, too, had spent their childhood in the valley, some of them having been born there. Like me, they had been forced by circumstances to leave and ever since had longed to return there.

The room was now filled to capacity and buzzed with conversation. Suddenly, the forty years, and many more for some, seemed as if they had never been. No longer was the gathering just one of the renewing of old friendships and the making of new but the re-uniting of members of the one big family, the family of the little village that to us would always be home.

Addendum

Since the first edition of this book the vision in 1982 of a Welsh Language Centre in the valley has become a reality. It is now a registered National Language Centre, the only full time residential Welsh Language Teaching Centre in Wales.

The challenge to achieve this dream was formidable faced with a village of derelict buildings, no accessible road other than the rough steep winding track up the mountain, no electricity and no water as the old reservoir was beyond repair. Money was scarce but determinedly the Trustees fought on to realise their dream. Some members contributing money, their services and their time without payment while other members undertook the responsibility of raising funds. A group of supporters was then formed and over the years this group has contributed crucial financial and inspirational support.

Renovated village as it was in 2014

As enthusiasm and determination grew, other bodies such as the Welsh Office, Prince of Wales Committee, Welsh Development Agency, Industrial and voluntary groups gave substantial assistance which enabled the work to progress at a much greater pace.

Today the village is as new. The buildings whilst preserving their outward appearance, internally provide every modern convenience and comfort. The little Chapel once again holds services as well as meetings and music festivals (Cymanfaoedd Canu). Bay View now houses an interesting museum, book and souvenir shop and the Plas houses the teaching block and library of Welsh and other European lesser used languages. The outbuildings that housed our poultry are now unrecognisable as a smart little restaurant that provides delicious home-made fare.

The Screw Hill has, in most parts, disappeared under the tons of rocks blasted out of the mountain to build a new road. Sadly, the little hawthorn tree that so badly frightened

Caffi Meinir at Nant Gwrtheyrn

Nant Gwrtheyrn with Yr Eifl in the background

Mr Barlow has also gone. A number of ex-residents as well as some visitors to the valley believe that the disappearance of the Screw Hill has taken away a degree of the mystique of the valley which undoubtedly affected everyone who laboriously climbed up and down the track. Nevertheless, a fine new road now leads down to the valley and although steep allows vehicular access.

The success of the Language Centre is reflected in the fact that to date over 13 thousand students have attended Courses. Recently a creche facility and outside play area has been provided. Plans are now afoot to accommodate even greater numbers of students in the next few years.

Undoubtedly, the valley is alive again, host to a thriving industry. Surely, these facts deny one of the monk's curses, yet, there are some who say that this is not so, as this is a transient community not an isolated community dependant solely on the valley's resources and upon each other.

Whatever one's views, all agree that an almost impossible dream has been realised and for us the children of the valley our old homes and our culture have thankfully been saved.

Part 3:

Biography

A moment of relaxation for Eileen after the initial book launch in 1983

Biography

Being asked to write a biographical synopsis of Eileen's life, a brief, I thought was impossible. Casting one's mind back on all the stories I have heard from others about Eileen, the stories she told me and my own life's story with Eileen, the difficulty is where to stop! I question – was Eileen an Actress, a Clairvoyant, a Teacher, a teller of stories (fact or fiction, whether to young or old), a Confidante. All aided possibly, by her exceptional memory. What was it with every situation, crisis, adventure, Eileen was able to steer it through without seemingly taking charge. She was courageous, intrepid is the word I think best describes Eileen, yet she always doubted and questioned her own ability. To write a synopsis, the picture would not be truly painted – I will try a condensed version only.

The Early years and an American Venture

When Eileen was born on the 9th October 1928, her family – Mum and Dad, brothers Garnie and Will and Ethel (Will's wife) – at that time were living in the village of Corfe Castle in the county of Dorset. Eileen's father, a mining engineer and geologist owned nearby a quarry and a fleet of Lorries, from which he successfully quarried and distributed the decorative "Portland stone" for a further two years. Then the recession of the 1920s took hold and the business could no longer be sustained, her father had no choice but to close the industry at considerable financial loss.

The family moved back to Wales where her father took over the management of Nant Gwrtheyrn. In chapter VI Eileen describes that day as being the day (the move to Nant) that she awakened and became aware of life around her. "This Valley Was Ours" tells of the following years of her life, the life of a child in this idyllic setting. Then in 1939 war threatened, this led to the inevitable closure of the Porth y Nant Quarry, the sea being the only commercial access to the quarry.

Nant Gwrtheyrn although only a short period in Eileen's life, remained the most dominant, so great was the captivation of the valley that when the family left and moved to Nefyn it broke her heart, she vowed to her father, if they did not return to Nant that she would never again speak in Welsh. This vow she kept even though her love for the language was great. In 1954 I think this vow was shaken when we were told, that a transient group of hippies had ripped out the wood from the houses and used it as firewood. Eileen began to acknowledge that without financial means the village was destined to become a ghost village and that her father had had little choice other than to leave the valley. I know that it was some years later before she held again a conversation in Welsh. The sad part I have been told by many was that her Welsh when heard was pure and grammatical.

Eileen attended Nefyn School and made new friends. Her best friend in Nefyn was Madge, an adventurous girl, who willingly listened with great interest to Eileen's stories of the magical valley over the mountain, of the people and of her best friend Annie Mair, and how, when they were leaving Nant, everyone there had said that they must come back as they would always be welcome. The pair hatched a plan. They would leave early one Saturday morning, an explanatory note left on the kitchen table as to their whereabouts, then they would set out and in true Dick Whittington style – their belongings, some bread and cheese, all wrapped up in a big red spotted handkerchief (this they couldn't find, a piece of cloth had to do) tied to a long pole. The day arrived and the plan was put into action.

Today this would seem hardly an adventure, but in the nineteen-thirties when transport and communication was very limited this was indeed a venture of some magnitude especially for two primary school girls. It took them some hours, their route was over rough terrain. When they arrived the welcome was not quite what they expected. They did not enter the valley down the screw hill but scrambled down the mountain side by the chapel, to be met by many people including their anxious and then angry families as by this time the news was out, search parties were being organised and the police had been informed. Poor Madge was blamed because she was older than Eileen and should have known better. I cannot remember what Eileen said their punishment was but I do know that she did not get off lightly.

When the Second World War was declared, it was decided that Garnie would stay in Nefyn with Will and Ethel, and Eileen with her parents would go first to Whitley Bay, whilst awaiting clearance to enter the USA, as her father had secured a position in America as a Mining Consultant with Ingersol Rand the Company with whom he had been articled.

They sailed outward bound for the States on a Cunard Liner. Their Naval Escort was released when they cleared land as Cunarders were very fast and considered therefore not threatened by U-boat attack. This particular voyage had few passengers, Eileen and her parents were honoured by being seated at the Captain's table. In a very short time Eileen was on friendly terms with the Captain and for a joke she quietly suggested that if they slowed down a bit perhaps they could do some fishing from the stern of the ship. The Captain pretended to go along with this and asked over the loudspeaker system if any of the crew had any fishing tackle with them. It ended quite hilariously.

Their stay in America was for about three years travelling

throughout the States, residing in thirteen States and Mexico for longer periods. When in New York they stayed at the Waldorf Astoria. It was there, when travelling in an elevator (lift), a lady dripping with diamonds spoke to Eileen asking her where she came from. Eileen replied 'Wales in Britain': the lady exclaimed "My! An' you speak English so well". Eileen was somewhat bemused. Their longest stay I believe was in Oakland, over the bridge from San-Francisco. The school she attended in Oakland was very keen on athletics, music and dance. Eileen had learned to ice skate previously when in Michigan so took advantage of this, to learn pair dancing on ice, and to her surprise managed to take a third prize in an amateur skating competition. She also became a very good ballroom dancer. Whilst there, they visited Los-Angeles and Hollywood where they met Spencer Tracy, the film star. Eileen was photographed sitting on his knee, unfortunately the photograph has been lost.

Because of their travels Eileen attended many different schools and when they learned that she had come from Britain, would ask if she could tell the school what wartime conditions were like in Britain. Eileen's limited experience did not deter her, and she would describe the horrors of war and the shortages particularly of food, on some occasions this led to an officially organized collection "food aid for Britain". She hoped that she was excused and forgiven for perhaps slight exaggeration. She never knew how many of these collections were successfully delivered because they never stayed long enough in any one place for feedback.

It was in Tennessee that Eileen had her first confrontation with racial discrimination. The school she was attending was a girls school. On her way home from school one afternoon she chanced to be walking alongside a black girl, so she opened up a conversation and they had a lengthy exchange about each of their lives, and then their ways parted. The following day at assembly the school was informed of the disgraceful conduct of a pupil, "Would Eileen Salmon report to the Headmistress's Study." Naturally she did as she was told although very confused to be confronted by an irate headmistress – that her conduct had been disgraceful , should she wish to continue her studies at the school she must cease fraternising with black people. Eileen was shocked, bewildered and then angered. Fortunately their stay in the area was of short duration and their move a very short time after was to Boston Massachusetts, where no such racial discrimination existed in the school there.

Return to UK – life in Fishguard

They returned to Britain in 1943 travelling homeward bound in a troopship with over two thousand G.I.s (American Soldiers), they were the only civilians aboard. A huge convoy of ships had been formed stretching as far as the eye could see, spaced out in an orderly fashion with escort vessels dashing around like well-trained sheep dogs. To lessen the risk of a co-ordinated attack by a "U-Boat Pack" (a number of German Submarines hunting together) the convoy took the long route up to the Arctic Circle via Newfoundland. Passing close to icebergs, superbly sculptured by nature, presented a spectacular sight especially in the eerie semi-darkness, their luminous shapes reflected in the black oily sea occasionally illuminated by the flashes of an Aldis lamp. This together with the dark silhouettes of the many ships, was an awe-inspiring experience that left an impressive mark on Eileen.

On their return to Britain they went directly to her father's hometown, Fishguard, in Pembrokeshire where

Will had now moved to. Garnie was married, had a baby daughter Julie and had joined the R.A.F. Her father, nearing retirement, took up employment at the Royal Naval Armaments Depot Trecwn. He bought a fishing boat named 'Sissy', for leisure and to supplement food supplies, but she was requisitioned by the Admiralty and has her own story to tell. Her replacement was a smaller elegant and seaworthy craft, the 'Touleena'. They obtained permission to fish, and were given a chart of the layout of the sea-mines in the bay which Eileen memorised. Eileen regularly went out on her own to lay the lobster pots but never to retrieve them, for safety this needed two people especially if a mine was adrift. She diversified by using her solo trips to visit the Naval small craft in the harbour – MTB's (Motor Torpedo Boat's), Miniature Submarines and Air Sea Rescue launches – and ran errands or messages for them. This was to help the war effort she told her father.

She became aware of the stress that the mothers and children in Lower Town were under. They rarely went anywhere and their husbands, almost without exception, were away in the services. They needed a break! She successfully organized a talent contest for the children, then a show by the children to raise money for an outing, and then the outing itself laying on buses etc. There were a few hiccups but a most enjoyable day was had by all.

With the arrival of the GIs, she knew that here was a lot of hidden talent, and with local singers the town needed a get together, a talent contest for the grown–ups, and this she did with the help of the Camp C.O. Major Hightower. To achieve her goal Eileen had to be very astute. Her father was very strict and to go out in the evening needed a good reason. With the help of her mother a story was concocted and the problem was resolved, and after a discussion with Ethel she was able to go openly to the army camp and invite the C.O. to Will's for tea. From thereon it was plain sailing. It was a huge success with the Towns people and servicemen alike. Amongst the contestants was a GI. Slim Whitman a folk- singer who became renowned, known worldwide. But Eileen publicly could not take any of the credit for the success of the event, as she was under age, and a girl, so was frowned upon by the" local watch" (busy bodies) who from behind drawn curtains were quick and ready to condemn and spread malicious gossip.

Eileen hated authoritarianism, the use of power without consideration or thought for the individual. An example that comes to my mind was of an occasion in Fishguard. A Gymkhana was held on the County School sports grounds. It was a very hot summer's day and tragedy struck. A little toddler was trampled underfoot by a horse. A GI, a Medic, rushed forward to give medical aid. In his endeavour his cap fell off, so he thrust it under his epaulette. His efforts were to no avail, the soldier was badly shaken at not being able to save the little boy's life and people were trying to console him. The tragedy so shocked everyone that the Gymkhana was brought to an end. Entering the crowd of people came two Snowdrops (American Military Police, nicknamed so because of the white helmets that they wore). They walked up to the Medic, grabbed him roughly by the arms, and bundled him into the back of their jeep that was parked nearby, then drove off in the direction of the Army Camp.

Eileen witnessed this and was incensed. She went as fast as she could to the camp, running most of the way; she ignored the challenge of the armed guard at the gate and ran straight for the Commandants Office (she knew its location having been there previously in connection with the Talent Contest). She burst in and demanded to see the Commandant, by now the camp was in an uproar. He saw her almost immediately and listened quietly and patiently as she told him in no uncertain terms what she thought of the M.Ps. He then had the prisoner and the two M.Ps in to tell their story. Eileen was asked if she would mind going into the ante-room for a while. The charge by the way was 'being improperly dressed'. She then heard a distant voice being raised. The prisoner and M.P s marched out, and she went back in, received a profound apology and was offered a cup of tea with biscuits which she politely accepted and then enjoyed a lift back into town in a jeep with the now ex-prisoner who thanked her profusely for coming to his rescue. Eileen made one friend and two enemies on that tragic day.

In chapter XXV Eileen mentions her virtuoso ability on the piano. Unfortunately she never had the opportunity to have piano lessons but instinctively she was able to play by ear, and even more so when Will allowed her to borrow his 120 base accordion which she soon got the hang of. There were many fine musicians and singers amongst the Americans so Eileen got a group together including Slim Whitman and they played in the evenings, above the Slade overlooking Lower Town Harbour. The sound of music drifting across the water in Lower Town I have been told by townsfolk was heavenly and eagerly awaited.

Eileen at this time secured a position as a junior clerk in a Solicitors Office even though she had no experience. This she found quite challenging as she had no shorthand knowledge. Fortunately with her superb memory and being innovative and unflappable she was able to cope. The Solicitor who was somewhat absent minded had forgotten that Eileen was only a junior and early on called Eileen in to take a letter; the head clerk was off sick. She grabbed a pad and pencil went into his office listened to his dictation making up her own shorthand, then went and typed her interpretation. He read it, smiled and said" ah yes- well done" and signed it. After that she was often called in. Some of the legal jargon was difficult to comprehend, so from time to time needed to consult the Law books which fortunately were in the office. She even attended County Court twice employing her home-made shorthand system, it was nerve wracking but nobody complained, the court was unaware that she was not a trained shorthand typist.

Life was not free of sadness for Eileen, and one of those times that left a never healing scar was the traumatic death in 1945 from leukaemia of her little niece Julie who was only two and a half years old. Eileen had some magnetic quality that drew children to her, and I have been told by many of the people of Fishguard that Little Julie was no exception, she became almost inseparable from Eileen and it was a rare occasion if one saw Eileen without Julie. She was an intelligent little girl and Eileen has told me that one could hold a conversation with her, but she couldn't say Eileen only Arnie.

V.E. day came, with the news that the war had ended in Europe. Eileen knew that there would be celebrations and so with her usual spontaneity and indomitable spirit and not knowing where the money was coming from, immediately hired by phone, a disc jockey from Milford Haven complete with all equipment and also, a company to rig coloured lights for a V.E. night celebration in Lower Town. She then went from door to door cap in hand asking if they would like to donate to the cost of what she was proposing for that evening. She also asked if they had anything in the way of food stuff to make a cake or something. She got help to set up the trestle tables that she borrowed, and the two local Inns to supply free pop for the children, then finally to ask the nearest householder to the venue if they would allow the electricity for the lighting system to be taken from them should the need be. Everything fell into place. The money collected miraculously covered the cost almost to the penny and the evening was a huge success with singing and dancing and great joy, but not forgetting those who would never return, and that the war in the Pacific was yet to be won.

Eileen had become quite proficient in playing the accordion and so was asked to stand in at the local hops (dances), in the church hall, when a lead instrument player was unable to attend. The agreement was that she would play half the time and then she could dance for the other half, no fee no charge. It worked after a fashion but the band did sound somewhat muted when she was dancing. She was also invited and played as a soloist at a local R.A.F. camp. Later In 1948 Eileen received a letter from Hughie Green (BBC presenter) asking if she would play the accordion in a possible forthcoming show that was being arranged 'Opportunity Knocks'. She declined as she thought that she was not good enough.

I was in the Fleet Air Arm and in 1946 was stationed about 24 miles from Fishguard. We chose Fishguard as favourite for its warmth and friendliness towards us and for its good dances. It was there that I met Eileen at a dance in the Drill Hall. My favourite film star was Ginger Rogers and when I saw Eileen as she entered the dance hall, I thought "it's Ginger Rogers except she is blonde". The first dance she danced was with her friend, Eileen taking the male part. I could see, yes, she can also dance like Ginger Rogers. The next dance was a quick step, my favourite. So, I asked Eileen – 'May I have this dance' and we just danced the rest of the evening away – I felt like Fred Astaire.

Eileen seemed to have the ability to make people relax and be drawn to her. This magnetism also applied with animals. I tell briefly the rather unusual story of the only chicken egg that did not hatch in a batch of eggs in an incubator. She held this egg in a cloth in front of an open fire for about two hours, then to have a rest she placed the egg wrapped in the cloth next to her on the settee, the cat came in and immediately jumped up and snuggled in close to Eileen. Ten minutes later there was a chirping sound, the cat got up – low and behold – a tiny yellow ball of fluff, a cute little chick. From there on the little chick stayed constantly at Eileen's side, or in fact in her pocket. This continued until Georgie as we called him became fully grown although he was more like a bantam (a small breed of chicken) or even smaller in size. If she left him, the noise he created was piercing and disturbed everyone, so she even had to take him in her coat pocket with his head sticking out when going to town, he would stay quite contented for however long it took and became quite a celebrity in the shops. I think that probably by now you are thinking that this is no ordinary chick. I think the following possibly bears this out. The corner shop in Lower Town was about one hundred and fifty feet from Eileen's home front door to the corner, sharp turn left, and then sharp left again into the shop. Georgie's first venture to the shop was purely accidental and unintentional. Eileen had reason to go to the shop so Georgie was shut up in the house. Somehow he got out. Eileen was being served and waiting behind her were two other lady customers. All of a sudden there were gasps and exclamations 'look!' Eileen looked around, the two ladies were pointing towards her feet. Eileen looked down and there was Georgie standing perfectly still between her feet. She scooped him up and then explained the situation to the people in the shop. How he found his way to the shop is a mystery. From thereon he was allowed to follow her to the shop. If you have seen the 'Road Runner' Cartoons, then you can picture Georgie. To keep up with Eileen his legs were a blur (at high speed) and to turn the corner where the surface was very fine chippings he would skid in a cloud of dust, legs moving fast just like the Road Runner's, then into the shop to stand unperturbed between Eileen's feet until she was ready to pick him up. It was worth seeing. He was eventually persuaded to live with the other chickens outside in the Hen House. Many months later there was a commotion in the hen house with a lot of noise. We rushed out fearing the worst that a Fox or some other animal was attacking the Hens. To our relief and astonishment we found Georgie running around in circles and shrieking – having just laid an egg, and this was to be the only egg that Georgie, then re-named Georgina, ever laid

In our courting days life was never dull. Eileen would still find adventure, and I briefly relate an incident. A large two masted yacht anchored alongside the quay wall in Lower Town crewed by only two people. Odd in itself. To handle a yacht of that size with any degree of safety would need at least a crew of four. The crew went to the Ship Inn and there, spoke to Eileen's father who was the Honorary Representative. for the Ocean Yacht Club. They casually asked about the tides and weather in the Bay of Biscay. Strange he thought as they were under manned for such a voyage, and later he mentioned this to us, Eileen then pointed out that she had noticed that the sails were furled and lashed, so they must only be using engine power. They were obviously not yachtsmen, this raised suspicion. About 11.30 PM that night we were taking a last stroll down the quay when we noticed a large limousine quietly drive up near the yacht, two men with cases got out and went aboard the yacht. We were in the shadows so they had not seen us and there was no one else about. Eileen quietly said to me, "no arguments, I'll give them quarter of an hour then I'm going aboard to try and see what they are up to. You wait at the foot of the gangplank in case I need you". With the time gone, she crept aboard onto the far side of the yacht and disappeared. I waited for about three minutes which seemed like three hours with heart in mouth, when she popped up and waved for me to follow her, which I did. She pointed to a port hole where the curtain had not been properly drawn. I looked through and saw a table that looked to be covered in diamonds. I felt a tap on my shoulder from Eileen to depart noiselessly. We then went to the phone booth and I phoned the police, then back to the shadows to await events. We waited for what seemed about twenty minutes, then a police car came from the town, did not turn down the quay but went up the road and then stopped out of sight, this we thought was the time to report back to father and call it a day. Next morning the yacht had gone, departed on the first tide. The police must have guessed who had phoned them because of my English accent even though I did not give my name, as some weeks later Eileen's father was told by the police that the couple had been apprehended in Gibraltar.

Eileen's nautical experiences did not stop there, two further incidents will provide an insight into Eileen's adventurous spirit; she was instrumental in saving an Irish girl and possibly a Swansea girl from being abducted. She also single handed saved a small unmanned yacht that was adrift in a heavy sea having dragged its anchor and was in danger of being dashed against the rocks. She secured a tow and brought it into the Inner Harbour. She did not claim salvage rights however as the owner was an Ex-Serviceman just de-mobbed.

We were married in May 1948. A week before the Wedding Eileen's mother had a bus accident and was admitted to hospital. She insisted that we did not postpone the wedding so we celebrated part of the wedding in the hospital. When her mother recovered we went to live in my home in Surrey for me to continue my studies. Her mother later became ill so we moved back for Eileen to look after her. Her mother then suffered a stroke which affected her memory; she developed an obsession. Night or day wanting to know the names and addresses of people they had known many years before not only in this country but abroad in Germany, Finland etc. Again Eileen's memory came into action recalling names and addresses of people that she had never met, perhaps only seeing it once when reading it on the way to posting a letter for her parents. She also remembered names from conversations her parents had in the past, she then spent hours cataloguing the names and addresses. In May 1950 her mother died, a fortnight later our son Allan was born and then Margaret, Garnie's wife died leaving a little five year old boy Serry. Will and Ethel were now living in Salisbury, Southern Rhodesia. Eileen had to deal with everything, a task with so much pressure and sadness, at the time seemed almost insurmountable.

The later years – caring for others, efforts to return to Nant and the writing of *This Valley was Ours*

We decided that we would go back to Surrey for me to continue studies, and take Serry with us. Her father insisted that Serry stayed with him and Garnie. This worked well for a time but eventually Eileen had to fetch Serry to live with us as her father was ailing. He died in 1951 and Garnie came to live with us for a short while.

Eileen was intrepid, regardless of consequences. I remember the occasion when coming out of Croydon Railway Station on a Saturday with Allan in a push chair and with Serry holding my hand. Across the street were five teddy boys laughing and having fun by rocking and bouncing up and down an Austin Seven car, inside a terrified old man sitting in the passenger seat. There were

Village in ruins

crowds of people around but nobody intervened. Eileen said, 'excuse me a moment' and swiftly walked across the street, touched the arm of the Teddy boy who appeared to be the leader. He turned, and she stepped up to him and said something close to his ear. He gestured to his friends that they stopped rocking the car. They all then walked slowly away. On her return I said to her, 'what did you say to him', her reply 'oh, nothing much'. We then went shopping.

Eileen had not forgotten the Valley. She would tell of its wonders and of the people. It was in 1951 that we finally made it to Nant. Yes, it was just as she described it. As we started our descent down the Screw Hill, peace and tranquillity surrounded us, the mystique of this valley was only too apparent, and then, a sadness on finding a virtually deserted village with only three inhabitants. A man was squatting in Tŷ Canol and I believe a Mr William Owen was living in one of the Sea View houses, his sister was looking

Back of Mountain View

Village and Chapel 1970

after him, he had refused to leave and wanted to stay until he died.

Our aim now was to return or to get as close as possible to this valley of enchantment. My roots were in the South and commercially safe, the task was considerable as there was little industry close to Nant. The closest I could get was Shell at Ellesmere Port, we rented a bungalow in Llanferres in Denbighshire, and then we moved to Yr Wyddgrug (Mold) in Flintshire. It was in 1954 that I think that she realized that her dream of returning to the valley was not to be. Since our first visit the houses had been gutted. All the wood had been torn out, it was said, by hippies and used as firewood. She had an idea that perhaps we could buy it. So we approached Amalgamated Roadstone and met the Managing Director who informed us that they would not sell because of the mineral rights. We asked if they would inform us should any propositions arise. Yes they would but they thought this would be unlikely. Eileen's hopes were dashed, the idea of perhaps finding all the people that had lived in Nant to form a co-operative was shelved, it was only a pipe dream and would have taken an enormous amount of money, at that time we only had one contact, and together we thought we were probably the only persons who had this feeling for the Valley. Our hopes were raised when I had a position offered to me with an engineering company in Penygroes, but it was short lived and the offer had to be withdrawn. They had not followed procedure and gone through the correct channel for advertising the vacancy. A number of things blocked our way, and then in 1967 I had an unexpected offer of a job in the U.S. They gave me six months to decide whether to accept or not. Serry would not be coming with us as he was now married and had set up home in Mold. To get things in order and make the final decision we moved to Hastings in East Sussex. The Vietnam

Nant Gwrtheyrn in 1974, a view from Benclog with Caernant jetty in the background

War finally was the deciding factor for us to stay in the U.K. and to settle awhile in Hastings with our thoughts still of North Wales and the Valley. Allan was able to continue his studies and later got married setting up home in Hastings close to us.

Hastings is a coastal resort where many people decide to spend their retirement thus making a community with a high proportion of elderly people. Eileen soon became aware of this, finding that many of these people apart from loneliness needed help in many ways.

Much of Eileen's time was taken up by giving this help. Here is an example, a rare one I must admit and a situation where Eileen's ability was put to the test – a married couple who were stone deaf from birth and so naturally had great difficulty in communicating, were having an altercation with their neighbour a Polish couple who spoke very little English. Eileen had met both couples briefly, just a passing greeting. Eileen got involved when she responded to a loud banging on our front door, she opened it to find the deaf gentleman frantically gesticulating and beckoning her to follow him. This deaf couple when in conversation always had a pad and pencil to hand to write down a message or word. In this case the Polish neighbours were unable to understand what was written on the pad so things were hotting up. I believe the dispute was about a boundary fence. Why Eileen was chosen to referee one does not know, but it proved to be a wise choice. Eileen somehow although she did not know either sign language or Polish, improvised, made up her own sign language and the problem was

Rear view of Sea View Terrace with Carreg-y-Llam in the background

resolved amicably. The story does not end there, she later received a phone call from a doctor asking if she would act as an intermediary as he was about to make a house call at the deaf couples home, by the way the doctor's first language was not English. This became a regular event amongst many other tasks that she carried out for them to the extreme. The Polish couple also were now aware of Eileen's attributes and she became the wife's confidante and also her doctor's intermediary. But there were also a number of other ladies who without imposing were grateful for the help that Eileen was able to give them. Eileen seemed to be collecting more people that needed help in many ways, and they were in different parts of the town. Eileen began to acquire some medical knowledge and was given two textbooks by a doctor to whet her appetite, which it did, but unfortunately she was unable to extend this study.

I mentioned in the first paragraph of this biography, asking the question was Eileen a clairvoyant. I will now explain. It was about this time that we were re-introduced to an albeit rather contrary elderly lady- a friend of the family of many years before, when Eileen was young. It became the norm that this lady would visit us once a week. On one of these occasions she casually asked if we had heard of an Ouija Board, she had just been given one and she would show it to us. The next week she arrived with this board and bullishly set it up on the table, then told us how to play it, the board had the alphabet around its perimeter; in the centre you placed the shuttle on which one gently placed their forefinger. The shuttle would then move about to different letters spelling out a message, a party game full of laughs because people cheated and pushed it around. Of course we did the same. Then we became more serious to see if it really would work. We waited for a while then it slowly began to move with an introductory message. We then questioned who moved it? And then gave up for that night. She brought it with her the next week, this time it moved faster and we knew that this was real thing; it began to move so fast that our fingers slipped off, we then realized that Eileen's finger

View of part of the village from Cae Mawr showing results of vandalism

was the only one that stayed on. It now moved so fast that one person had to call out the letters while the other person wrote them down. We then blindfolded Eileen but it made no difference, it was almost too fast. For many weeks this continued, it was becoming apparent that the lady was becoming obsessed. When we had messages that referred to the near future which proved to be true, I agreed with Eileen that it was time that we fake the messages and close it down without the lady knowing. I am not disclosing any message contents, for one I have forgotten most of them, and secondly the reams of paper with the messages on them have been destroyed.

Eileen was asked if she would be interested in joining the Samaritans. She went for training and eventually became a Samaritan. However, she found that she was not entirely at one with them, that in addition to the concept of giving emotional support to the caller, some of the callers did not know where to turn and needed additional help to guide them for their next step forward. She found that at the end of day in case discussion she received adverse comments and was admonished, especially when one of the callers left a lovely bunch of wild flowers (which must have been picked from the hedge rows) and some sweets as a thank you for her practical help. Eileen carried on for a while but found it hard to comply with the restriction.

The Inception of *This Valley Was Ours*

In 1979, Eileen received a letter, and a news-paper cutting requesting anyone interested in attending a forthcoming re-union in Pwllheli for the children of Nant to contact Mrs Phyllis Roberts or her brother Gwilym. She immediately contacted Phyllis. As the date grew near we had a build-up of great excitement and speculation. Would anyone remember me? What shall I wear? I think this was probably the first time that I had seen Eileen in a real flap.

What an event it turned out to be. At first there was hesitancy and then catch up time, the talking became incessant as if they were transposed back forty years or more. Even later in the evening when the time came for official photographs the press photographer had a tough job on his hands driven almost to a point of desperation to stop everyone from talking to allow him to do his job. At last the group – paused – ready for the take, although their physical appearance had changed over the years, the spirit of Nant could not only be clearly seen but also felt. In chapter 1 Eileen describes the start of our journey to the reunion, and the last two paragraphs of chapter XXX the reunion. Oh! What a day, not just a re-union of her generation but a social – historic event of the people of Nant.

At the reunion, Eileen discovered that the spell that had

Annie Mair presenting a silver bowl to Phyllis, a thank you to Phyllis and her brother for initiating and organising the reunion

Eileen receives a presentation from Phyllis, a thank you for writing the book

Eileen holding up presentation – a Welsh slate etching

been cast over her, but for one exception, was cast over the other children of the valley. This included previous generations. They all suffered this unending yearning (hiraeth) this invisible bond forever drawn to the valley, this extreme longing to return. We heard of the untrue stories told of the people of the valley, of poverty, the women struggling over the mountain for a crust of bread. This picture was conjured up to colour the articles in the national press and magazines of the ghost village on the Llyn Peninsula. There was a consensus that someone had to tell the true story of the people of Nant Gwrtheyrn; it was suggested that Eileen would be best suited for the task, 'she must do it'! She agreed to take on the responsibility and recognised that it would be a great challenge and that she hoped she would do it justice.

She then set to work, three years of hard work and memory coming into play, cataloguing virtually everything that happened when she was in Nant, verifying if possible every detail, contacting shipping companies and ships' captains, newspaper records in London and Caernarfon the County Offices, church records, libraries, and personal visits to the surviving elder members of the Nant community. From time to time she had moments of doubt as to her own ability but when the book was published she was thanked by John Kelly (ship owners) Belfast for writing a true picture of shipping in the stone trade (chapter XXIV. Distribution); she was made an honorary Captain and given a shipmasters tie. We were told that other than Captains of John Kelly's she was the only person ever to be given one. She was also offered a voyage on one of their vessels around the coast of Britain.

In 1983 *This Valley was Ours* was published. Eileen received letters from different parts of the world thanking her for giving them the opportunity to gain an insight into life in the valley, answers to questions that must be on the lips of every person that had the temerity to venture down the torturous screw hill into the idyllic setting of Nant Gwrtheyrn (Porth y Nant). There were people who had only read the book and found that they must see this valley for themselves. Eileen made many new friends through the writing of the book.

When Prince Charles visited Nant, Eileen was invited to meet him together with her publisher. I was told afterwards by the publisher that Prince Charles and Eileen wandered off into Cae Mawr deep in conversion and after ten minutes or so they had to be politely reminded of the time. In his speech to the assembly he thanked Eileen for the copy of her book and said that he would read it at night when in bed.

During the writing of the book and for many years before and after Eileen continued helping the old folk, then she became ill. Our doctor had just gone away for three weeks so

Police check point – Eileen and Mrs Parry (original publishers) prior to meeting Prince Charles

Eileen being interviewed for S4C television after book launch

she was attended by a doctor who also practised Homeopathy. She rapidly deteriorated. I went to the surgery, saw another doctor and asked urgently for a second opinion. Our doctor must somehow have been informed, immediately flew back from wherever and took charge and was almost in constant attendance for about three days until she was out of danger, giving her injections every few hours. Miraculously she started to recover, he then handed over to another doctor. We never knew what the cause was, but when Eileen had regained her health our doctor laid down the law telling her that she must stop the help she was giving to people, otherwise she could be facing dire consequences.

Almost all our annual holidays were spent in Wales together with Allan and his family (Pal his wife, and daughters Laura and Allanah), in places that we had not been before both in the North and South. Eileen always felt whether North or South that she was nearing home (Nant), I also felt the friendliness and warmth of the welcome wherever we were. We also visited Southern Ireland to recapture Eileen's memory of her stays with her Auntie when Eileen was a child in Nant, and we paid further visits making close friends in Tralee

On one of our visits to Wales we stayed at a hotel in Criccieth. We were sitting in the lounge talking to the proprietor; somehow or other the subject of feet came up, he mentioned something about his partners feet. Eileen jokingly said that she knew everything about feet, you can tell a person's character by looking at their feet, it's the same as if you read their palms. She then pointed at me and said "he's got sneaky feet". The proprietor went away and came back with his partner. Take your shoes off and let Eileen look at your feet. This was done, he then turned to Eileen, 'well what do you see'. Eileen then in a serious tone read his character and his fortune. They looked at one another in amazement "Oh gosh- that's true! Would you read other peoples' feet?" Eileen without thought said 'of course'.

The next day when we came in for dinner that evening, Eileen was told that people from outside the hotel might be coming for a free foot reading on Friday night. There were many unfamiliar faces in the Hotel that Friday night. A queue formed and Eileen carried out the task explaining that she was not qualified in any way as a clairvoyant or medium, this was purely entertainment. This did not deter anyone. Her readings seemed to be taken seriously as they talked amongst themselves, and we know of at least one person to whom it gave strength to carry his grief, an elderly gentleman who had lost his wife some months before. He and his daughter were guests at the hotel. His daughter was despairing, her father had hardly said a word since her mother had died and the stay at the hotel being a change of scene she was hoping would help relieve the grief. We had noticed throughout the week that at breakfast he did not respond to the usual morning greetings. This Friday evening was for them the same as every other evening sitting in the lounge without saying hardly a word except that all around them people were discussing their foot readings. When the evening had almost drawn to a close he removed his shoes and socks and approached Eileen, quietly asking if she would read his feet. This must have taken terrific willpower and strength for him to make that approach to Eileen. She sat him down and talked to him in a whisper inaudible to the people around them. I think she then helped him with socks and shoes and then his daughter came over with a look of surprise and bewilderment, the evening ended. Next morning at breakfast he thanked Eileen and the daughter gave her a big hug. I think there were others that it helped, when we were in the town a lady came up and thanked her. I asked her how she had known different peoples individual

Ex Nantites at book launch

life patterns. "I don't know" she said, "I think somehow they tell me and then it all fits into place", and then she laughed and said "you're sneaky and you've got sneaky feet".

In 1996 Eileen was invited to give a talk at the University of Bangor on the Valley of Nant Gwrtheyrn. The University offered a course known as ELCOS (English Language for Overseas Students) and as part of their extra-curricular programme gave students the opportunity to study local places of historical interest,they felt that the talk would be a cultural supportive addition to their programme.

Eileen as always was efficient in preparation enquired as to the nationality of the students who would be attending. This would give her the opportunity to learn the formal greeting in each tongue, and then greet each group of nationals or individual national respectfully. This she did at the opening of the talk. Spanish, Italian, Russian, Arabic, Chinese etc. She then asked whether she had rudely omitted

Eileen with original publisher Gareth Maelor, Tom Puw, Nan Parri and Harri Parri

any national. A Japanese lady student stood up, Eileen apologised and asked if she would kindly tell her the greeting so that she could then greet her in the proper manner. Eileen listened and then repeated the greeting with a courteous bow. This met with applause and the talk was off to a very good start. What was supposed to be an hour's talk turned out to be two hours and even then had to be brought to an end by the University staff. The students showed great interest with a barrage of questions. At the end Eileen received spontaneous applause and almost all of the students came forward individually to thank her for such an interesting presentation. The students wanted to know how they could obtain copies of *This Valley Was Ours*. Little did she know that her talk was going to be so well received as only three days after this talk a letter arrived in the post from the University thanking her and I quote "Thank you very much for the fascinating talk ……..it was very much

Eileen holding 1st edition for press photographer

appreciated" asking her if they could have a copy of the typescript "... to exploit the talk to the maximum".

I think that corresponding with people in different parts of the world and reading of inclement weather conditions in different climates sparked off her interest in Ecology. She joined 'The Workers Education Programme' attending lectures held once a week, run by Sussex University. This gave her concern as the lectures forecast the environmental situation up to two thousand and twenty and the situation that we have today.

It was in 2002 that Eileen was not feeling up to the mark.

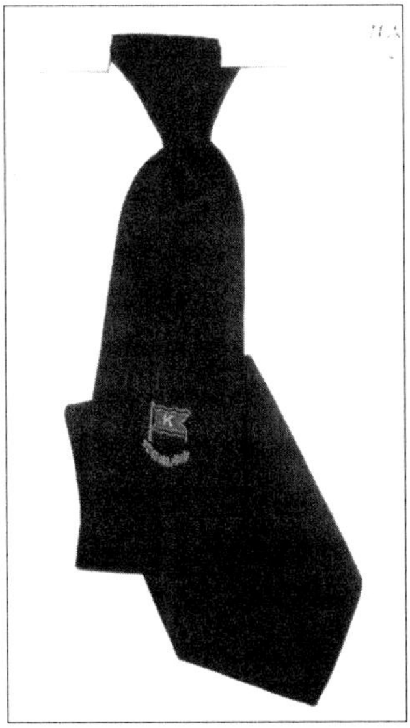

Kelly's Master Mariners Tie presented to Eileen in recognition of her accurate and fair portrayal of the part that shipping played in the transportation of stone

For a year she was back and fore to the doctors, repeated blood tests repeatedly showing no infection. It was a bank Holiday; Eileen again was not well so phoned the N.H.S. help line. Immediately she described her symptoms the doctor on the phone told Eileen to instruct her doctor to arrange an immediate specialist consultation. Within days she was admitted to hospital having to have a Kidney removed as she had a Renal Carcinoma. As we were about to leave the hospital the Nursing Sister passed us a leaflet, saying that Eileen had M.R.S.A. the leaflet gave the medical instructions. From thereon Eileen's health deteriorated, she did manage to fight it for just about two years, but it had destroyed her immune system and she was diagnosed with terminal cancer. She was confined to bed and for further three months, fought always with a smile and an apology for creating problems. She passed away peacefully in her sleep in the morning of the 29th September 2005.

Those last three and a half years of Eileen's life although suffering from ill health, she bore this with fortitude, helped by the great support given by our family and by 'The Darvell Christian Community' in Robertsbridge East Sussex (a Bruderhof Community). I will explain – In 1995 our eldest granddaughter Laura was a student at Robertsbridge College. Miriam a classmate from Darvell invited Laura and family to a Carol Concert. This we accepted and had a thoroughly enjoyable evening. We then visited on other equally enjoyable occasions. When Eileen was told by the Consultant that her illness was terminal, the shock was so great she was devastated. Pal knowing that Eileen found Darvell a place of comfort suggested that we drive there directly. We were met with a genuine welcome, concern and understanding. This had an uplifting effect on Eileen and when we left there she had a smile and the fortitude to carry her load. When confined to bed over the three months, the Community without hesitation sent a young lady Amelia to nurse Eileen throughout the day. She has since become a doctor. Also on occasions a small group would visit and sing to Eileen at her bedside. Pal and Allanah were also in almost constant attendance giving personal care. Laura was away at University.

During the last three months of her illness when she was confined to her bed she in fact did reflect on her life and asked me if I would act as her scribe as she found that she was unable to hold a pen, that she wished to dictate her life story. Sadly and ironically the exceptional memory that had served her so well throughout her life and had helped many people was being destroyed by the insidious cancer and would not allow her to expand her thoughts causing her great frustration and anguish. We tried again on a number of occasions and then I believe and I hope managed to persuade her that her medication was the cause and was only temporary that we try again in a few days. It was not mentioned again.

Eileen's funeral service was held at The Baptist Church. Our dear friend the Reverend Gareth Parry led the service, a friend made through the writing of the book. Many friends from Darvell were in the congregation. At the graveside on the interment the voices of Darvell sang a most beautiful arrangement of the twenty third psalm. Gareth, a true Welshman and therefore used to hearing lovely Welsh harmony was as moved as I was. I feel sure Eileen was listening.

Ever since Eileen's passing in 2005, a number of people having read *This Valley Was Ours* have enquired whether there is a symbolic monument of some sort to honour her for enabling the modern generation to have a glimpse back into how life was in bye-gone days. To acknowledge her endeavour in providing us with a wonderfully written account of the social history of this captivating place, hopefully in the near future, something will be erected not only to remember Eileen but also all the other children of this unforgettable valley.

To the best of my knowledge I have tried to portray an accurate, albeit a brief account of my dear wife Eileen's life which was sadly shortened by the dreadful cancer. I hope that I have not offended anyone in my recounting, or in omitting, any fact inadvertently. If I have, I apologise unreservedly.

Acknowledgements

I wish to express my thanks and gratitude to all those who have supported me during the writing of this biography:
Rev. G. Parry. Mrs A. Mair Williams. Eryl & Beryl Jones.
Cliff & Hazel Roberts.
Sam & Sue Mc Loughlan.
Not forgetting my very supportive family.